# THE HOME CARE EXPERIENCE

D1070221

# SOME OTHER VOLUMES IN THE
# SAGE FOCUS EDITIONS

# THE HOME CARE EXPERIENCE
## Ethnography and Policy

Edited by
**Jaber F. Gubrium**
**Andrea Sankar**

**SAGE** PUBLICATIONS
*The International Professional Publishers*
Newbury Park   London   New Delhi

Copyright © 1990 by Sage Publications, Inc.

All rights reserved. No part of this book may be reproduced or utilized in any form or by any means, electronic or mechanical, including photocopying, recording, or by any information storage and retrieval system, without permission in writing from the publisher.

*For information address:*

SAGE Publications, Inc.
2111 West Hillcrest Drive
Newbury Park, California 91320

SAGE Publications Ltd.
28 Banner Street
London EC1Y 8QE
England

SAGE Publications India Pvt. Ltd.
M-32 Market
Greater Kailash I
New Delhi 110 048 India

Printed in the United States of America

Library of Congress Cataloging-in-Publication Data

Main entry under title:

The home care experience : ethnography and policy / Jaber F. Gubrium,
    Andrea Sankar, joint editors.
        p.   cm. — (Sage focus editions ; v. 119)
    Includes bibliographical references.
    ISBN 0-8039-3527-7. — ISBN 0-8039-3528-5 (pbk.)
    1. Frail elderly—Home care—Cross-cultural studies.   2. Frail
elderly—Home care—United States—Case studies.   3. Frail elderly—
Home care—Great Britain—Case studies.   I. Gubrium, Jaber F.
II. Sankar, Andrea.
    HV1451.H63   1990                                                    90-8223
    362.6—dc20                                                           CIP
**FIRST PRINTING, 1990**

Sage Production Editor: Diane S. Foster

# Contents

# Introduction

JABER F. GUBRIUM
ANDREA SANKAR

The deinstitutionalization of medicine is underway. It is being accomplished by reimbursement systems that encourage the early discharge of patients, often with high levels of acuity, and by advancements in home-based technology and pharmacology that have enabled acutely ill patients to be cared for at home. A growth in the number of chronic care patients who must be cared for in the home parallels the introduction of acute care into the home. The aging of the population, especially the increase of those over 85, has been accompanied by growth in the number of those suffering from the combined effects of age and chronic disability. The majority of these people, even those suffering from severe mental and physical disabilities, are cared for at home. This combination of factors is converging on the household and family to produce the predominant setting for health care delivery.

The home care experience is only dimly understood. Policymakers, insurers, health care planners, and professional home care providers appear to conceptualize the home as a kind of black hole into which a range of medical services and conditions can be transferred. Little is known about *how* care is delivered in the household or *how* the family copes with the increased level of responsibility. Few in fact have even posed the question of whether the family should be expected to cope with the life-and-death responsibility often associated with this level of caregiving.

Indeed, the simple task of defining what is caring—how it is variously understood by those concerned—seems to be furthest from the minds of most researchers. Concepts have been defined, variables selected, hypotheses formulated, measures and scales constructed, samples selected, inquiries conducted, and data analyzed—all as if the basic meanings and concepts of the home care experience were known. Few, if any, have bothered to ask whether care, caring, and caregiving have different meanings to those directly or indirectly involved in home care. None seem to have wondered whether caring and caregiving are the same or contrasting orders of experience. Rarely, if ever, has anyone even raised the question of whether there might be different versions of the home's goings-on as a sickroom, which would imply that measurement would necessarily produce multiple, possibly contradictory, "figures."

### Existing Research

Existing research on the family in home care has involved large, statistical studies (Soldo & Manton, 1985; Stone, Cafferata, & Sang, 1987) or multivariate analyses of what Gubrium and Lynott (1987) call the "care equation," namely hypothesized covariations between such caregiving attitudes as perceived burden, felt stress, and the institutionalization decision (Gwyther & George, 1986; Zarit, Orr, & Zarit, 1984; Zarit, Reever, & Bach-Peterson, 1980; Poulshock & Deimling, 1984; Morycz, 1985). There is little work on the actual dynamics and processes of home care or what we call the "home care experience." The few studies that have been undertaken have explored how the household's interpersonal relations figure in the behavior of children (Henry, 1985; Bermann, 1986; Kantor & Lehr, 1977), alcoholics (Steinglass, 1979), and mentally-impaired adults (Laing & Esterson, 1964; Anderson & Bagarozzi, 1983; Bagarozzi & Anderson, 1982; Reiss, Gonzalez, & Kramer, 1986; Leff & Vaughn, 1985). These studies were focused on elucidating possible pathological processes, not on understanding the complex response of a family to the task of caring for a member who is acutely or chronically ill. Further, these studies were primarily focused on the interaction of young children, adolescents, and their caregiving parents. In contrast, much of current home care involves relationships between elderly parents, spouses, and older adult children in which the problem of redefining the family of origin or priority involves different developmental issues. Studies are needed to evaluate how families at various points of development react to the increase in the scope, intensity, and competing loyalties of caring.

Yet the prospects for work in this area seem equally problematic. In a recent editorial in *The Gerontologist,* Zarit (1989), a pioneer in studying the social psychology of home care for the elderly, questioned the usefulness of continued research on caregiving. He pointed out that numerous studies had affirmed that caregiving is a stressful undertaking and that the sources of this stress are multidimensional and the relationships involved are complex. Zarit noted the move beyond bivariate studies to sophisticated explanatory models, but he doubted the feasibility of large-scale testing for these models. From these observations, Zarit went on to discount the utility of self-report data, which he criticized as inaccurate, in the reporting of the magnitude of events (p. 147).

Frustrated by the complexity of the problem, Zarit advises researchers to "control" those complicating factors and move toward more precise measurement. In contrast, this volume is expressly devoted to the appreciation and documentation of that complexity. By its very nature, caregiving is complex, involving concepts of self; familial and gender roles; cultural and social values and expectations; the symbolic spatial dynamics of the home context; economic and political factors which promote or inhibit the ability of the caregiver to care; relationships with professional caregiving institutions; and perhaps most significant, the meaning of the experience for the caregiver, the person cared for, the family, and significant outsiders. Clearly, it is not possible to incorporate all these factors into an analysis. To fully comprehend the dynamics of the care experience, however, an appreciation of their salience and interactive quality must be present.

Caregiving may defy meaningful measurement, (that is, informative and conceptually accurate measurement). If meaningful measurement is possible, however, then it will only be after far more basic research on the phenomenon has been conducted. Zarit is correct in highlighting the complexity of the problem; but the solution is to delve into that complexity so as to *understand* it, not control for it.

## The Emerging Ethnography

A small but growing number of researchers on both sides of the Atlantic has chosen to examine the home as a dynamic context of caregiving. They have oriented to several analytic understandings. First, because of the "native informality" of the household, relatively unstructured methods are being used to examine interpersonal relations and circumstances. Some have conducted participant observation in the home (Henry, 1965; Sankar, 1986, 1987, 1988), while others have utilized open-ended interviews with family members (see LaRossa & Wolf, 1985; Rubinstein, 1987). Still others have focused on the household/institution nexus for its diverse interpretations of domestic order and familial responsibility (Gubrium, 1987, 1988). Much of what goes on in the home as a caregiving setting does not allow access through standard testing and measurement procedures. The latter would tend to spoil what might be said to be the household's most natural characteristic, namely the family "at home" (Skolnick, 1983). Thus ethnographic methods and analytic techniques appear to be the most effective means of constructing an accurate and insightful understanding of the home care experience.

Second, because the home has not been extensively studied in general, and certainly little understood as a care setting in particular, those currently engaged in research have permitted themselves to *explore* its social organization. It is important to keep in mind that, when little is known, there must be provision for open investigation lest the unknown be shallowly conceived or prematurely standardized into a research entity. There is much speculation and popular opinion about the household and home care. What is lacking is "basic" research—that is, research into the basic concepts and understandings of caregiving.

Third, since there are few, if any, guidelines for conducting social research on home care, methodological standards have not been selected that are appropriate to home care's social characteristics. As a step in this direction, the existing ethnographic research has plied new ground in as reasonable a fashion as possible, developing procedural insights and rules as it moved along. This is characteristic of any new orientation to a field of study. The assumption is that we are only beginning to have the means to evaluate the quality of related research and the basis for comparison.

Fourth, because little basic research exists, home care policy should be developed and initiated with considerable reservation. If policy considerations move too far ahead of what is solidly known, the search for basic knowledge will be hampered by unrealistic definitions, views, and expectations. Policy initiatives run the risk of inappropriate targeting, inadequate implementation, and unrealistic goals.

Taken together, these understandings suggest the broad outlines of an emerging, ethnographic research agenda. It is important that studies of the home care experience be flexible enough to explore, be open to the natural characteristics of the home as a setting, and aim for the kinds of analyses befitting the native dynamics of the household and the institutions to which it is linked. Findings from this type of research can provide the basic information required for effective policy development and implementation.

## Plan of the Book

As a point of departure for developing a pertinent analytic discourse and public debate on the nature of home care, researchers in the United States and the United Kingdom whose work is guided by the preceding understandings were asked to contribute to a collection of original papers on related issues and policy. We believe the resulting collection—*The Home Care Experience: Ethnography and Policy*—provides a useful context within which to address the area's important questions and critically assess its existing answers. Needless to say, the collection is relevant to the classroom too, especially in such disciplines as nursing, family practice, social work, and the medical social sciences, which are rapidly moving in the direction of training an informed generation of home care practitioners and professionals.

The chapters herein fall into three parts. The first part, "The Home as Sickroom," deals with the culture and social organization of the household as a care setting. Focal are its adaptations, ritual borders, cultural variations, crisis resolutions, interpersonal histories, and dynamics of affection. Steven Albert's chapter, "The Dependent Elderly, Home Health Care, and Strategies of Household Adaptation," introduces us to the home as sickroom by showing how members variously adapt to caregiving demands and parental impairment. Albert argues that adaptation strategies often evolve to prevent the radical reorganization of the household, to maintain traditional allocations of space and time. Robert Rubinstein's chapter, "Culture and Disorder in the Home Care Experience: The Home as Sickroom," focuses on a clash of expectations: the tensions between household order and developmental strivings on the one hand and the disorders of sickness and chronic convalescence on the other. The chapter presents ways families differentially resolve the clash. The chapter by Juliet Corbin and Anselm Strauss, entitled "Making Arrangements: The Key to Home Care," features the surprisingly adept management strategies of the household to show how informal arrangements can make the household both a sickroom and home rivaling the ostensible efficiency of formal care settings. The fourth chapter, "The Defiance of Hope: Dementia Sufferers and Their Carers in a London Borough," by Joel Savishinsky, shows how variable the sickroom is that home caregivers offer, associated with different experiences in obtaining household help for themselves and a demented member of the family.

Part Two, "Patterns of Caregiving," reveals the diversity of caregiving relationships. Highlighted are the various "others" who enter into the care experience, ranging from family members and distant kin to neighbors, friends, and ostensible strangers. Judith Barker and Linda Mitteness's chapter, "Invisible Caregivers in the Spotlight: Non-Kin Caregivers of Frail Older Adults," zeros in on a category of caregiver commonly labeled "other" in many studies. The authors inform us that what is otherwise virtually dismissed in reports of research findings reveals a complex and significant configuration of assistance in home care. In contrast, the next chapter, "Support Systems for the Familyless Elderly: Care Without Commitment," by Lucy Rose Fisher, Leah Rogne, and Nancy Eustis, cautions us that while "others" (namely, non-kin caregivers) may offer assistance, they are not as formally compelled by the normative commitments of filial responsibility, which raises the issue of the long term in home caregiving. Clare Wenger's chapter, "Personal Care: Variation in Network Type, Style, and Capacity," reveals the diverse networks that set the background for home care, informing us that the type of network is as important as the number of social ties for the provision of personal care. Using a life-course perspective, Myrna Silverman and Elizabeth Huelsman's chapter, "The Dynamics of Long-Term Familial Caregiving," interprets case histories to show how experiences and behaviors prior to the current caregiving situation differentially pattern the meaning of caregiving. Chapter 9, "Daughters Caring for Elderly Mothers," by Emily Abel, describes how the dynamics of affection mix with interpersonal history among very significant others, creeping into the daily routines of home care to convey caregiving's manifold feelings and oscillating intergenerational meanings.

Part Three, "Service Provision: Definitions and Decision-Making," takes us outside the household proper and its front-line domestic workers to examine broader contexts that serve to define home care. While the focus is the same—the home care experience—we find that the meaning of home care roles, actions, and events are bound up with diverse organizational, professional, and public policy interests and agendas. James Holstein's chapter, "Describing Home Care: Discourse and Image in Involuntary Commitment Proceedings," instructs us about the place of language and professional image in the interpretations of household events and domestic order. In a useful caution against too naturalistic an ethnography, Holstein argues that being in the home is no guarantee that one succeeds in "accurately" defining the organization of caregiving. The next chapter, "Transformations of Home: The Formal and Informal Process of Home Care Planning," by Ann Dill, extends the argument to show how perspective produces facts otherwise considered to be undeniable features of domestic life. Taken together, the Holstein and Dill chapters indicate how definitional and decision-making issues intertwine, regardless of the age of care receivers and caregivers. Finally, in a chapter entitled "Policing the Family? Health Visiting and the Public Surveillance of Private Behavior," Robert Dingwall and Kathleen Robinson raise important public policy questions concerning the borders of household care and its privacies on the one hand and, on the other, the increasing demand for surveillance by a welfare state bent on quality assurance in the care of its citizenry. While centered on the surveillance of home care for the young, the chapter is broadly suggestive of looming issues in home care for all ages.

Although research in home care is virtually exploding, we hope this collection will persuade practitioners, researchers, and policymakers to pause to consider guiding assumptions and taken-for-granted concepts before moving ahead. As the onus of care is increasingly placed on families, significant others, and the home, they deserve to be understood in their own terms, against the complex and varied backgrounds that both influence and articulate the caregiving effort.

## *References*

Anderson, S. A., & Bagarozzi, D. A. (1983). The use of family myths as an aid to strategic therapy, *Journal of Family Therapy, 5,* 145-154.

Bagarozzi, D. A., & Anderson, S. A. (1982). The evolution of family mythological systems: Considerations for meaning, clinical assessment, and treatment, *Journal of Psychoanalytic Anthropology, 5,* 71-90.

Bermann, E. (1973). *The scapegoat.* Ann Arbor: University of Michigan Press.

Gubrium, J. F. (1987). Organizational embeddedness and family life. In T. Brubaker (Ed.), *Aging, Health and Family,* (pp. 23-41). Newbury Park, CA: Sage.

Gubrium, J. F. (1988). Family responsibility and caregiving in the qualitative analysis of the Alzheimer's disease experience, *Journal of Marriage and the Family, 50,* 197-207.

Gubrium, J. F., & Lynott, R. J. (1987). Measurement and the interpretation of burden in the Alzheimer's disease experience, *Journal of Aging Studies, 1,* 265-285.

Gwyther, L. P., & George, L. K. (1986). Symposium. Caregivers for dementia patients: Complex determinants of well-being and burden. Introduction, *Gerontologist, 26,* 245-247.

Henry, J. (1985). My life with the families of psychotic children. In G. Handel (Ed.), *The Psychosocial Interior of the Family* (pp. 51-66). New York: Aldine.

Kanter, D., & Lehr, W. (1977). *Inside the Family.* San Francisco: Jossey-Bass.

Laing, R. D., & Esterson, A. (1964). *Sanity, madness, and the family.* Baltimore: Penguin.

LaRossa, R., & Wolff, J. H. (1985). On qualitative family research, *Journal of Marriage and the Family, 47,* 531-541.

Leff, J. & Vaughn, C. (1985). *Expressed emotion in families.* London: Guilford Press.

Morycz, R. K. (1985). Caregiving strain and the desire to institutionalize family members with Alzheimer's disease. *Research on Aging, 7,* 329-361.

Poulshock, S. W., & Deimling, G. T. (1984). Families caring for elders and in residence: Issues in the measurement of burden. *Journal of Gerontology, 39,* 230-239.

Reiss, D., Gonzalez, S., & Kramer, N. (1986). Family process, chronic illness, and death. *Archives of General Psychiatry, 43,* 795-804.

Rubinstein, R. (1987). The significance of personal objects to older people. *Journal of Aging Studies, 1,* 225-238.

Sankar, A. (1986). Out of the clinic into the home: Control and communication in patient-physician relations. *Social Science and Medicine, 22,* 973-982.

Sankar, A. (1987, November). Home observation: A qualitative and quantitative approach. Delivered at the annual meeting, Gerontological Society of America, Washington, DC.

Sankar, A. (1988). The home as a site for teaching gerontology and geriatrics. In M. Lock & D. Gordon (Eds.), *Knowledge and practice in medicine* (pp. 155-174). Holland: Reidel.

Sankar, A., & Becker, S. (1985). The home visit as an educational tool for the medical student's decision-making in chronic illness and geriatrics. *Journal of Medical Education, 60,* 308-313.

Sankar, A., Newcomer, R., & Wood, J. (1986). Perspective payment: Systemic effects on community care for the elderly. *Home Health Care Services Quarterly, 7*(2):93-117.

Skolnick, A. S. (1983). *The intimate environment.* Boston: Little, Brown.

Soldo, B. J., & Manton, K. G. (1985). Changes in the health status and service needs of the oldest old: Current patterns and future friends. *Milbank Memorial Fund Quarterly Health and Society, 63*(2):286-319.

Stone, R., Cafferata, G. L., & Sang, I. J. (1987). Caregivers of the frail elderly: A national profile: *The Gerontologist, 27,* 616-628.

Steinglass, P. (1979). The home observation assessment method (HOAM): Real time naturalistic observation of families in their homes. *Family Process, 18,* 337-354.

Zarit, S. H. (1989). Do we need another stress and caregiving study? *The Gerontologist, 29* (2):147.

# PART ONE:


# The Home as Sickroom

# 1

# The Dependent Elderly, Home Health Care, and Strategies of Household Adaptation

## STEVEN M. ALBERT

## Introduction

Ethnographic research has shown how household organization plays an important role in a wide variety of health contexts, such as sanitary practices, nutrition, responses to morbidity, decisions to seek medical care, and the interpretation of symptoms. In particular, anthropologists have stressed the ways that variation across households *mediates* the effect of disease transmission or attempts to improve health. For example, variation in task allocation and the organization of work within households makes some households more efficient in preparing food and securing adequate nutrition for family members (Pelto & Pelto, 1984). The anthropological emphasis on household organization is equally relevant in assessing the ways that households marshal resources to meet a health crisis, such as acute illness or chronic disability in a family member. Mobilization of the material and psychological

AUTHOR'S NOTE: The research reported here was supported by an NIMH program project grant (MH43371) to the Philadelphia Geriatric Center, "Family caregiving and the dependent elderly," M. Powell Lawton, E. Brody, and R. Pruchno, principal investigators. I thank Elaine Brody and Robert Rubinstein for allowing me to use transcript materials from earlier pilot interviews with caregivers, and Jay Gubrium and Andrea Sankar for comments on an earlier draft of the paper.

resources required for such caregiving also differs across households; one task from an ethnographic perspective on the home care experience is to document the range of variation in this *household production of care*. How do households meet the disruptions in family life associated with illness? What makes family caregivers more or less successful in coping with these challenges? What adaptation strategies emerge within households for managing care demands?

A wide range of research has shown that the household is the key element in the organization of care for the chronically ill and impaired elderly. Families, organized as households, provide 80 to 90 percent of the medical and personal care required by the elderly (Brody, 1985). This is true even for severely impaired, older adults whose functional limitations and care needs are virtually identical to those of the institutionalized, nursing home population. For example, nearly one quarter of the elderly in the United States are functionally disabled and require assistance with personal care (bathing, dressing, toileting), help with the instrumental activities of daily living (shopping, cooking), and nursing care of the kind typically provided by a skilled nurse or health aide (changing dressings, administering oxygen). Yet only one in five of these elders receives care in a nursing home; the other four are cared for at home (Doty, 1986). Use of the formal support system of nursing, homemaking, and counseling services is usually delayed until family resources have been stretched as far as possible; even when formal services are engaged, households always combine formal support with family supports. Likewise, nursing home placements are normally an option of last resort. Among the small number of families that do institutionalize an elder, nursing home placements are usually sought only when the elder's health declines dramatically (and quickly, before a family has had time to adapt), or when some change in the household (divorce, illness of the caregiver) affects the capacity to render care. As Brody puts it, "the family, virtually unnoticed, had invented long term care well before that phrase was articulated" (Brody, 1985).

Given the deep-seated commitment of families to care for impaired parents at home, it would be valuable to know more about the ways households adapt to the demands of caregiving. In accommodating household organization to the needs of an impaired elder, families make a continuing, often implicit appraisal of the *disruptiveness* of an elder's impairments and the caregiving demands bound up with them: Is my mother's condition such that caregiving can be peripheral to normal, ongoing household activity? Does giving her effective care now require that the household be thoroughly reorganized around caregiving tasks? It must be stressed that this appraisal process is only partly determined by the severity of an elder's impairment. The bedridden elder who is moved to the first-floor living room certainly becomes newly prominent in household activity, as patterns of interaction, contact with friends, and utilization of space are all altered. Yet it is striking that in some households the same living rooms are hardly altered and remain the focus of family life despite the presence of the elder. Caregivers and their families continue to gather there to watch television at night, to converse, or simply to relax. Other households respond differently, either by refusing to relocate the parent to the center of the home or by taking the living room out of circulation once the parent has been moved.

This chapter reports on ethnographic data gathered within caregiving households to explore variation in adaptation to caregiving demands and parental impairment. A major finding of the research concerns the importance of particular *adaptation strategies* that evolve within households and which allow them to render care more effectively. As we will see, such strategies in fact often evolve explicitly to *prevent* the radical reorganization of the household that is threatened by over-whelming caregiving demands. In a phrase that recurs again and again, caregivers say they "draw lines" between caregiving tasks and the noncaregiving component of the household. After a brief discussion of the source of these data, we shall explore the nature of parental impair-ment as a disruption of household organization and the ways house-holds prepare for such disruption, and actual strategies used by care-givers to adapt household organization to caregiving demands. We conclude with a discussion of the ways that knowledge of such adaption might be useful in designing interventions to help caregivers.

### Subjects and Method

To pursue these above-mentioned questions, semistructured inter-views with a pool of 75 caregivers were conducted. These interviews typically lasted 90 to 120 minutes. A smaller sample of 15 households participated in repeated interviews stressing adaptation to caregiving. These were conducted once a month over a 6 month period, with two interviews conducted in the respondent's home and three conducted as follow-up telephone calls. The interviews drew on a "care diary" that caregivers filled out to keep track of their parent's changing health needs and their own caregiving responses. Unfortunately, the diary was only partly useful as a source of data. Many caregivers found it onerous to record what seemed to them to be "more of the same old thing"—doctor's visits for chronic minor illnesses; successive alterations of medications; and continued bouts with a parent's constipation, refusal to drink water, sleeplessness, etc. The result was that only few households produced reliable data on the frequency of changes in household routine. However, the diary elicitation was useful in stimulating caregivers to think about the ways they respond to caregiving demands.

The interviews were part of a larger, ongoing study of caregiving as a cultural system (Albert, in press), which represents the ethnographic portion of the Philadelphia Geriatric Center's program project on caregiver mental health and the dependent elderly. Subjects were recruited through word of mouth; public service announcements; and fliers sent to caregiver support groups, adult day care centers, and related social service and medical facilities. In addition, tapes and transcripts from two prior studies conducted by the Philadelphia Geriatric Center were reviewed. Interview material was supplemented by direct observation of household organization and material culture.

For this study, we restricted caregiving households to those of daughters, daughters-in-law, and sons of the impaired elder. We did not require that caregivers and impaired elders be coresident. Also, a number of caregivers reported on caregiving that had taken place prior to a nursing home placement or death of the parent. We reasoned that a degree of distance from the caregiving might allow retrospective insight on the ways the household had changed in response to caregiving demands.

The interviews yielded a great deal of verbal transcript material concerning caregivers' progressive socialization into the role of caregiver, their interpretation of when they had become a caregiver, and their perception of key markers in the periodization of their caregiving career. A number of open-ended questions were also asked of informants specifically to elicit caregivers' perceptions of household adaptation to caregiving demands. These included the following:

1. Do you have any special tricks or techniques that make caregiving easier? What are they? Can you remember how they first got started?
2. Would you say your caregiving has gotten easier with time? What has gotten easier? What has made it easier?
3. Are there certain family routines that seem to have emerged in response to the demands of caregiving?
4. What has gotten you through the hard times of caregiving? What do you do when you feel you need to get away from it all?

## Parental Impairment as a Disruption of Household Organization

In what sense do caregiving demands disrupt a household? Beyond the obvious, changes in the utilization of space in a home and alterations in a family's activity patterns are more subtle and complex forces of change. Relocation of a newly impaired parent to a caregiver's home is both more and less disruptive than one might expect, or more accurately, it disrupts the different components of the household regime to varying degrees.

### Household Preadaptation

The unexpected rapid decline of a parent, who then lands in the lap of a family unprepared for the event, is quite rare. Households begin their adaptation to caregiving demands long before acute illness forces a relocation of the impaired elder (or the relocation of a caregiver to the parent's home), just as households continue to care for a parent who has been removed from the home and placed in a nursing home. Sensory and cognitive deficits, functional limitations associated with chronic illness, and loss of the parent's informal support system (e.g., through the death of a spouse) usually precede the acute crisis that results in the actual relocation of the parent. This gradual decline leads future caregivers to alter schedules and begin their socialization into the role of caregiver *before* caregiving demands precipitate major changes in the household. With such increasing parental dependence, we find that caregivers and impaired parents begin to form *quasi-households:* For example, a daughter's occasional food shopping or preparation of meals for her mother becomes a regular feature of the week; after the death of her father, an unmarried working daughter begins to stay at her mother's house on weekends so that trips back and forth are less onerous; occasional visits with a daughter's family become more frequent and begin to lengthen in duration, so that when the heater at the parent's house finally breaks, it seems easiest and most appropriate to formalize the relation and admit that the parent really lives with the daughter's family.

When the impaired elder suffers a health crisis that finally precipitates a family gathering to discuss, as one caregiver put it, "who's gonna do for Mom," the outcome of these meetings is mostly decided in advance. One adult child has usually already assumed the role, though such people, on reflection, are often surprised to see how much they have altered their household routine even before they finally define themselves as caregivers. This moment of recognition—the realization that one is a caregiver rather than someone who simply helps out once in a while—is quite complex. Research shows a great deal of variation in the thresholds of such self-definition. A parent's deficits are compared to his or her prior level of competency, which also changes over time. Caregivers find themselves comparing the parent's current disability to a more restricted functional competency. This allows caregivers to deny that the parent is as impaired as he or she really is. Many caregivers, particularly spouses, also cover up for the elder's deficits, often in ways not completely conscious to themselves. Since in some families a father never cooked or did laundry, or a mother never balanced a checkbook or paid bills, a standard for pre-impaired competency may also simply be lacking. Of course, when an adult child finally recognizes herself as a caregiver, she may have to admit that the parent has irrevocably changed and that the relationship between them has been fundamentally altered. One daughter, for example, reported that she knew she was a caregiver when her father collapsed and her mother stood by confused and unable to take action; the daughter realized that she alone possessed the wherewithal and concern that could keep her parents alive. It is significant, however, that a great many caregivers reach this point only after a long history of adaptation and selective recognition.

Another source of such preadaptation involves caregivers' *self-selection* to the role of caregiver. While many say "there was no one else" in explaining why they became caregivers, quite often there is in fact someone else. This yields another clue as to how households preadapt to caregiving demands. Research reveals that one child becomes the primary caregiver, and that being female, single, nonworking, and living near the parents all predict selection to the role of caregiver (Ikels, 1983). This has been shown to result in a bias toward youngest adult children, who may still reside with the parent when functional limitations become apparent and who may delay a move out of the home because of anticipated caregiving obligations. Less often remarked in the process of caregiver selection is the active role of one child in excluding siblings who might also become caregivers. While active competition between siblings over who will become the caregiver is rare, our research reveals that the child who becomes caregiver often pre-selects him- or herself by taking a greater interest in the parent's welfare, by staying near or moving near the parent, and by preparing her household in advance for the parent's eventual relocation. These adult children are not always the favorite children of the parents; in fact, some seek increased intimacy with the parent through such overtures. Preselection in this sense ranges from quite conscious planning to a more or less implicit coadaptation within families, a relationship in which a set of siblings allocates different caregiving responsibilities among themselves while reserving primary responsibility for the one who has already shown the greatest interest. The pre- or self-selected caregiver often is motivated by a desire to provide the parent with a *family,* quite apart from caring for the parent's needs or illness.

This exclusion of rivals and stress on the family links caregiving to other processes in which a single family member makes a sacrifice for another family member. A striking parallel, for example, can be seen in the case of kidney transplantation. Research by Simmons and her colleagues has shown that the person who donates a kidney to a family member often takes actions that give other potential donors an excuse to bow out (Simmons, Klein, & Thorton, 1973). Likewise, a family member feels a greater obligation to donate when he or she is the only one available (as determined by medical evaluation), when he or she has fewer family obligations, and when he or she adopts the spontaneous norm-directed decision style that is consistent with commitment to family as a paramount value. Thus the caregiver who states that she offered to have her mother join her household without any concern as to whether her siblings would make the offer is behaving quite similarly to the kidney donor. This caregiver has already taken a series of antecedent steps that has given her siblings an opportunity *not* to provide care.

The upshot of this preadaptation to caregiving and the formation of quasi-households involving the elder is that the transition to caregiving is less disruptive than one would expect. The majority of caregivers in our sample *expected* to share their household, once they noted that their parents were beginning to need help. And, as we have seen, many alter their routines in anticipation of doubling up with a parent, going so far as to take actions that give their siblings an opportunity not to get involved.

### The Limits to Preadaptation

While the decision to become a caregiver appears to be relatively easy and straightforward in its implications, putting a limit on such care—that is, knowing when one has done enough—is not so easy. Rendering care *to* a parent quickly becomes a sign of how much one cares *about* a parent. Caregivers assert that if you care for someone (definition one, if you love and show concern for that person), then you must be caring (i.e., you provide nursing care for that person when he or she is infirm). Since care (definition two) is normatively unbounded, many feel that being caring must be similarly unbounded, even when it exceeds one's resources and affects the health of the caregiver—even, we might add, when the demented recipient of such care bears only the most remote relation to one's mother or father. For many, to do anything less means that one's care for the parent was not deep enough or true. The anxiety caregivers feel on this score is summed up well in an adage often recited by caregivers: "A parent can take care of many children, but many children can't take care of even one parent." The shift in meaning between the two senses of *care* is elided.

Intensive interviews with caregivers reveal that this uncertainty regarding the limits of one's obligation to render care is perhaps the greatest source of disruption in household organization. If one is always on call, always expected to do more, and never sure one is doing enough, it is impossible to plan for the future or maintain any interest outside caregiving. Caregiving in this case absorbs all household resources. The caregiver who can say, "I know I've done all I can possibly do, a 100 % plus," is usually one who has allowed her household to be maximally disrupted by caregiving demands. The same caregiver, for example, also claimed that she was continually unsteady on her feet because of the loss of sleep and daily fatigue brought on by caregiving demands. Even caregivers who do expend all their resources on care-giving may doubt themselves. For them, the impaired parent must die at home; otherwise the child's loyalty to the parent and commitment to caregiving are suspect.

Preparing oneself to become a caregiver in the ways outlined above does not seem to be associated with an ability to set limits on such care once one has become a caregiver. This ability to set limits must be learned. However, if caregivers are differentially predisposed to learn how to set these limits, one significant factor predicting their ability to do so appears to be their own status as parents (Albert, in press). Caregivers who are parents themselves are evidently more likely to set limits on what is enough in caregiving. It would seem that being a parent is associated with some degree of psychological distance from one's own parents, or perhaps having children leads to a greater sense that one has obligations that rival commitment to parental care. More research is required on this point.

Having made the choice to care for a parent at home, how do caregivers set limits to caregiving demands? Our research shows that households have evolved two broad sets of strategies for limiting the disruptions caused by caregiving demands. The first involves establish-ing *routines* for caregiving tasks, a strategy that limits disruptions of temporal and spatial order. The second strategy involves *role redefini-tion,* which limits disruptions of social organization. The two together allow members of caregiving households, as many say, "to balance our lives," to establish a boundary for their obligation to render care. In practice, this means imposition of a routine for caregiving tasks and a redefinition of one's relation to a parent.

### Routines and Ritualization of Caregiving Tasks

One can easily imagine the value of a *routine* for performing care-giving tasks. Imposition of a routine means fixity in timing, place, and sequence—in short, more certainty with respect to what the task con-sists of and a clearer sense of when it is complete. A routine for bathing, feeding, or administering medications establishes regular borders and patterning. It makes caregiving more finite: something is done in a certain way, it is then completed, and one can go on to other things. Such routinization is an obvious candidate for limiting the disruptiveness of unbounded caregiving demands. Many caregivers measure their mastery of the situation by the routines they have established for getting the job done.

It is curious, however, that caregivers often speak of these routines in other terms. Rather than stop with talk of efficiency or expediency, many go on to speak of the *rightness* or even special *efficacy* of doing the task just this way. They may feel that the care routines actually have a medical effect or restorative power. They adhere to the routine even when the parent's condition has changed significantly and thereby made the routine inefficient, a sign that the routine has a meaning *apart* from its function in getting the job done. When these conditions remain, routine gives way to *ceremony* or *ritual*. The routine becomes a symbol of something else and begins to carry its own set of meanings.

Why routines, which have a clear value in limiting the disruptiveness of caregiving, should shade into ceremonies that may not do so is an interesting question. One respondent, a son caring for his mother, is worth quoting at length on this issue because his case illustrates how these routines shade into rituals in ways that are not always conscious to caregivers. He speaks of his routines as "shortcuts," or efficiency techniques, that benefit both his mother and himself, the former because such care prevents skin breakdown and additional illness, the latter because the routines allow him to concentrate his energies and complete the task efficiently.

> As time went on, and my mother became more physically deteriorated and less conscious about me and her as far as her dignity was concerned, it became more a matter of fact, or routine, for me to do things: A, B, C, D, or 1, 2, 3, 4, everyday. It's probably more boring because of the routine. You get up an hour and half earlier in the morning, make the breakfast, wash her, change her, diaper her. . . . It was just my response of what I had to do. I had to attend to her with tunnel-vision precision. The more I would do, and the more consistently I would stick to my routine, the greater it was not just to my mother's benefit, but to mine too.

While this attitude toward the scheduling of care tasks may not sound like ritual, it is only a small step from such a routine to notions of magical causation and symbolic efficacy. For example, this caregiver goes on to describe a bathing-exercise ritual that he felt made his mother look younger and which rejuvenated her skin.

I would pull her forward, massage her back; then I would take each arm separately, or both together, and exercise them. . . . I would take my jacket off, roll up my sleeves, and I would start to perspire. The sweat would run down my forehead. I would massage her legs with the washcloth, then her feet, and I would go through each individual toe.

It does not seem wrong to describe this last routine as ritual, first because it increased the amount of time required for caregiving and second because the caregiver ascribed great, possibly magical, regenerative power to it. We might also add that he performed it *after* his mother was admitted to a nursing home and when she was already almost completely comatose.

The transformation of routine into ritual is prominent as well in the power caregivers ascribe to "going through the motions" of normalcy in the care of an Alzheimer's patient. Caregivers are counseled to find meaningful activity for the Alzheimer's victim or to surround him with objects (e.g., photographs) that anchor him to his former identity. Some caregivers recognize that such advice is largely wishful thinking for the advanced Alzheimer's patient, but others persist in the routine long after it could plausibly have such an effect. Some caregivers go further and feel that a *pretense* of autonomy for an impaired parent may have this effect. To foster such normalcy, caregivers devise systems for reminding the impaired parent where he or she is and what he or she is supposed to do. This may take the form of notes in large print placed at strategic points in the house. Caregivers may also purposely keep leases or accounts in the parent's name to encourage such autonomy, as the following quotation indicates:

I had tricks. I always wanted things in Mom's name, to give her control. But I had to coach her on the phone. Later, I used paper plates [for] notes to my Mom, in big black magic-marker letters. It would say, "Stay inside. Do not leave." I'd put them in several places. . . . Everybody in my neighborhood knew that my mother was impaired, but for the longest time I wanted to hide it. I coached her. The utilities and lease are in her name. I believe in the theory, "if you don't use it, you lose it." If you teach them and have them go through all the motions, you can keep them going through the lapses. It comes back.

Thus while caregivers clearly understand the benefits of routinizing caregiving tasks as an adaptive strategy, there is a tendency for these routines to take on a life of their own in the form of ceremonies that may rival the caregiving tasks in their disruptiveness.

Even routines that do not take on a ceremonial quality can become a problem. The routines may still gain a life of their own, which again interferes with caregiving. In such cases, the caregiving routine becomes more important than the object of such care, namely the elder whose needs mandate such care. For example, one caregiver actually spoke positively of the gastrectomy her mother had to undergo and the introduction of parenteral feeding for her. "The feeding tube makes care for Mother easy, a real breeze." On the one hand, the gastrectomy did in fact make caregiving easier. This caregiver's experience reminds us that when the impaired parent is *less* incapacitated, caregiving may actually be harder. An impaired parent who can walk may require more observation, emotional support, and cognitive guidance; an impaired parent able to swallow may require more time and effort to ensure proper food intake. On the other hand, in this caregiver's case, a caregiving routine seems to have displaced the goal of securing maximum health and independence for the impaired elder. Is such a caregiving routine adaptive when it distorts the reasons for rendering such care in the first place? We take up this point below.

### Caregiving and the Redefinition of Roles Within the Household

Caregivers render care for parents who are no longer capable of fulfilling the parental role and who may, in fact, appear to be reverting to earlier stages in the life-course; in such instances, the adult children begin to make decisions for them and, in extreme cases, may even diaper an incontinent parent. Consequently, caregivers often speak of their parents as "regressing" to childhood. The situation is further complicated by cognitive impairments, such as Alzheimer's disease, which may lead some parents to address their own children as a parent or spouse. This is especially unsettling to caregivers. Some caregivers to parents with Alzheimer's disease have taken the idea of regression a step further and claim that the final stage of the disease results in a parent assuming the fetal position once again, completing the imputed regression to childhood in an extremely vivid form.

It is not surprising, then, that a second set of adaptive strategies has emerged within caregiver households that revolve around the redefinition of roles within the family. Daily acts of personal care, such as bathing, diapering, grooming, and feeding, seem to be the most charged in this respect, since they force an adult child to assume a relation of parental intimacy with his or her own parent. Exposure to a parent's nudity is perhaps the greatest challenge to cross-sex caregiving, as when a daughter must diaper her father, or a son his mother. In such cases, the spouses of a patient may feel that this parent-child intimacy violates their own spousal intimacy. While daughters who are on very intimate terms with their mothers do not seem to chafe at the confusion of roles implied in such caregiving, other caregivers find that they need to redefine the role of parent and child in such situations.

One response to this home care situation is the *infantilization* of the parent (that is, speaking of the parent as a child) and the associated idea that this stage of life is characterized by "role reversal," in which children become "parents" to their own parents. A second strategy is to reconceive the parent as a *patient* and the caregiver as a nurse or doctor. A third strategy common among our sample of caregivers is simply to reconceive the parent as *someone else,* a stranger, someone who "used to be" Mother or Father.

### Infantilization: The Impaired Parent as a Child

If the parent is no longer a parent but is instead a "child" or "infant," then the threat to prior adult-child relations bound up with caregiving is circumvented. One caregiver's comments will speak for many:

> You know their whole physical make-up. You get real intimate. It's like taking care of a baby. You have to clean them up, dress them, remind them of things they have to do. . . . We needed to reassure her, give her compliments. It's like with a child. You reverse roles. She even called me Mom when she first got sick.

This redefinition of roles obviously builds upon strong similarities between care for the impaired, incontinent parent and care for a child. It is notable, however, that caregivers who make such statements are clearly aware of the ways caring for such a parent is *not* like caring for a child. They selectively emphasize certain elements, choosing to ignore, for example, the different contexts for such incontinence and the different outcomes for the dependency of child and impaired parent.

This selective emphasis points to the importance of the quality of the relationship between the parent and child in determining the caregiver's recourse to this strategy. Infantilization as an adaptive strategy appears to be linked to issues of control on the one hand, and to the attempt to recapture (or perhaps create for the first time) an intimacy associated with the caregiver's own childhood on the other. Thus many daughters report that they enjoy being with a mother more *after* they become caregivers. Many report a return of an idyllic childhood warmth to their household.

**The Elderly Parent as a Patient**

The conversion of a parent to a patient is an alternate strategy in redefining the role of parent and child. While not incompatible with the infantilization of the parent, this strategy emphasizes the *illness* of the parent rather than functional limitations, as the following excerpt shows:

> As time went on and my mother's situation got worse, little by little I adjusted [the bathing routine]. I would have to be there all the time. I was afraid she would drown. My feeling changed. At the very beginning, I still mentally maintained a strong mother-son identity, when it would come to the feeling of dignity. As my mother's physical and mental state deteriorated, my mother almost became a patient, and I became a doctor or nurse. . . . I was very much aware of this psychologically. I [now] saw her as a person who had an illness and needed care. That became more so as her situation deteriorated.

By emphasizing the sickness of the parent, the parent is redefined as a patient. In this way, the disruption of parent-child relations is again circumvented as roles are redefined. The use of this adaptive strategy appears to be linked to the caregiver's prior exposure to nursing and medical experience. For example, the caregiver quoted above served as a paramedic in Vietnam and explicitly drew on this experience in thinking about the care for his mother.

**The Impaired Parent as a Stranger**

The final adaptive strategy related to redefinition of parent-child roles involves the conversion of the parent into some other, perhaps only distantly known, person. Here caregivers admit that they "pretend" the impaired parent is someone else, "a person," as one caregiver put it, "who I visit a few times a day." They may say they are unsure if their mother or father is still the same person.

One case in our sample is particularly striking as an illustration of this strategy because here household caregivers were able to view a parent as two different people: one who was still the parent and another who was someone else. The impaired mother fluctuated between two conditions, a relatively docile state, "the old Maggie," and a more frightening, irrational state, "the other Maggie." The caregivers even mention the analogy to Dr. Jekyll and Mr. Hyde, though they invert it.

> She turned into Mrs. Jekyll. She wouldn't go to bed. She started to holler and really carry on. We would say she turned into the other Maggie. When she was the old Maggie, she was quiet. When you talked to her, she answered. . . . But when she went into the other Maggie, she would get very agitated. Her fingers would go like this. Her eyes would be going back and forth. And she would start talking. It would all be in the past. She would imagine there were people downstairs. She would call out for dead relatives. It would go on all day and into the night. Then she would sleep a day. And then she would be the other Maggie, say, for so many weeks. Then she would change again.

In the one condition, she is the mother; in the other, she is not. Denial that this second "Maggie" is the parent is evident in a distinct name given to her. This division of the mother into two people according to the fluctuations in her condition is an extremely important illustration of the caregiver's ability to view a parent as someone who is both a parent and a stranger to them. In more extreme cases, caregivers are driven to deny that "the person upstairs," as one spoke of her father, really is a parent.

## Conclusion: Adaptation Strategies and Interventions for Caregivers

In this chapter, we have briefly reviewed the ways households reorganize to meet the caregiving needs of an impaired parent. We saw that even before the relocation of parent and caregiver to a common household, households "preadapt" to caregiving demands. Quasi-households emerge as caregivers prepare for the eventual move of the parent. Equally important, adult children who will assume the major caregiving responsibility select themselves to the role. If they do not actually exclude rival sibling caregivers, they give their siblings opportunities for not taking the initiative in caregiving. The pre- or self-selected primary caregiver often feels a need to provide the impaired parent with a family, as well as with the care that only a family can provide.

Given this concern for the parent's well-being, the major problem for caregivers is to set limits in the obligation to render care, for caregiving demands can easily overwhelm a household. Since care *for* a parent quickly comes to be seen as a measure of how much one cares *about* a parent, setting limits is not easy. Even caregivers who have undertaken heroic self-sacrifices for an impaired parent still wonder if they have done enough. For some, only the death of the parent at home offers a guilt-free release from the obligation to render care. Thus drawing a boundary between caregiving tasks and other obligations, wants, and needs becomes an overriding necessity.

Caregiver households erect such boundaries through adaptation strategies. Two such strategies discussed here are the use of routines for caregiving tasks and the redefinition of parent-child roles. Routines for personal and nursing care make caregiving tasks more discrete. The tasks become a distinct part of the day, which can be marked off and considered complete. Other parts of the day are thereby defined as noncaregiving time. Likewise, routines for care establish a division of space within the home. Care demands are performed in a certain place, at a specific time, and in a certain way; these define the tasks as separate from other household and personal activities. Redefinition of roles sets limits to caregiving obligations in another way. The parent is redefined as a child, patient, or stranger. These redefinitions all have the same effect: If the parent is no longer viewed as a parent, one's obligation to render care is attenuated. Redefining the role of the parent also allows caregivers to perform tasks that would normally be seen as inappropriate, such as bathing, diapering, or simply taking control of decisions regarding the parent.

These adaptation strategies evolve within households in an unplanned fashion. They emerge in response to concrete caregiving demands and through a great deal of trial and error. For example, while it is unclear how long it takes a household to establish routines for completing caregiving tasks, our research shows that some households achieve such routinization early on and quickly master caregiving challenges. Other households go through a period of false starts and continual recalibration of tasks and routines until they reach an adequate arrangement. Still other households never seem to reach a level of routinization for care tasks and find themselves in a situation of unending "crisis management." One focus for intervention, then, would be programs to teach caregivers how to establish routines for caregiving tasks. It should be noted that an informal network for sharing ideas on caregiving routines is already in effect by caregiver support groups, which disseminate information on successful management of caregiving tasks. This model should be extended more generally as an adjunct to hospital and adult day care programs.

Based on our research on the routinization of caregiving tasks, an intervention geared to the promotion of such routines should have two goals. First, successful routines for caregiving should be disseminated. Caregivers who have had success with routinization of caregiving tasks should be encouraged to share their experience. One case resulting in the successful dissemination of such a routine is worth mentioning here. One caregiver was at a loss in regard to her mother's continual bouts of severe constipation, which required enemas and suppositories, and made relations with her bedridden mother more difficult. In a Children of Aging Parents (CAPS) support group in Levittown, Pennsylvania, she learned that a daily breakfast involving a mixture of unprocessed bran, applesauce, and prune juice spread on bread was a great help in promoting regularity. The caregiver incorporated this routine into her overall morning caregiving regime. This sort of practical information on ordering caregiving tasks would go a long way toward reducing a caregiver's burden.

The second goal of such an intervention is more difficult. As mentioned above, caregiving routines often take on a ceremonial or ritual sphere, and this ritual component may interfere with the goal of such routinization. Caregiving rituals may make the caregiving tasks more burdensome rather than less, and they may even displace the overall goal of such caregiving. In the latter case, performing the ritualized routine may become more important than actually caring for the impaired parent. The case of the caregiver who welcomed her mother's gastrectomy and parenteral feeding is a case in point. Thus a second goal of such an intervention would be to make caregivers aware of the tendency for such routines to become ritualized. Caregivers may need an outside perspective to tell them when the routine has become an oppressive or inadequate ceremonial. This may be more problematic, as the case material cited above illustrates. If a caregiver feels his routine of washing rejuvenates his mother and he is willing to spend the extra time this ritual requires, should he be dissuaded from doing so? While the goal of the intervention is to make caregiving easier, we must be careful not to upset stronger, more profound beliefs that allow caregivers to take on so fundamental a commitment.

The role redefinition strategy could also be taught to caregivers, perhaps in a similar support group environment. While this recasting of roles seems to come naturally to caregivers, at the very least caregivers could be counseled not to feel guilty about their inability to see the demented parent as a parent. More radically, caregivers could be encouraged to regard the impaired parent more as a patient than a child or stranger. This redefinition may be most appropriate in later stages of impairment, since it avoids the enmeshment characteristic of parent-child role reversal and the guilt associated with viewing the parent as a stranger.

## References

Albert, S. M. (1990). Caregiving as a cultural system: Conceptions of filial obligations and parental dependency in urban America. *American Anthropologist, 92*(2).

Brody, E. (1985). Parent care as a normative family stress. *The Gerontologist, 25*(1), 19-29.

Doty, P. (1986). Family care of the elderly: The role of public policy. *The Milbank Memorial Quarterly, 64*(1), 34-75.

Ikels, C. (1983). The process of caregiver selection. *Research on Aging, 5*, 491-509.

Pelto, G., & Pelto, P. (1984). Anthropological methodologies for assessing household organization and structure. In D. E. Sahn, R. Lockwood, & N. S. Scrimshaw (Eds.) *Methods for the evaluation of the impact of food and nutrition programs* (pp. 204-225). Tokyo: The United Nations University.

Simmons, R. G., Klein, S. D., & Thorton, K. (1973). Family decision-making and the selection of a kidney transplant donor. *Journal of Comparative Family Studies, 4*, 88-115.

*2*

# Culture and Disorder in the Home Care Experience:

## The Home as Sickroom

ROBERT L. RUBINSTEIN

An important and neglected aspect of the home care experience is the experience of *home*. For many people, feelings about home are strong. Moreover, developmental, psychological, and sociocultural meanings may be embodied in the home environment. Such feelings and meanings become especially significant for the caregiver and the care receiver in a home care setting. It is the case that intensive care and close monitoring may best be enabled only when the caregiver and the care receiver share a residence. In the case in which a spouse is no longer available for caregiving tasks, as is frequently the case with impaired older women, the challenge of care falls on an adult child. A fundamental dilemma for the child is that by inviting a demented (and to a lesser

AUTHOR'S NOTE: Data described in this chapter were collected in two research projects, "The meaning and function of home for the elderly," supported by the National Institue of Aging (RO1 AG05204) and "Senile dementia patients: Mental health of caregivers" (M. P. Lawton, PI) supported by the National Institute of Mental Health (MH 37292). The support of these institutes and of Dr. Lawton is gratefully acknowledged. I am also indebted to the editors for their comments on the various drafts of this chapter.

I am indebted to the caregivers who spoke with me about their lives and situations. All were middle-aged children caring at home for a parent with severe symptoms of senile dementias. All names here are pseudonyms and, in some instances, specific details have been altered to preserve anonymity.

degree, a frail) parent into the home, the child admits a degree of disorder to his or her carefully constructed domestic world. If the home environment is a projection or representation of the persons who have made that space, then the presence of disorder in that environment in the form of a demented parent may have significance for the caregiver beyond the caregiving tasks.

Fundamentally, the home represents both a cultural (shared) system for order and each person's interpretation or version of shared community values about space, organization, and being. Therefore, the home represents each person's continued developmental strivings (Rubinstein, 1989a) as each seeks both to enact and represent identity, growth and change.

This chapter concerns the meaning of home to elders who have Alzheimer's disease or related dementias, who are cared for at home by middle-aged caregivers and the meaning of home for these caregivers themselves. Some meanings attributed to "home" by a sample of middle-aged persons will be described, as will the experience of home by middle-aged children caring at home for a demented elderly parent along with their reports concerning what their demented parents feel about their homes. Some salient aspects of the experience of home when it has been transformed into a sickroom will be outlined and related to the issue of developmental strivings of both the caregiver and care receiver. Thus instances when order, disorder and developmental strivings come into conflict will be discussed.

Data reported here were derived from two research projects. Fourteen persons age 40 to 60, as well as approximately equal numbers of persons age 20 to 30, and 65 and older, were interviewed over a two- to three-hour period in a semistructured format as part of a larger project entitled "The Meaning and Function of Home for the Elderly." Data from this project are reported immediately below, and additional data are reported in Rubinstein (1989a). The remainder of the data reported here derives from ethnographically based, in-depth interviews with seven middle-aged children who cared for a demented parent at home. Additional material on this project is reported in Rubinstein (1989b).

### Defining Home

The term *home* is one of the richest symbols in Western culture with seemingly endless attributional valence. Home is a key cultural symbol that has a wide range of meanings, and a seemingly endless possibility for usage and extension. It exists both as a focal cultural image, as the independent dwelling enclosing the nuclear family and in the family's wide variety of actualities. Basic to the meaning of home are the various elements of control, security, family development, independence, comfort, protection, feelings, and the presence of people. Despite (or perhaps because of) the increasing medicalization of significant events in American life, to keep a sick person at home means, in essence, that the person is not fully "sick." In comparison with other alternatives, to be at home represents a more active personhood. The function of the home as protector and familiar, may play an important part in modulating illness or redefining a situation as not being one of illness.

Part of the research project on the meaning and function of home considered the meaning of home to middle aged persons. Asked whether his dwelling was home and why, a 52-year-old man said,

> Yes, it's home. . . . It's comfortable, it belongs to me. I own it. I can do what I want. . . . All the people and things that I'm used to. . . . that I like, I love, are here.

A 48-year-old married woman noted,

> Yes. It's home. There's a lot of good feelings here. My husband and I enjoyed building our life together here. Our children were born here, they were here when they were young. My family has been in this area for a very long time. . . . We've been through a lot here.

The idea of the family in terms of generations may also be emphasized. A 49- year-old married woman noted,

> It's the good times we've had here. . . . the good memories. My kids, my husband. Proud memories of my daughters and my son. They're all wrapped up in this place. . . . It's the things with the kids. [The meaning is] the love we have for one another, the acceptance of one another . . .

A married woman, age 53 related,

> It's home. I had my kids here. We've been here for 25 years. My kids come back now. It's the kids coming to a place that makes it home . . . [The

meaning is] the family. If I was a woman without children, I wouldn't want
to be here. The meaning of the place is the people.

If the meaning of the place—that is to say, the home—is the people,
then the place is inexorably tied up in the lives of individuals as they
are born, age, and die. Additionally, because home is a key cultural
symbol, the meanings attributed to home may be multiple, situational,
and malleable.

As will be shown in the cases below, the home, as a sickroom,
expresses three sorts of meaning in terms of caregiving. These are the
home as an arena of both moral and tactical concerns, the home as
embodying various models of family and generation, and the home as
a stage for the personal tasks of caregiving.

The moral and tactical meaning of home pertains to two key aspects
of the experience of home in regard to the caregiving task. Home may
be defined in terms of coresidence and thus as the setting for the more
practical, tactical aspects of caregiving. The impaired person is close
at hand, and care tasks may therefore be performed parsimoniously.
Alternatively, home may be defined in terms of a moral function. The
home expresses love, unity, and caring and is believed to have a curative
or restorative effect above and beyond its technical role in facilitating
care.

Related to these factors are a number of models of home that are held
singly or multiply and conflictually by caregivers. These models relate
to developmental strivings (see below), and are often in the background
to the meaning of life as a whole in the caregiving effort. The first model
sees the home as the setting for the young nuclear family, comprised of
parents and preadult children; in this instance, the house is a setting for
the developmental work of raising these children and maintaining ties
to them as they go out into the world. In this model, the home is
nurturant and derives value in how it compares to other, similar homes,
but it is separate from them and therefore exclusivist. The charter myth
of this home is of the family as pioneers, as beginning anew with each
generation. In contrast, an alternative model of the home is as multigenerational and inclusive of three or more generations, nurturant, and
of a single mind across the generations. The charter myth of this home
is the belief that in unity the family survives. The third and final model
is of the home as collaterally organized: Although centered around an
apical ancestor, it is laterally organized around several siblings who

define one location as a central place although they may all maintain independent households. The charter myth of this home is the inviolability of the sibling set.

Finally, the home may be viewed as a stage for the personal tasks of caregiving. In this instance, there is a central paradox. The first element in this paradox is the caregiver's role in maintaining the independence of the impaired person and thus enhancing the quality of life that he or she loves. A long standing separation of households or decades of geographical distance in the caregiving dyad are negated as the impaired elder comes to reside in the caregiving child's home. Even if the elder has never lived in this home, there is a familiarity and warmth of people reflected in the place.

The second element is the need to contain the demented person's irrational or destructive behaviors within the context of the domestic order created by the caregiver. The domestic order is the reality of home life: the home as a physical place, the use of space, and the role of routines and procedures in daily life. Order implies defining and organizing space, making and following rules, and restricting disorder. With home care come changes in the household, as the home in whole or in part becomes a sickroom. Changes occur in space use, daily routine, wear, noise, odor, and so on.

When the caregivers are children and the care receivers parents (as in the cases described below), the situation is additionally complex in that a third element—that of developmental striving—intervenes. Individuation is often incomplete, and tasks of individuation continue over the life span. While parent and child may have lived apart for decades or had little contact, a relationship will be renewed and redefined in particular ways through coresidence.

There are two scenarios to consider here. The first is the case in which the caregiver has in some way used the home to establish a sense of order in the world. One important meaning of home is as a haven or refuge from the world. The home thus serves to order the world into the safer domain, that which is defined, controlled and managed, and the outside, which is more problematic. A major psychological predisposition is embodied in the way the home is defined with respect to the world. There is little doubt that the individual who defines the home in this way will significantly feel the disorder inherent in the presence of a demented person. The second, and probably more common, instance is when the home is defined as the aggregate of ongoing life events, and aspects of the home, including possessions, decor, and routines represent who the person is and, in contrast to future organizations that may be planned or contemplated, who the person hopes to be, and his or her ongoing developmental strivings. Caregiving may lead to an interruption or alteration of developmental strivings as represented in the home. As one's life is "put on hold" when caregiving, a task for which the end is largely unpredictable, the home, as a representation of personal development and change, is similarly put on hold.

In a sense, the goal for the caregiver is to increase independence, express love, offer care and give dignity to a person whose increasing disorientation and disease may bring disorder and intrusion, requiring restriction. The line between enhancement and containment, mediated by pressures on personal and familial development, becomes increasingly problematic. An end point or limit of tolerance must eventually be defined.

Because a home is symbolically more than the sum of its parts, there are two additional points that should be mentioned here. In choosing to define the home in terms of people, family, or generations, the home is recast with a temporal dimension. It may encode a time span as well as a place. It is as if the home becomes a story of a family's generations: the actual physical space and the tenure, be it of short or long duration, become unimportant. Rather, the story is reframed as births and deaths, the ushering in and out of generations (Rubinstein, 1989b).

Related to this is the important quality of home as a cultural symbol. Home represents not only the mundane daily details of everyday existence but a framing or distancing device. To put questions about a life in terms of home (as a narrative technique) leads to a telling of the story from a distance, with hindsight, or reflectively. On the one hand, alternative perspectives are represented in the home as specific individuals and their realities and, on the other hand, the home as a collective representation—the home as a narrative of lives and generations. This latter perspective serves as a device for the long view, a frame for standing back.

### Three Cases

In the next part of this chapter, I discuss examples of caregiving by middle- aged children to senile elders that reflect a variety of themes of culture and disorder. These cases illustrate the moral and tactical meaning of home, various models of homes and issues of enhancement, containment, and conflicts over developmental strivings when the home has become a sickroom.

### Case 1. Bob Lewis

When I first interviewed Mr. Lewis, 43, he lived with his mother, 79, who was senile and severely ill. She was on a waiting list for a nursing home and would enter one several months after our interview in 1986. I met with Mr. Lewis again, about 6 months after his mother's placement. Mr. Lewis, who was from an Irish working-class background, was unmarried and worked as a salesman in a bookstore. He lived with his mother in a row house in northeast Philadelphia. Because he worked, he had a companion from church to take care of his mother, who stayed with her from 8 AM to 7 PM, five days a week. Despite the low amount he paid the companion, this arrangement was a financial strain for him. He had one sister, married with no children, who lived about half an hour away from him.

A series of incidents marking his mother's downward trajectory began about four years before our interview and included a possible stroke on Christmas Day, 1982. Mr. Lewis described the period between 1982 and 1984 as one of "a progressive loss of function." A major transitional incident occurred in October 1984. Mr. Lewis noted,

I was out with my girlfriend from about 4:30 in the afternoon till about 10:30 at night. . . . [When I left], my mother said that she was going to wash her hair that day. So, I went out with my girlfriend. I came back later that night and I couldn't get in the door, the cellar door that I usually come in. So I called into her, "Come on down and open the door." [She replied,] "I can't. I'm on the floor." So I get in through the front and she's there lying on the floor. She complained that the kids [from the street] were in there and terrorized her. She was incoherent, suspicious. Then she started changing her stories about the kids and cursing them out. The stories constantly changed. Then finally she said, "I want to go home." I told her that she was home and she couldn't believe this was her home. She had lived here for 26 years. . . .

She was ok after that for a couple of months, but by December I needed someone to come in and sit with her half days and by 1985, all day. In 1985, she was increasingly incontinent. One time, we were eating dinner and she put her arms in front of her and waved them wildly about. I asked her, "What's the matter?" There was no answer and then her head fell forward. We thought she had died! Then she was incontinent. We called the rescue squad, but when they came, she was eating her dinner as if nothing had happened.

The mother was cared for primarily by Mr. Lewis and the companion. Mrs. Lewis spent most of her time in a small room on the second floor of the two- story row house. Meals were brought to her, and she needed help in the bathroom. The companion, who came in daily, cared for the mother all day, prepared dinner, and ate with the family. Mr. Lewis had to leave his mother alone while he drove the sitter home.

Care of his mother had come about at a time of tremendous personal growth and need for personal freedom for Mr. Lewis. He felt that his personal development had been delayed. He noted, "I refer to my situation as one of 'marginal socialization.' " He began therapy with a psychologist in 1983, prior to the onset of the worst incidents of his mother's illness. Thus it was not the illness that precipitated his seeking help, but rather his need to face his own issues, "my own fears and depression. These things went back quite awhile." He described his family pattern as he was growing up as one of fear and isolation. When I asked him what the hardest thing was for him when caring for his mother, he contrasted his family style with the situation of his girlfriend:

The worst thing is that I'm restricted socially. Anyway, I'm naturally restricted. She's spontaneous. We're poles apart on this. When I was growing up, we didn't have a car. We were always afraid of the world, our family. In fact, this is one of the things I'm working on in therapy. If we went somewhere, we always had to plan. Her [girlfriend's] parents were the type that decided to go to Ocean City, just like that.

One impetus for his therapy was the fact that his sister and her husband had started therapy, and seeing them do so convinced him to begin. But the therapy has also helped him to cope with the stress of his mother's illness: "Because of it, things are better, socially better." The illness, "has been the topic of many, many, many [therapy] sessions."

In our interview, Mr. Lewis turned several times to the incident when he came home and found his mother lying on the floor, unable to get up. This event was implicated in the history of his relationship with his girlfriend, and thus in his own development: "That was our first long date, the very day my mother disintegrated." He still feels a certain degree of guilt that he was out that day for as long as he was:

> That week, I was out three times. I went out with my girlfriend to the mall, and I was taking a special college course at that time and I was out at night for that, and there was a third thing I was away for that week. My sister posed this as a question for me [did being out so much lead to the incident with the mother?]"

The decision to place his mother in a nursing home had engendered guilt and has firm family antecedents: "When we were growing up, we lived two doors away from the Fairtop Nursing Home, which was closed down for numerous violations. We used to hear loud noises coming from there. There were things like patient abuse and things like that which I guess wouldn't help our attitude now. This was a while ago. We left that neighborhood in 1968, and the place was vacant for several years, five or six years, before that."

Mr. Lewis's devoted care for his mother had him on the horns of a dilemma. He knew that he would have to institutionalize her as a matter of course, since he could not do all that total care requires. He felt guilt about this decision. And, he is making up for lost time in his own life. He realizes that his personal history has been unusual and he is late, for a variety of reasons, in his development. He is actively, consciously trying to change his life and at the same time to honor the requirements of his role as son that were defined long before the need for change in his life was apparent.

With his concern for personal growth occurring at the same time as his mother's illness, the home had begun to take on new meanings for Mr. Lewis. When his mother was well, it was the center for the family and represented the family's ability to survive: They had finally managed a move from the undesirable neighborhood where he had grown up. As his mother's illness progressed, the place became more difficult for him to inhabit. Though he was devoted to his mother and to family ritual, he had an increasingly hard time being himself at home. Although his life development was delayed, the home began to embody new meanings for him. Indeed, his definition of home began to switch from a multigenerational one to a nuclear one. Mr. Lewis hoped for his own family, with himself as the head. During the transitional period, he was no longer tied to his home as he had once been, but was increasingly interested in exploring the world outside. The house was increasingly his possession, and he thought about making changes in the layout and decor, which he began to do after his mother moved into a nursing home. He recognized that making changes while his mother was still living there would be detrimental to her own cognitive and emotional well-being. A feeling that she was somehow not at home was a frequent feature of her demented ideation. He also began to think about the house as a place to live when he eventually married, as he now felt he would.

Mr. Lewis could no longer accept his life as being on hold. Ironically, as this feeling increased, caregiving tasks tied him down to a single place that at best represented difficulties and family myths about development and success that no longer applied to him.

### Case Two: Mrs. Dahlia Smith

Mrs. Smith is a 45-year-old black woman who is caring at home for her mother, 82, who is severely demented and on a nursing home waiting list. Mrs. Smith, one of four daughters and two sons, who now in her view should share responsibility for their mother's care. I interviewed her in her present home, a small, two-story row house in central North Philadelphia, a largely poor and working-class black neighborhood. Neighborhood housing stock is old, featuring attractively maintained row houses alternating with burned-out and abandoned properties.

Four years before the interviews, the mother suffered a severe stroke that left her partially paralyzed. Over a two-year period, she significantly recovered so that she could walk, cook and clean. About a year before the interview, she became very sick and confused and was unable to speak. She was sent to a hospital and then a rehabilitation center and was able to talk a little bit. Upon her discharge, she temporarily entered a nursing home while the family applied for a state grant to support her.

> We placed her in there because all the girls [daughters] worked; they all had jobs. Now my brothers could cook and clean for her, but they couldn't provide personal care. So, she was fine for awhile. Finally, we got the state grant, but it wasn't for the kind of care she needed: The grant didn't cover

skilled care and we couldn't afford to pay the difference, so we decided, or I should say I decided, to keep her at home.

Approximately 9 months before the interview, Mrs. Smith quit her job and moved into her mother's small home. The experience of caring for her mother at home has engendered four areas of difficulty in her life. She has had to leave her own home in another area of Philadelphia and some of her older children who remained there in order to move to her mother's house to be with her. The caregiving work is difficult, and she has been unable to work for pay outside the home, which is her major goal when her caregiving work is completed. She has also experienced considerable disappointment in her siblings, who promised they would help care for their mother but have not, in Mrs. Smith's view, come through. She noted:

I have three sisters and two brothers. The brothers don't really come to see her. Now, Bill, he stops in every day, but he doesn't help out. Bob, he doesn't come at all. He's been here only twice since I've come back here. . . . He's angry. He was staying here [with the mother]. When I decided to come up and stay here to take care of her, he wanted to stay here, for personal reasons, mostly to get her [Social Security] check. . . . But it was worse with the sisters. They all promised they'd come and take her weekends and relieve me, give me time off, but they haven't. Selma [one of the sisters] says, "It's not fair. Mom's with you. She should stay with you. It's too confusing for her to leave [to go to Selma's house for the weekend], until she goes in a home. I'm looking after Mom's best interest." Well, she works eight hours a day, but I work 24 hours a day!

Despite all these difficulties, it is clear that her mother's well-being is paramount. I asked Mrs. Smith what her mother is like nowadays. She replied:

She's not herself. She often hollers, swears, bangs. I have to clean her. We never really anticipated [all] that. . . . at least I didn't. . . . And she's confused. She refuses to believe she's here. She wants to go home. Home to her is being. . . . she wants to cook and she wants to clean, and unless she cooks for herself and cleans for herself, she's not home. She'll never be "home" unless she can do these things.

I asked her where home was for her mother. She replied:

Well, it's here, on this street. But "home" to her is getting up and coming downstairs in the morning and cooking. And I can't stress to her [enough] that she is home. I must say a thousand times a day, "You're home, but you can't get up and cook for yourself." [I say,] "You can't cook here!" She says, "No. I want to go home!"

The care Mrs. Smith is providing for her mother has precipitated profound family conflicts and has seriously troubled the course of her own life. Leaving her home, moving into her mother's house, leaving her older children in her own house, and bringing her younger children with her have been temporary but assimilated changes.

More profound is the frustration she has experienced in being unable to continue with her own work-for-pay. She had lined up a job in a day-care program that had received government funding but had not yet begun. It was very clear that having this job was an indicator of independence and maturity for her and that the money was needed for her family.

The unwillingness of her sisters to help out as they had promised is in part due to economics: Each has a good job with a government employer. They live in somewhat better neighborhoods. Much of Mrs. Smith's comments about them indicated a sense that they may have gotten too big, too full of themselves, and had lost authenticity and feeling for the family. There was an inner conflict in her caregiving. On the one hand, moving into her mother's home, on the same small street on which she had grown up after coming north, had a moral centrality to it. Family unity was centered around her actions. She had literally taken the mother's place in order to care for her. On the other hand, her desire to place her mother, resolve her situation, and return to work, while relating to her own efficacy in the world, found a foil in her sisters' greater success, their better jobs, and nicer neighborhoods. Her brothers, who had been chronically unemployed and who also did little to care for their mother, represented an alternative but equally unsatisfactory arrangement in her view. While her view of home remained multigenerational, the events surrounding caregiving had forced a change away from the collateral view of home. The death of the mother would, no doubt, bring about a profoundly felt generational succession and might lead to increased dissociation among the siblings.

**Case Three: Tom Moore**

A 39-year-old engineer, Mr. Moore lived with his wife, a phone company manager, and his mother in a suburban Philadelphia ranch-style house. In our discussion of his mother's illness, he noted that his mother's mother had displayed many of same traits as his mother. Because of his first-hand experience with his grandmother's illness, he felt he was more habituated to his mother's symptoms, such as stealing and combativeness, than he might otherwise have been.

He was considering nursing home placement for his mother.

Some people say that it's cruel to use a [nursing] home, but that's the typical reaction of those without experience. They have no sense of reality. My mother, or someone like her, will require full time custodial care, or else they will hurt themselves. Toughing it out? That's not for me. Up till now, my mother is still lucid at times, she can enjoy us, and we can enjoy her sometimes. . . . Placing her is a pretty horrible decision to make. We could tough it out, but that's the easy way out, cause you never have to make the decision.

Home consists of two settings for Mr. Moore: the suburban home that he shares with his wife and mother, and a house on the New Jersey coast that his family has owned for more than 40 years. The environments make a big difference in the quality of life for his mother. There is a degree of social isolation in the suburban home that is not present at the shore. In the suburban home, the houses are placed far apart in the development, a car is required, and Mr. Moore described a high degree of social isolation there. And while his mother is still able to talk lucidly at times, she does so, "especially if she is at the shore. And there's no one there to worry about upsetting." Although the number of contacts at the shore is few, the network is dense. His mother's lapses of memory and erratic behavior do not produce fear, stigma, or labeling. This is in contrast to the social isolation of suburbia, where relationships are newer and untoward or erratic behavior is unwelcome and stigmatized to a degree. But the shore home is different from the tract house:

It's smaller. The whole environment is smaller. The whole town is smaller. You are able to walk to the store. We do the shopping for her, my cousin, my brother, my wife and I, when we go down. . . . There are three neighbors, long-time neighbors, that she talks to. They watch out for her, as does the agent who rents the apartment in the house. She has friends there that she doesn't have here. . . . She has more warm memories of that place in her life than she has of this place, certainly. Here it's new to her. If you'd say to her where is home, she'd probably say there.

Her intent was to retire there. My father worked two jobs to retire there early, if possible. So, that may still be in the back of her mind. She's been around there for so long, she knows the neighbors, and even the police are aware of her situation. They check on her twice a day when she's there. If there's any problem, they got my work number and my home number.

At this point, while Mrs. Moore's illness is advancing, she still has many periods of clarity. She takes walks, bathes herself, and watches TV. She can usually be left at home when her son and daughter-in-law go to work. But since she has few friends there, she must be monitored daily by an assortment of phone calls and by family members stopping in. Mr. Moore noted that he monitors two conflicting elements or trajectories: what his mother can do all the time, frequently, or rarely; and the increasing numbers of things she cannot do. The point of seeking nursing home placement will come in the next year, he believes. He noted, "The thing is that she's in relatively good [physical] health. I'm afraid the same thing will happen to her that happened to her mother. When she goes into a home, she'll lose it. She'll just go . . . pffft. I really think that's what will happen. So I'll try to put it off as long as she can get by."

Both Mr. Moore and his wife are well established in careers and are now turning to having a family. The burden of caring for his increasingly confused mother is a constant preoccupation for him. They realize that their house will eventually become a danger zone for the mother and that her lapses of memory will lead to potential difficulties and disruptions. They have begun the long transitional project of monitoring her well-being and searching for residential alternatives.

Mr. Moore appeared to have little overt conflict about institutionalizing his mother, noting that it was horrible but had to be done. He was certain that institutionalization was a proper alternative for someone whose illness had progressed dramatically, and he was also sure that institutionalization led directly to a terminal decline. Mr. Moore felt that he was not hard-hearted about this, but rather just practical and realistic.

In fact, underlying this presentation were two models of what a home should be. The first model was multigenerational, represented in the home in which he grew up: a three-generational household that included his grandparents, his parents, his brother, and at times, aunts and uncles. In this model, the family worked as a unit, achieved goals together, and made plans for the future, as in the case of his father's retirement. An accomplishment by one was an accomplishment for all. In a sense, the unity of the family made the deferring of gratification easier. This model was embodied in the shore home, at which the mother was most comfortable. It had been something his father worked hard for, and had been the fun place for all the relatives, including uncles, aunts, and cousins, as well as family friends. The second model was nuclear and neolocal: There he was the apex of the family, and energies were directed to having and developing children, rather than to siblings and parents. This was the model of home embodied in the suburban tract house that so alienated his mother. This house was one of many with small nuclear families in the idealized form, a home in which there were few older people and in which the focus was on the activities of children.

Because both he and his wife were in their late thirties, they were increasingly concerned about their ability to have children. They wanted children, but had delayed so that both could pursue education and careers. They had done so successfully and were both well established in middle-management positions.

The change to the second model of home had been engendered by two sets of pressures. First, the old model had failed. The father never lived to see much of the fruit of his work. The mother was increasingly senile. And the brother was felt to be more of a burden than the mother. Mr. Moore described his brother, a man about five years younger than him, as one who failed to get "on track." He could not hold jobs or stay in school, and was in constant need of money. Mr. Moore had taken responsibility for him, helping him financially and with employment, but had now reached the end of his toleration for his brother's waywardness. He felt his brother should grow up, just as he had done and was continuing to do. However, the change in the model of home was more directly energized by the Moore's desire to have children and the recognition that the time to do so was short. This did not mean that Mr. Moore did not wish to care for his mother or that he would place her prematurely. However, this change in the models is consonant with the apparent lack of conflict and the "realistic attitude" Mr. Moore displayed towards placement.

### Analysis

The culturally idealized version of home is one with a family, most often a younger married couple and their children. The American dream is seen as a single, freestanding dwelling. The three examples cited above deviate substantially from this cultural ideal. In the first instance, a man who views himself as developmentally delayed in marriage and in other social and psychological ways struggles to make up for lost time while confronting the drastic changes he sees in his elderly mother. In the second, a working-class black woman in a ghetto neighborhood struggles to maintain her mother and to keep her own life in order while continuing to define herself with respect to her own accomplishments and those of her siblings. In the third case, a young married man, who has no children and is economically comfortable, confronts the inevitability of his mother's decline while utilizing two meanings of home to bracket the caregiving experience.

Personal tasks of caregiving for a demented elder involves at least three dimensions that by definition must engender conflict as the home or its parts is transformed into a sickroom. These, discussed below, are personal development, containment, and enhancement.

### Personal Development

One dimension concerns the personal development of the caregiver and impaired person, respectively. One side of this dimension, the caregiver's life course, may be viewed as an expansion that takes place in a setting—a home. The home mirrors or can contain multiple and conflicting definitions of who the caregiver is and who he or she wants to be. Home can be a place, people, or a time of life. The cases above demonstrate that people may hold conflicting or ambiguous definitions of home and that these definitions are quite sensitive to developmental work and conceptions and expectations about self. The home is not a neutral background; rather, it is an organic entity that finely represents and embodies a variety of meanings at different scales. Thus

Mr. Moore's conflicting models of home clearly represent two quite different stories about who he is and who he might be in the world.

A second aspect here is the life course of the impaired person. We know little about how impaired persons view themselves. However, we do perceive much of their agitation, discomfort, and pain. It is well known that many older demented people say that they want to "go home." Wherever their residence, it does not seem to them to be home. At whatever level of cognition, there is a feeling or sense of home that is widely different from that which the person experiences. The human dimension of this tragedy, of this homelessness, is appalling.

The developmental strivings of the caregiver may come into conflict with the elder's illness. While the elder may be mentally impaired, the irrational content of a demented person's behavior may produce a kind of developmental "spillover" that may have a reactive reading by the caregiver. The caregiver may intellectually realize that the parent is not responsible for her utterances, but, of course, in many ways still sees that person as a parent, seeking her approval and validation. For example, Mrs. Simon, another caregiver in the study, saw her demented mother's acting out on the day of her daughter's wedding as a major transitional point in her mother's illness and in her own reactions to it. She noted:

> I wasn't angry at my mother. I was more frightened by her violence. I didn't know how bad she could get. On the day of my daughter's wedding, I was wrestling with her, trying to get the [house] key out of her hands [the mother had taken it and wouldn't return it]. After all, I'm younger and stronger, and I was able to open her hand to get the key . . . so in order to stop me, she bit me. At that moment, I wondered what more she could do [laughs]. Pick something up to actually do me bodily harm? I don't know if she would be capable of that.

Also on Mrs. Simon's mind is the question of why her mother chose this special day to act out or have a major episode. The question of timing was also raised by Mr. Lewis about his mother.

## Containment

The second dimension is the containment of the impaired elder that must be done by the caregiver. With the progression of the disease and an increase in the capacity of the impaired person to hurt herself or others comes the need to control that person. Ironically, then it may be said that containment leads to enhancement. Strategies of containment may engender changes at home. Significantly, the life space of the impaired person may decrease dramatically. Journeys outside diminish, as in the case of the elder Mrs. Moore who, while given wandering privileges at home, was beginning to have significantly restricted access to the world outside, the exception being the shore house. While it was clear to Mr. Moore that increased stimulation through social contact might have been beneficial to his mother, there was a chance that freedom would lead to various difficulties, and the setting of the home was not especially conducive to such contact. The potential for disorder inherent in a fuller degree of independence may lead to further restriction, eventuating in full-time occupation of a single room, as in the case of Mrs. Lewis and Mrs. Smith's mother who spent most of their time in a small bedroom.

Caregivers are sensitive to such restrictions in their management of disorder. Restriction of space is inherently at odds with wellness and certainly not part of a definition of home that is multigenerational and nurturant. The use of binders and ties to keep the impaired person from falling out of bed or hurting herself may be culturally associated in other contexts with punishment and considered a recourse only when the potential for disorder is too great. The extent to which the sickroom may be spatially defined or controlled in its effects on the overall conduct of family life is also important. Mrs. Smith dealt with this issue by generally restricting her severely impaired mother to one room, most often permitting her to go downstairs when others were not at home.

Despite spatial restriction, spillover occurs. Banging and yelling are disruptive, seep outside of the sickroom, occur day or night, and act to destroy the regularity and routine so important to creating order. All the caregivers discussed here experienced such spillover, although Mrs. Moore was in greater command of her faculties. There was a continual fear that she would leave the range on and start a fire.

*Enhancement*

The love that motivates care eventuates in attempts to enhance the life of the elder. Enhancement of the quality of life may include increasing the number or type of events that the elder appears to like, increasing stimulation, or decreasing situations that lead to agitation.

Caregivers believe that their own care will improve the quality of life of the impaired person. This belief exists regardless of any sense of guilt that may have brought about the caregiving and despite a rational recognition of the immutable course of the illness. The fact that a person is cared for at home as part of a family or within a familiar place is considered integral to the routine of caring. In the case of Mrs. Smith, in which the daughter moved into the mother's home, seems rather unusual. The cases of Mr. Lewis, in which the mother and son had been lifelong coresidents, and of Mr. Moore, in which the mother moved to the child's home, are more typical of caregiving arrangements. The fact that the impaired person has never lived in the child's home (although certainly she had visited) does not appear to be singled out as a move with a potential for disorientation. Interestingly, Mrs. Smith noted that one of her sisters cited just this argument, that the mother would be disoriented by spending the weekend at the sister's home, as a justification by the sister for not fulfilling her promises of filial care. While perhaps initially disorienting, the act of moving a demented elder in with a child, is ultimately viewed as a means of extending the familiarity and love of home into the everyday tasks of caregiving.

In the minds of the caregivers described above, home is contrasted with institutions, which ultimately lack "homelike" caring. To a certain degree, the home is posited to have curative or maintenance effects above and beyond other environments and above and beyond the fact that proximity makes hands-on care easier. To whatever extent possible, the home lets the impaired person "be herself."

There is a widespread belief by caregivers that nursing home placement leads to decline. The relationship is seen as causal, not coincidental. For example, one middle-aged caregiver in the study who had placed her mother, regretted it, and took her back home, noted:

That [nursing] home was the worst decision. She couldn't feed herself and she was in with everybody else. You know what I mean. There was no special care for her needs. The girls on the daytime were very good to her, but they had so much work. Each had fourteen patients. Like, if they had someone who could do things for themselves, they're all right. But my mother was total care. And when she was in that home, she was hospitalized three times in those four months [for various infections].

Despite the fact that the nursing home was a "good" one, the decline in physical care was inevitable, according to this caregiver, leading to poorer health, as the loss of identity. Her beloved mother "was in with everybody else."

The widespread notion that nursing home placement leads to decline, as articulated, for example, by Mr. Moore, is situated both in the perceived differences between the practical aspects of care of getting things done, facilitated by coresidence, and the moral aspects of care, centered in the love the home provides. All three caregivers discussed here cited practical limitations to care caused by the decline brought about by the illness that necessitated placement. Mr. Lewis, who evidenced the greatest degree of overt emotional attachment to his parent, was most openly concerned about the loss of a home as a moral umbrella for his mother's personhood. Although his mother was eventually placed, he had trouble some months later in remembering the events of the placement, noting that he had "blanked out" during the weeks surrounding the event. Mrs. Smith evidenced a conflicting sense of morality: She had gone far beyond the call of duty in caring for her mother, and placement was directly the result of her siblings' failure at commitment to the task. She rationalized away the moral authority of home. For her, the home was defined as multigenerational, collateral, and therefore as central, but it now lacked collateral dimensions. Mr. Moore was most explicit in both admitting to and denying the moral dimensions of home. He was most certain that institutionalization brought decline, but he also felt that those who did not see the need for placement were both nescient and amoral.

## Discussion

For the caregiver and possibly the parent, the home as a sickroom may become a place in which developmental meanings become magnified and intensified as events are scrutinized with the hope that they represent lucidity, with an underlying but unrealistic assumption that the course of dementia, as with some other diseases, is reversible from the perspective of someone who is always a loving child.

The above cases show how the home is not a passive setting in which caregiving happens to take place just because it is easier or because a child feels a responsibility. Rather, the home is a representation of the child's feelings about who she is in the world, and often is an embodiment of conflicting representations. The need to control a parent whose behavior may be increasingly destructive and the desire to enhance the quality of life of the elder are complex; they are intertwined with the notion of home as a place of living and of meaning. The home, as a symbolic construction and a symbolic representation, may be one language in which the content and emotional tone of caregiving is expressed and which is the only means of expressing certain feelings and events, especially those concerned with developmental strivings.

## References

Rubinstein, R. L. (1989a). The home environments of older people: A description of the psychosocial processes linking person to place. *Journal of Gerontology, 44,*: S45-S53.
Rubinstein, R. L. (1989b). Themes in the meaning of caregiving. *Journal of Aging Studies, 3,* 119-138.

## 3

# Making Arrangements:

## The Key to Home Care

JULIET M. CORBIN
ANSELM STRAUSS

When one thinks of managing illness, the hospital and all its drama and high technology first come to mind. Yet hospitals provide only a small proportion of care to the ill, their part being limited to the management of acute phases of illness. Most of the day-to-day management of illness, in fact, takes place in the home, a nondescript and nondramatic place when compared to the excitement of a hospital with its modern equipment.

Since the daily ongoing care takes place at home, we have come to view the home as the center of care in chronic-illness management (Strauss & Corbin, 1988). It is the hub of activity, while other institutions and services, such as hospitals, clinics, and home health agencies, are the spokes that support it. Unlike hospitals, though, the home is not an institution expressly established for the purpose of caring for the ill. When it takes on this function, its members must learn the skills, gather the equipment, find the services, and carry out the work as best they can. One man caring for his paralyzed wife expresses the sentiments of many caretakers like himself, when he says:

> When my wife says, "You didn't do this, you didn't do that," I say, "Give me a chance. If you were in the hospital, you would have three or four attendants, one to make your meals, one to take care of you, and so on." I

have to lift her out of the bed and onto the commode. I have to make sure of where the catheter is and the drainage bag. I say, "Honey, I only have two legs, two arms, and one mind." I can't afford to have someone living here full time. I would have to mortgage my house. Some of the bills I receive from the doctors are unbelievable. (Excerpt from interview of a husband caring for wife, who is suffering from paraplegia due to an injury.)

How is it, then, that this caregiver and others like him are able to care for their ill members at home, given the constraints that they face? Basically, they do so through a process we have termed the "making of arrangements." In this chapter we will describe what we mean by arrangements and explore their role in the care of the ill at home. Before doing so, however, we will briefly review the work involved in caring for the chronically ill at home.

This chapter is based on the results of a study of 60 couples managing chronic illness, of one or both partners, at home. (See Corbin & Strauss, 1988; Strauss & Corbin, 1988.) It is also based on the many years of experience the authors have in working with the chronically ill and in teaching nurses and others to care for the chronically ill.

## *The Work of Home Care to the Chronically Ill*

Home care of the chronically ill is aimed at keeping the illness course stable and managing any associated disability. Because the home is not a hospital, home care must also provide for the comfort of ill persons and take care of their sentimental and affiliative needs, all within the context of daily living.

Keeping an illness course stable is not necessarily easy in the hospital, never mind at home. It involves carefully following a regimen, monitoring and dealing with symptoms, and preventing and managing crises and complications (Strauss, Fagerhaugh, Suczek, & Weiner, 1985). Unless these various tasks are carried out, a stable condition could easily pass into one of instability, acuteness, crises, deterioration, or even death. (For a more detailed description of the phases of chronic illness, see Corbin & Strauss, 1988.) Thus even managing an illness places considerable burden upon the ill person and/or caretakers.

Then, too, there is the handling of associated disability (Locker, 1983), which can range anywhere from mild to severe. The more severe the disability, the more care will be needed and the more the home will have to be arranged to meet needs. Hospital beds, wheelchairs, lifts, handrails, and other equipment may need to be obtained, installed, and kept in working order. Rooms may have to be rearranged and the use of stairs eliminated for the patient. Schedules may have to be set in order to accomplish all that there is to do in one day and to make the most of a person's ability such as during periods of peak energy. There is also the task of providing for the ill person's comfort. Ill persons may have difficulty handling heat or cold. They may have to be moved from bed to chair and back to bed, be cleaned and have clean linen, have meals they can tolerate and enjoy, be mentally stimulated, and so forth.

Since illness can hit a person's identity and sense of self (Bury, 1982; Charmaz, 1980, 1983; Corbin & Strauss, 1987, Schneider & Conrad, 1983), providing ways for ill persons to feel good about themselves and and feel a part of family life are also important. The ill also need caring and affectionate touching that goes beyond that of mere handling, as in caretaking.

In order to carry out all of these various tasks, arrangements are needed. It is to these that we turn next in our discussion.

## Arrangements

When we speak of the *making of arrangements,* we are referring to the process by which agreements are reached and maintained between persons for carrying out the tasks associated with home care. Just as the home is the center of care, arrangements are the heart that allows that center to function. What kinds of arrangements are necessary? Who makes them? How? Under what conditions? What happens when arrangements are in place, when they are not, or when they break down? To understand these matters, it is best first to conjure up an image of how a family unit ordinarily functions.

### Arrangements for Ordinary Family Functioning

A family has a number of "standing arrangements" necessary for carrying on the activities of daily life. Thus the family's division of labor—who does the shopping, who carries out the garbage—rests on domestic agreements. Every kind of everyday activity, whether it be child-rearing, cooking, house cleaning, house repairing, or whether it is less onerous and more pleasurable or sentimental, rests on agreements. These concern the best ways to carry out the activity, when, by whom, and even where. Arrangements are not necessarily fixed in concrete, but may be flexible depending on circumstances, and open to renegotiation. On occasion, they are supplemented by "temporary arrangements," as when a marital partner is called away for two or three days and a relative or paid helper is called in to help.

## When Temporary Illness Strikes

This set of standing, flexible, and temporary arrangements can be thrown into considerable, albeit brief, disarray if a family member becomes stricken with the flu. Suppose, say, that a key member of a youthful domestic unit, the mother, becomes so weak as to be put to bed. This event will not disrupt the family's routine too much; but if the illness lasts much more then a few days, the performance of this person's tasks must be "covered," thereby necessitating a cluster of temporary arrangements. Some of these arrangements have to do with shifting the family manpower resources to carry out what would normally be her tasks. When the patient recovers, the usual arrangements can resume and life becomes normal.

## When Chronic Illness Strikes

What does the domestic picture look like when someone has a chronic illness? This tends to vary depending upon the severity of the illness, the regimens needed to control it, and the degree of associated disability. When an illness is relatively mild, few arrangements may be necessary. Those that are arrived at will probably have less to do with the shifting of tasks and more to do with the working out of agreements between the couple on how, when, and where certain regimens will be carried out especially if they are considered somewhat offensive or disturbing to the other partner.

Consider what happens when a husband has a mild condition such as chronic bronchitis and related chronic sinusitis. To sleep soundly, he does posturing (lying on the floor for perhaps ten minutes, in order to cough up accumulated phlegm) and uses a machine that clears out his nasal passages, a process that takes about ten minutes. There is an understanding between this busy husband and his wife that he will do this regimen early enough so that her last minutes before sleep will not be disturbed. Moreover, there's a silent understanding that he will do his coughing in a room other than the one in which she's sitting. Otherwise, this household operates exactly like any other, with all the usual cluster of domestic arrangements. The arrangements necessary for managing his illnesses are just, in a manner of speaking, "there"— they do not particularly interfere with ordinary daily activities.

It is quite different, however, when someone has a chronic illness so severe that it disrupts the flow of normal life—whether it be that of the ill person or other persons with whom he or she is living. Yet life must go on: People must eat, bathe, sleep, and perhaps go on raising children, work outside the home, and socialize.

What happens is that the arrangements necessary for managing the illness are brought into the web of ongoing everyday arrangements. However, arrangements needed to deal with the situation are not merely added: Bringing them in is not necessarily done without turmoil or without altering or destroying some of those previous arrangements. An intricate combination of arrangements for illness management and everyday life management must be worked out through the use of agreements and understandings. Undoubtedly, trial and error and per-haps astute planning may be involved.

In effect, when an illness becomes extremely intrusive, the home is turned into a kind of small institutionalized hospital. As with a real hospital, a lot of work has to be done, resources are needed for the work, and arrangements are needed to obtain and maintain the resources. Those arrangements must be securely in place and working. (In the instance of some people in serious decline, even their simplest activities may require careful arrangements. Sometime considerable thought goes into conceiving and maintaining them, down to the careful placement of tissues, bringing in special telephones, leaving sufficient time for slow transport of the ill person from bed to chair, and other factors.) As in a hospital, services and resources must flow in and out of the home—not merely the usual household supplies and services, but the supplementary human resources, medications, and other resources re-lated to illness management. Standing agreements may be made with the physician so that he or she can be called at night if need be. Friends may offer to take spouses shopping once a week for the heavier items in order to ease their burdens.

Services must also be available through human resources internal to the household, notably by marital partners or caretaking children. Certain services are maintained in routinized ways. Bedpans are placed at the bedside at night. Telephones are placed near the ill person when the spouse leaves the house. Husbands learn to give diabetic wives their daily insulin shots and help to monitor their blood-sugar levels. Temporary arrangements are also made to bring another caregiver into the home—making him or her internal to the home for a short period—as when caretaking spouses decide to travel for two or three weeks because they just need to get away, or when they just enjoy traveling.

## Classification of Arrangements

As is suggested by the above examples, arrangements can be usefully classified into two broad categories: standing, or routine, and temporary.

### Standing Arrangements

These types of arrangements are those that are in place. With them, there is no need to work things out each time such resources are needed (unless the conditions on which they were based have changed and then new ones must be negotiated). For instance, a person may go to a large medical center every two months for a routine check-up, but sees his local physician in between such bimonthly visits and for emergencies. There may also be a medication protocol arranged for handling symptoms. Plus, there are all sorts of other small arrangements that are necessary to ease the burdens that illness can bring. For instance, a couple who must travel to a distant medical center may agree to spend the night at a motel near the hospital because doing so is less tiring than making the trip all in one day.

In addition, the spouse of a chronically ill person may have to assume supportive agentry roles: assisting with the carrying out of the regimen, acting as a protective agent to prevent medical crises, and monitoring symptoms.

A partner may also do identity and sentimental work by keeping the ill person involved in the daily household activities and decision-making and by attempting to cheer their mate when he/she becomes depressed. There may also be arrangements for a home health aide to come in to help with daily routines (bathing, dressing), and for a nurse to visit in order to monitor blood pressure, change a catheter, or perform other medical-related procedures.

Such standing arrangements are, of course, paralleled in the lives of other couples or families when someone is severely ill. Even people living alone will make similar arrangements with friends, professionals, and paid employees to supplement what they themselves cannot do. If they are repeated often enough, emergencies result in domestic routines for handling the dangers. For instance, the spouse of a diabetic becomes skilled not only in monitoring for signs of insulin reactions, but also in acting appropriately when a crisis occurs. The wife of one diabetic said that: if her husband becomes physically violent during a hypoglycemic episode, she calls an ambulance. "I imagine that [has happened] a dozen times," she says.

*Temporary Arrangements*

These agreements for service or care must be worked out each time they are needed or desired. Thus arrangements may be made for Meals on Wheels when a wife is temporarily ill. Likewise, couples make a temporary agreement with friends to reschedule a social visit if the ill person is not feeling well. When the ill person is outside the confines of the house, a marital partner may in an emergency utilize whatever temporary arrangements are immediately necessary (for instance, asking a man to go into a public bathroom to check on a husband with severe cardiac disease if he stayed in the restroom unduly long.

**What Arrangements Are All About**

In the case of the severely ill, most arrangements have to do with securing and maintaining the manpower and other resources necessary to obtain and maintain the equipment and supplies, provide for a division of tasks and continued motivation necessary for the long-term management of illness and associated disability at home; and to provide for the performance of all the other household work that has to be done.

**Resources**

There are two basic types of resources needed to manage illness at home: structural resources and supportive agents.

*Structural Resources*

Structural resources are so called because they provide the structural foundation for the home management of illness. They include such elements as time, information, devices of all sorts, human resources, soft and hard technology, energy, money, regimens, skill, services of various types, and advice and counseling. One can easily see that without these, home care would be difficult—if not impossible. Also part of the structural resources are the different institutions such as hospitals, clinics, and respite and nursing homes, plus services such as Meals on Wheels and home health agencies.

These latter act as backstops to home care. In other words, they fill in when the home is inadequate to meet the ill person's needs, the need for caretaker relief, or the arrangements that are in place break down.

The amount and kind of resources needed at any given time will vary by living and illness conditions. Take for instance, the element of information. One may need more information at the beginning of an illness than later, such as how to fill out forms for Medicaid, the nature of the condition or the drugs used to treat it, where to go to obtain and learn the cost of medical equipment, how to follow a regimen, and how to contact self-help groups.

The need for resources may increase or decrease over time, with one type (say, money) being needed more than another (like special equipment). Yet, overall, one can assume, since the conditions that we are speaking of are chronic ones, that the demand for resources will be generally consistent.

On the other hand, the availability of these resources may change over time. Resources, like money in the form of savings, can be used up. Others, like energy, equipment, or manpower, may no longer be available, wear out, break down, or be insufficient. This indicates that not only must resources be obtained in the first place, but they must be maintained and replaced according to need.

*Supportive Agents*

We have termed persons who help to sustain home care through their supportive actions as supportive agents, of which there are two types: the professional and the lay.

Professional agents include doctors, nurses, social workers, therapists, home health aides, and counselors who work with the chronically ill. The nature of their work is well known. While their roles in helping to manage and live with stable illness are very important, one can described them as being on the periphery of home care. That is, these agents are not likely to be involved in the everyday work of caring for the ill and the home except in certain cases where there is twenty four-hour nursing care. Instead, they tend to move in and out of the management arena over the course of a day or with need.

The lay agents who consist of spouses, family members, kin, and friends of the chronically ill, tend to be more directly involved in the day-to-day illness and home management activities. For example, spouses and other family members often act as caretakers (Cantor, 1985; Chester & Barbarin, 1984; Corbin & Strauss, 1985; Eckberg, Griffith, & Foxall, 1986). They also assist with regimens, monitor symptoms, watch over the ill person and protect him or her. Along with other kin and friends, they may shop for the ill person, provide transportation, and run errands (though in some cases professional agents may do this also).

Like structural resources, supportive ones may come and go with time. Someone may become dissatisfied with a physician and desire a change, a spouse may die or become ill, and friends can also become ill or move away. Thus by means of arrangement-making these resources, too, must be obtained, maintained, and replaced with changing conditions. Unless such is the case, the home care (management work) may be difficult and even impossible.

*Properties of Arrangements*

When considered in the terms mentioned above, the number and types of arrangements needed to obtain and maintain resources to perform illness and household tasks under conditions of chronic illness make the home somewhat akin to a small hospital. However, it can also be conceived of in terms of another metaphor: an acrobatic act! Arrangements are analogous to the men and women who form a pyramid, standing on, above, and next to one another in intricate delicate balances. So, too, are arrangements; they also are interlocking, are interdependent, and in a fragile and complex equilibrium. Some are more pivotal than others: When these go out of kilter—when the resources they maintain thereby become affected—the entire structure of both illness management and daily life is threatened, or even destroyed. For instance, if a family's savings get used up so that available funds are in short supply, the family may have to go on Medicaid. When this happens, they may have to, albeit reluctantly, send their ill member to a nursing home because it is easier to justify this expense as opposed to those associated with home care. Among the most precarious resources to maintain are the services of friends and professionals. Every family with a severely ill member knows that many friends tend to fade away in the long stretch despite their generous offers to help when illness first appears. Even those professional helpers who evince much concern and care may show far less of those qualities after their clients' physical conditions stabilize.

As for the intimates, including marital partners, their energies may wax and wane, and finally decrease permanently. Many a caring partner could echo one who said, "He is tearing me down because you are always on the lookout: How is he, does he need something?" And then the impact becomes reciprocal: "I feel like, oh, my word, this dear man, he is pulling me down; I am pulling him down." (Excerpts from interview with couple, wife caring for a husband with diabetes and heart disease.) Aside from lowered energy, there can be decreased commitment to the relationships—and its obligation to supply labor and services—if interpersonal relationships between the caring partner and the ill individual deteriorate. This sometimes happens when the ill, as is sometimes stated, "change personality" even though their physical conditions are well stabilized.

Moreover, arrangements with outside agents may have to be renegotiated. For instance, if an elderly wife is called upon to take her husband's pulse accurately and she finds this too trying, she may have to renegotiate performance of this procedure with her physician, who might suggest an alternative. When physicians do not heed a wife's warning that her husband's deteriorating condition is perhaps due to an experimental drug, she might renegotiate a change in the therapy with one of the residents.

### Arriving at the Arrangements

While many of the arrangements are based on clear negotiations, persuasion, and even coercion, others are more in the nature of implicit understandings. That is, the parties more or less have come to ways of acting toward each other—thus supplying services and doing respective tasks—without having clearly verbalized their agreements and attendant arrangements. For example, when Mr. Bell disappears from a gathering, his wife goes looking for him. If she notices that he seems to be having trouble with his angina, she says nothing but gives him his emergency medications. (Excerpt from fieldnotes, couple in which husband has severe heart disease.)

However, the parties may be aware of their reciprocities. The well partner, for instance, may consciously do a lot of reassuring, touching, telling of jokes, kissing, and saying, "I love you," to keep up the spirits of the sick person. One man in an interview told us: "I love her to death. I go in there and I look through the bars, [of the bed] and she says 'hello, baboon.' I tell jokes. I woke up the other morning and said, "Will you marry me?" (Excerpt from fieldnotes, husband caring for a wife, who suffers from paralysis.) On the other hand, the ill have to show appreciation and do their best to be as cheerful as possible. Sometimes however, the partners are not even aware of some of their understandings until one does not adhere to them. Paraphrasing one diabetic wife: She wishes that she and her husband would sit down and talk about how she often gets bratty when her sugar gets low before meals, and she would like him to recognize that more clearly. (Excerpt from interview of a woman with diabetes.)

Since a home is what it is (unless it consists of only a single person), interpersonal relationships underpin the shared, interlocking, and even different but related activities. Some arrangements are affected by changes in those interpersonal relationships (as implied in the previous sentences about domestic commitment). When the arrangements do not seem to work, when they seem inefficient, inconvenient, or unfair, they get renegotiated. Since that isn't always possible, they may get rearranged by persuasion or coercion. For instance, spouses have to be convinced that they should no longer drive the car, or be ordered not to drive. Unsatisfactory arrangements put other family members, especially spouses, in the uncomfortable positions of acting too frequently or openly as control agents, reminding the ill of what they are supposed to do (such as carrying out regimens promptly or correctly). The control agents may be told they are nagging, or just feel like they are doing this: "So [when] I push him, I become a nag." However, if the partners are reasonable, they may be able to work things out anyhow: "I become a nag. He knows that, he knows what I am doing. We are both aware of this play. But I think we have worked it out pretty well." (Excerpt from an interview of a wife, whose husband has Parkinson's disease.) Even when domestic relationships are firm, marital partners run up against the boundaries of the ill person's tolerance for control, though it is clearly in their own interest. Thus one husband, a well-known authority in his field, accepted two speaking engagements before telling his wife. She displayed disapproval at "overdoing" but told us: "He still wants to feel needed and necessary, which I understand also. But . . . if I insist that he doesn't go, then that is putting him down. Though why, why? . . . I tried to talk to him about that, but it is a rough area. He doesn't want to really face it [retirement]. It is like the driving—he hasn't been driving for at least five years. He still says, 'Why don't you let me drive'? I keep repeating: 'Honey, it is not safe for you to be behind that wheel.' " (Excerpts from interview of a wife, whose husband has Parkinson's disease.)

On the other hand, because so many domestic agreements are unspoken, even virtually subliminal, there is a high probability misunderstandings will occur when domestic stress is precipitated or enhanced by long-term severe illness. This is true even when the physical conditions are relatively stable. If the misunderstandings deeply affect the domestic relationships, it is likely that the illness itself will become destabilized.

### Recommendations

In summary, arrangements must be made and functioning properly in order for home care to take place at all, let alone effectively. It is through these arrangements that the necessary resources for managing an illness are obtained, utilized, and maintained. With intrusive chronic illness, these medically oriented arrangements inevitably become inter-twined with others: the usual, garden-variety ones that make everyday living and its activities possible. Combinations of both types of arrange-ments rest ultimately on interpersonal relationships, domestic and oth-erwise. Of course, these relationships sometimes deteriorate under the strains of prolonged chronic illness. Yet, if the illness itself is to be kept stable, it is because both types of arrangements are effectively function-ing. Good medical/nursing care by itself is not at all enough to keep an illness stable.

Health professionals (whether they be nurses, social workers, physi-cians, or others) might well find this way of *systematically* thinking about stability useful. Of course, skilled home care workers do recog-nize when their clients are "managing well or badly" and that they have set up a variety of means for effectively, or not, carrying out regimens, monitoring symptoms, and keeping the ill mobile. The practitioners will also pick up the prevailing moods, complaints, difficulties, and satis-factions. These are all indicators of the underlying arrangement/re-source/work scheme we have outlined in this chapter. It is our belief that what the practitioner ordinarily notes can be made additionally useful if thinking about these matters can be made both more explicit and systematic. To that end we recommend the following.

It is important to put together an accurate picture of the current arrangements that underpin the couple's or family's (or single person's) efforts to manage the illness. This means that very specific questions bearing on their current arrangements and resources should be asked. How have the arrangements been set up? Who took the initiative, or was it happenstance? With whom are these arrangements made? How stable do the arrangements seem to be, and at what points do they seem shaky or begin to break down? Have some not worked effectively, and, if so, in what regard? What resources are in hand and working for the ill and/or the family? What is the family short on or running out of, and why? Which kinds of work are suffering because of a lack of given resources (information, skills, energy, money) and why is this so? Note that these questions seek to get at effective as well as ineffective management: It is important to know "why" in either case, since even slight changes in arrangements/resources can impact how management works. It is this total picture of functioning and cause that makes for genuine understanding. The practitioner's ears and eyes should be used as effectively for this systematic purpose as for purely clinical or therapeutic ones. (An attempt should be made to translate the language of complaints into what has gone wrong operationally in terms of arrangements/resources and work.)

Besides asking specific questions, it is essential to be or to become a skilled interviewer. This does not mean merely that someone can collect data. He or she must genuinely listen for and elicit relevant information. Interviewers trained in behavioral or social science learn how to listen carefully, how to endure silences, how not to interrupt the flow of narration, and how to elicit information by special devices such as, "Mr. Jones tells me he manages to do it this way because . . . , what about with you?" These techniques and many others are useful. Practitioners need to have some training at these nonclinical and non-therapeutic, but equally subtle, kinds of interviewing and associated techniques. Furthermore, they need to accumulate wisdom about which arrangements seem to work, and under which *relatively specific* conditions. It would be well if they would act as gentle bumble bees, passing this information along to clients. After all, unless they belong to self-help groups, the ill and their families do not get many opportunities to learn about improving their care management because they often live and work in relative isolation from other ill people. Each practitioner, having observed and heard about arrangements from many clients, is in a position to think systematically about this information and to pass on appropriate selections of it to other persons. Practitioners might participate also, perhaps in making it fit instrumentally to new situations.

Although we have been referring exclusively to medically oriented arrangements, all our remarks are intended to apply also to the "whole ball of wax;" that is, to the inextricably combined total set of domestic arrangements that includes the nonmedical. What must surely often occur when practitioners give counsel, whether they are visiting the home or the ill/families are visiting health facilities, is that they give inappropriate counsel because it runs afoul of domestic arrangements. These are either not perceived or, worse yet, are misperceived. (Once, a public health nurse was observed unwittingly destroying the spatial arrangements of a relatively immobile client who lived in a tiny one-room apartment that was described as "a perfect mess." It was so because the arrangements were so effectively worked out that all resources were within arm's reach; indeed, the disarrayed arrangements were probably restored as quickly as possible.) Although this example is an extreme case of practitioner insensitivity, it might well stand as a negative exemplification of how much better a systematic understanding of a clients' arrangements, both medical and domestic, can underpin more effective home care by professionals.

## *References*

Bury, M. (1982). Chronic illness as biographic disruption. *Sociology of Health and Illness, 4,* 167-182.

Cantor, M. (1985). Families: A basic source of long-term care for the elderly. *Aging, 349,* 8-13.

Charmaz, K. (1980). The construction of self-pity in the chronically ill. In N. Denzin (Ed.), *Studies in symbolic interaction, Vol. 3* (pp. 123-145). Greenwich, CT: JAI.

Charmaz, K. (1983). Loss of self: A fundamental form of suffering in the chronically ill. *Sociology of Health and Illness, 6,* 168-195.

Chester,. M., & Barbarin, O. (1984). Difficulties of providing help in crisis: Relationship between parents of children with cancer and their friends. *Journal of Social Issues, 40,* 113-134.

Corbin, J., & Strauss, A. (1985). Issues concerning regimen management in the home. *Ageing and Society, 5,* 249-265.

Corbin, J., & Strauss, A. (1987). Accompaniments of chronic illness: Changes in body, self, biography and biographical time. In J. Roth & P. Conrad (Eds.), *The experience and management of chronic illness, Vol. 6.* Greenwich, CT: JAI.

Corbin, J., & Strauss, A. (1988). *Unending work and care.* San Francisco: Jossey-Bass.

Eckberg, J., Griffith, N., & Foxall, M. (1986). Spousal adjustment to chronic illness. *Rehabilitation Nursing, 25,* 19-29.

Locker, D. (1983). *Disability and disadvantage.* London: Tavistock.

Schneider, J., & Conrad, P. (1983). *Having Epilepsy.* Philadelphia: Temple University.

Strauss, A., Fagerhaugh, S., Suczek, B., & Wiener, C. (1985). *The social organization of medical work.* Chicago: University of Chicago.

Strauss, A., & Corbin, J. (1988). *Shaping a new health care system.* San Francisco: Jossey-Bass.

## 4

# The Defiance of Hope:

## Dementia Sufferers and Their Carers in a London Borough

JOEL S. SAVISHINSKY

### Introduction

Many myths cluster about the image of old age. One of the most persistent and pernicious is that of indifference and neglect by families. There is, however, ample evidence to show that most elderly people in the United States, Great Britain, and other countries, remain connected to their kin: They live either with or near them, and maintain regular contacts (Shanas, 1979). Families continue to care about—and care

AUTHOR'S NOTE: In conducting the research for this project, I have had considerable encouragement and support from many people. I would like to thank Dianne Willcocks of the Polytechnic of North London and Audrey Noble of Islington Age Concern for their assistance and advice. My research in London was funded in part by contributions to the Gerontology Program at Ithaca College and supported by the help of my wife and family. My greatest debts are to the carers themselves and the people in the voluntary and statutory agencies in Islington with whom I worked. While I cannot mention them by name out of respect for their privacy, they were generous of both their time and candor. Without their cooperation and considerable concern for the elderly and those who care for them, this project could not have been completed.

This chapter is an expanded version of an earlier paper (Savishinsky, 1989a). It draws on material contained in the full report of the research project presented to the Working Party on Dementia Sufferers and Their Carers, convened by Islington Age Concern (Savishinsky, 1989b).

75

for—their older relatives despite the stereotypes and the difficulties, reflecting the hope that neither age or illness will compromise an enduring set of relationships.

As people live longer and survive in the face of declining health, however, their kin may be confronted by new situations and decisions. Can an increasingly frail individual be maintained in the community? In whose home should he or she live? How shall family members apportion the personal and financial responsibility for providing care? What kinds of outside assistance are necessary and appropriate, and at what point should a transfer to a residential facility be considered?

Facing up to these issues can jeopardize or foster people's hope of maintaining their family ties. Such questions take on a special poignancy when an elderly relative develops symptoms of dementia. Responsibility then becomes heavier, and its boundaries shift. Issues of competency become as important as methods of caring. Though some dementias are reversible, many are not; in the latter situation, a family's hopes of a cure may yield to the more pragmatic hope of simply being able to cope. In a redefinition and sometimes a reversal of roles, spouses, siblings, and children become the caretakers of their peers and elders.

As increasing numbers of families find themselves thrust into such an unanticipated position, there is a compelling need to look at the human and financial costs of such continued care for frail, senile relatives. This chapter reports on the situation among caregivers in one area of England. It is based on anthropological research in the London borough of Islington, where a group of voluntary human service agencies have formed a Working Party, or task force, to consider the conditions faced by dementia sufferers and their family carers.

On the local level, the Working Party was examining a situation that affects millions of people in Great Britain. Estimates of the number of family or "informal" caregivers in the country ranged from 1.3 to 3.25 million individuals, even though health authorities and social service departments had no mechanism for discovering how many carers resided in their locality (Webb, 1987). An increasing proportion of carers are themselves elderly: Their mean age is 61 (Henwood & Wicks, 1984, 8-9). Furthermore, advocates for caregivers who were interviewed from local and national organizations argued that the burden of family responsibility has probably increased in recent decades because kin are now likely to be caring for much more heavily dependent individuals: As more people live longer, they are more likely to develop serious, debilitating illnesses (see also Webb, 1987, p. 11).

In the last few years, a number of charitable and voluntary bodies— including Age Concern, the Alzheimer's Disease Society, the Association of Carers, the Family Welfare Association, and the National Council for Carers and Their Elderly Dependents—have taken an increasingly active role in advocating on behalf of family caregivers. They have emphasized that the task of sustaining frail older people has also become more difficult because recent cuts in government budgets have reduced supportive services for carers during a time when the state has stressed more "care in the community" (DHSS, 1981b; McGwire, 1988). In particular, the National Health Service has been in a state of crisis, a situation that has had an especially severe impact on the elderly, who are its largest group of users (DHSS, 1981a; Lohr, 1988). A long-awaited government study of services for caregivers was released in 1988 (Griffiths, 1988), but its recommendations for restructuring the organization and financing of community supports for carers remain under discussion.[1]

Created in 1986, the Working Party in Islington became aware that its member agencies shared a number of clients and that the provision of services for them was not always well matched to people's needs and expectations. While I was a visiting Professor at the Polytechnic of North London's Centre for Environmental and Social Studies in Ageing during 1987 and 1988, the Working Party asked me to do some basic research on two related issues: the supports and services available for senile people and their families in the borough and the experiences that caregivers have had with their elderly relatives and service providers. Working Party members were sensitive to the vagaries of hope and hopelessness that informal carers experienced, as well as the frustrations of service personnel trying to assist them. In response to these concerns, the study also addressed the question of whether the image the caregivers had of themselves and their role was congruent with the way these were seen by agency staff. The ultimate purpose of the research was to utilize the data collected to formulate programs and policy initiatives to improve supports for people in Islington. The project was thus related to two of the central issues raised by other investigators of the home care experience: the use of qualitative research to inform social policy (e.g., Trager, 1980; Sankar, 1988) and the need to understand the interface between caregiving households and outside institutions (e.g., Gubrium, 1987; Gubrium & Lynott, 1987). Some of the main findings that came out of this study are summarized below.

## Community Services

In contemporary Great Britain, several social forces shape patterns of responsibility for the elderly, including the tradition of family support for the old, and a history of community care for the elderly and other dependent people. In the past, the latter emphasis has been expressed in church and voluntary-sponsored charities, and in such institutions as the Poor Laws, almshouses, public-assistance facilities, and hospitals. In the decades following World War II, the morality of caring took on a political form in social welfare legislation. Through the National Health Service and Department of Social Services, the national government and local authorities made provision for acute and long-stay hospital care, residential homes and day centers (nonresidential facilities providing social activities, meals, and recreation), community nursing services, Home Helps (who come into the homes of the elderly to help with domestic tasks), Meals on Wheels, special allowances and benefits, and aides such as wheelchairs, transportation, laundry, and other services (Means, 1986). Since the 1970s, there has also been considerable growth in the private sector development of nursing homes, and an increasing government emphasis on community care by families, friends, and voluntary organizations, rather than state-funded services (Willcocks, Peace, & Kellaher, 1987).

The situation in the North London Borough of Islington between 1987 and 1988 was a reflection of several of these trends. Medical services in the borough were divided up between the Islington District Health Authority and the Bloomsbury District Health Authority, which cared for the northern and southern parts of the borough, respectively. The Islington Department of Social Services had 24 Neighbourhood Offices (local offices) in various localities that provided the elderly with residential and day care, as well as social work, protective, and other services. There were no private nursing homes in Islington at the time, but there were a variety of voluntary agencies that offered the senile elderly and their families such assistance as care attendants, respite and relief schemes for carers, counseling and support groups for family members, and advocacy, advice, and rights information for the elderly and their kin. The array of supports was thus being derived from a combination of families, voluntary agencies, and government services at both the local and national level.

Caregivers and those who worked with them in Islington emphasized that locally, and throughout England, most people wanted to go on caring for their relative rather than place him or her in a residential or nursing home (Addison, 1986). This was regarded as being especially true of women who, it has been estimated, make up 75% of England's family caregivers (Peace, 1986, p. 87). The emphasis on enabling aged people to remain at home coincides with the desires of most older individuals themselves, reflecting the fact that community care is both an ideal and a reality for the vast majority of the elderly (Qureshi & Walker, 1986).

However, the details of that reality vary from area to area and from one household to another (Webb, 1987). The preceding inventory of organizations and services in Islington indicates what is available to people, but not how consumers actually utilize these resources or how they feel about them. A number of agency staff from the public and voluntary sectors in the borough observed that community caregivers were not always informed of their rights or the supports that existed for them, and that some of the people the caregivers went to for assistance were also not informed. At first, many families hoped to remain self-sufficient in providing home care, but they then wanted quick, sensitive responses when they did turn to others for aid. Furthermore, we found that the first attempts of carers to get help could affect their future attitudes toward community resources and that their feelings about the responses they got could shorten or lengthen the time it took for them to get meaningful assistance. The following case studies show some of this variability in experiences by examining the efforts of three caregivers to get help for themselves and a demented member of their family.

## The Experiences of Caregivers

### Rose Flynn

Rose Flynn was a 59-year-old Irish woman who had been caring for her husband Brian, a retired building tradesman, for four years. She had to quit her job in a local authority school (public school) in order to do so. Her husband was 69, and his dementia quite pronounced: It was marked by wandering, periods of agitation, very poor short-term memory, and double incontinence.

Brian's dementia became manifest after his retirement. He was dedicated to his work and loved it, never taking off on holidays. In retrospect, Rose felt she could detect signs of senility that had been there while he was still employed. He would sometimes wake up in the morning and ask her, in confusion, where he was supposed to go that day. "So it was coming on him then," she said, but she could not recognize it at the time. Now, each day, Brian's work ethic persisted. He insisted on sweeping the sidewalk and paths in front of their building each afternoon because he felt he had to be doing something to merit the old-age pension he received each month.

Rose remembered discussing Brian's case with the hospital consultant who first diagnosed his Alzheimer's disease.

> "You don't realize your husband could live for 10 years," he said. That was four years ago. He wasn't as bad then. I still wouldn't want him to get anything bad [enough to put him in the hospital]. Don't get me wrong. I mean, sometimes I give up. And I don't want to be a martyr or anything like that. He was a good husband for 37 years and I wouldn't like to not do what I could [for] as long as I could.

There were a number of supports and services that helped Rose to keep providing care for Brian while avoiding the anointment of martyrdom. A married daughter came to visit once a week and took their laundry home with her. Brian himself was out three days a week, attending a day-center [care] program for demented elderly people run by the Department of Social Services. The latter agency also sent a Home Help to Brian's home each week, as well as a volunteer to give Rose some respite on another day. A former Home Help even continued to check in on the couple, an act of concern that greatly touched Rose.

She confessed: "I couldn't do it if I didn't get a break because it's very wearying all the time—he's so restless." Rose was a member of two support groups for carers, one run by her local Neighbourhood Office, and the other by CHOICE, a voluntary charity supported by the Family Welfare Association. These groups were important as "an outlet" for her; she found them both distracting and comforting at the same time.

Rose had been fortunate in the sequence and sensitivity of helpers and professionals she had met. She had first contacted her general practitioner about Brian, and this had led to Brian's brief period of hospitalization and diagnosis. After his release, the hospital arranged for the community nurse to visit, and it was this woman who put Rose in touch with both CHOICE and a local social worker. The latter helped to get the services of a Home Help and found a support group for Rose and a place for Brian at the day center.

Over the years, Rose remained well connected to medical as well as social services. She received incontinence pads and monthly visits from a community nurse. When needed, she took Brian to see a consultant at the district hospital. She kept a pad on which she wrote down all the questions she wanted to ask him at their next appointment. During the preceding year Brian had developed a loud, constant growling noise, which the medical staff had finally been able to bring under control after experimenting with various drugs and dosage levels. Rose was satisfied with Brian's treatment, both as an in-patient and out-patient, but she was also reluctant to have her husband see the doctor too often because of the drugs he was given. She said: "I don't like to see him too heavily medicated, you understand," noting that the drugs diminished the degree of his reality orientation. And, she explained, the less he could connect to her and what was real and enjoyable in his life, the less meaningful it was for her to care for him.

Rose herself wondered whether Brian would be looked after more adequately in a residential institution, but she would counter her own thought by arguing that he was doing no one any harm by staying where he was. Once, during a visit, Brian joined us near the kitchen table and looked out their 12th-floor window and across a park to a small factory. He saw smoke rising from the chimney, and his face and eyes lit up. "It reminds him of his work," Rose said. He has "flashes of insight and awareness like that" from time to time, and this was one reason, she said, she did not want him in a home or under too much medication: It could take moments such as these away. "When he looks and smiles at me," she explained, "there's no way I could see him put away. Little things like that . . . and I couldn't take that away from him, not just yet, anyway."

## Simon Darmante

Reflecting on his experiences caring for his senile mother, Simon Darmante was more likely to invoke the image of the devil than the cloak of martyrdom. His widowed mother, Myra, had lived in her own apartment, only a five-minute ride away from Simon's place, but the strain on him could not be measured just in terms of distance. The daily journeys to her home had grown from one to two and sometimes to three trips. In the middle of the night, Myra's panicky phone calls woke Simon and his wife Ethel: "She'd cry she was having a heart attack" said Simon, "and I'd run over and she'd meet me at the door saying, 'You want a cup of tea?' " During the day, Myra's questions, repetitions of sentences and phrases, and disappearances grew in number. Simon would leave food for her, which she would then feed to the dog. He would be near her 10 minutes, he recalled, "and the tension would become diabolical." Where he once used to take one pill a month for his angina, he ended up swallowing four a day.

Simon said he stuck it out and asked for help only after he had "come to the end, the point where you can't go in and take it any more." He recalled that his father, a large, strapping man, had kept Myra's illness secret from the family for years and had then died from the strain of caring for her. "In her own way, she killed him. She loved her family, but she did do him in." Ultimately, Simon was nearly brought to the same situation. "She actually, literally, ruined your life. If you do care, if you're a caring person, it does ruin your life."

By the time a knowledgeable social worker came into the picture, Simon was 58 and his mother 83. He had already had some "disastrous experiences" trying to get help from doctors when his mother had had some surgery. The physicians he had met denigrated the efforts of social workers, but did not offer much in the way of help themselves.

They've got no feelings for people whatsoever. They just say "get 'em out of the hospital. I've done with 'em. I can't do nothin' about it" [i.e., her senility]. . . . They're not even concerned about the stress they're puttin' on the people they're with. Their attitude is: you've looked after 'em up to now. You can keep on lookin' after 'em. That is, until you come into the hospital in place of 'em.

The first social worker Simon saw was more sympathetic, pointedly critical of the doctors, but equally ineffective. Sweet but inexperienced, in Simon's view, her judgment was that his mother could cope. "I said to her," he recalled, " 'you must be joking.' But she wasn't. Hearing something like that makes the whole family crazier."

Turned off by these initial experiences, Simon did continue to cope for several more years. He was the only one of his siblings without children, and so the burden of responsibility fell to him. He eventually had to leave his job as a salesman. His sister, Doreen, did spend one day a week with their mother, and she and Simon took turns putting their phone numbers up for Myra to call so that he could get a break. But even on those days when his number was off the wall, he could not stop worrying. Their mother would complain to each child that the other was neglecting or abusing her, and so Simon and Doreen had to learn to check out these accounts or run the risk of destroying their own relationship.

Finally, in desperation, Simon contacted the Department of Social Services, and an active case worker came to see him and his mother. She sized up their respective states of mental health and arranged care for Myra so that Simon could get away for a few days. He later recalled that she told him, "If you don't get away from this for some relief, she'll kill you before you bury her." Simon felt that she was right.

The social worker helped to put in place a series of supports for Simon and his mother: There were Meals on Wheels; regular visits by a Good Neighbour (who checks in to see if everything is okay in the home on a day-to-day basis); an Attendance Allowance (financial aid to care-givers of the elderly and impaired at home); occasional visits by a doctor; and periodic sessions with Myra, Simon, and the social worker. Some other forms of relief were not feasible or worthwhile for Simon. Being a rather private individual, he declined to join any of the carers' support groups he was told about, and, for much the same reason, his mother refused to have a Home Help, to go stay with his brother for a week, or to move to a warmer, safer apartment.

When Myra's confusion became worse and she could no longer safely live on her own, the social worker helped to place her in private nursing home at council (local government) expense. Simon felt that the kinds of relief he had received and the human contacts provided for his mother had allowed him to keep her at home for as long as he had. It was the social worker who had kept him, as he said, from "becoming like my mother." He railed against the cuts that were being made in social service and health budgets. He felt they would make people suffer by leaving them to cope even more and more on their own. "The cuts will do that. Their message is: 'Help yourself; get on with your life. You'll be all right, Jack.' Well, like hell you will be." He urged other family carers to get all the help they could as soon as possible:

> Old people come out of the idea that they don't need outside help, but don't let that rule you. *You* need help—right at the beginning. Get the social workers, the Home Helps, the Meals on Wheels, the laundry, a nurse. Get everything that is due these people . . . Get all the help *you* can get. If it comes to it, as quick as you can, get them into a home. Make the council do this. . . . Don't go through what I went through. Because you've got to carry on for years until you break and you can't take no more. Don't matter how strong you are. Start at the beginning as I finished up at the end.

### Cora Greenman

Cora Greenman saw her current situation as the result of a "terribly old-fashioned life." She and her sister Laurie had always lived together, and for the last 21 years, since their mother's death, they had shared a council apartment in the same neighborhood where they and their five siblings had grown up. Neither Cora nor her sister had ever married. Work had also bound the two sisters: They were both secretaries in the same small, family-owned company, and for years they had traveled together to and from their jobs each day.

Laurie's dementia announced itself one morning when she got lost on her way to work. When she was found by the police, hours later, she was unharmed but unable to account for her day. Her disorientation grew slowly but progressively worse over the next few years. The company kept her on for as long as possible, giving her an early retirement when Laurie, older by two years than Cora, reached pensionable age. By her mid-60s, Cora had been "watching" her sister for seven years and been "fully responsible for her for the last three."

Though she liked to handle this commitment in a fairly independent and proud way, Cora also had several forms of help for which she was quite grateful. On the financial front, she received an Attendance Allowance even though the government had turned her down for one initially. A nurse and doctor visited on occasion. Except for a consultation when Laurie became incontinent, neither sister had so far required much medical attention. Cora had a few neighbors who were willing to watch Laurie when she needed to step out. Her four brothers lived too far from London to be of much assistance, but a widowed sister, Bette, came in from Surrey each Thursday and stayed with them through Saturday. This enabled Cora to get out, do some shopping, and attend the weekly carers' support group run by CHOICE. After joining the Alzheimer's Disease Society, which contacted CHOICE, a support group leader from the latter organization called Cora to invite her to participate in that group.

Cora had no Home Helps or volunteers from any agency, but that was her own decision, she emphasized. "Mind you, I haven't asked for any. . . . I'm sure if I asked [they would come]. If I couldn't carry on as I do presently, I'd want help and would ask for it. If I got up one morning and felt I couldn't carry on, I'd pick up the phone and call Bette or Social Services to send someone."

Cora had received no special training or guidance with her tasks as a carer. She noted that it was fortunate that Laurie was smaller than her; otherwise the chores of dressing and bathing her would be far more difficult. Her sister's slowness at eating meals alternated with agitation, restlessness, and wandering, and in that sense "it is never really that peaceful in the flat."

Of the many changes in Laurie's behavior in recent years, a few had hit Cora with particular force. Her sister now almost never spoke. "She used to be a great reader," she recalled. "Now she wouldn't know a printed page from the carpet." Laurie occasionally went through periods of crying for no apparent reason. Her temperament had grown milder, becoming, as a friend put it, "sweet." "You know," Cora admitted, "that's a way you'd never have described Laurie when she was well. She was a nice person, but she could be quite sharp, and didn't suffer fools gladly . . . . So it's been a new personality to live with."

Cora hoped "to go on caring as long as I have the health and strength to." She found her responsibility a combination of hard work, occasional humor, and sadness. Reflecting on her own experiences, she asked, rhetorically, "Is it worth it? Her brain's gone and, quite frankly, perhaps anyone could do it provided they didn't hurt her. I don't think it's mattered [to Laurie] that I've done it: She's none the wiser. Perhaps occasionally she might realize it."

Yet Cora said she would not put Laurie in a home as long as she could continue to care for her. Nevertheless, the cost to her of doing this work came out in a throwaway line, the half-joking confession that she would keep on "though I may go mad in the process." There were indeed moments that were indeed quite painful. Cora had recently come across some dress patterns that Laurie had once cut out and tacked up in preparation for sewing. They had lain in a closet for years, from a time when sewing had been one of Laurie's passions. "Everything was immaculate. Not a pin out of place . . . Meticulous . . . That brought tears to my eyes. When I think of the way she was. . . ."

### Analysis

The cases presented above suggest the variety of situations faced by carers. Their histories do not pretend to exhaust the possibilities, but they do highlight some of the unique and recurrent features experienced by carers. These are worth summarizing as a prelude to the analyses that follow.

### Case Characteristics

Though small in number, the cases described above have some inherent variety, including differences in living situation, gender of carers and sufferers, and the specific kinship relationships that connect them. In the cases of Cora and Rose, people were caring for a relative with whom they resided, whereas Simon had to travel back and forth between his own apartment and that of his mother. Two of the three carers were female, and one was a male. The same numbers applied to the gender of the persons for whom they cared. The relationships between primary carers and their kin included a son and mother, a wife and husband, and an older and younger sister. And at the time of the research, Rose and Cora were continuing to provide care at home, while Simon had placed his mother in a nursing facility.

Furthermore, family members who sustained an elderly, senile relative bore a burden of responsibility from which many others would shy. That does not mean that all caregivers had consciously or willingly chosen to take on this role. Some had done so, whereas others felt that they had no viable alternative or that a commitment to care was implicit in the nature of family ties. Both Cora and Simon, for example, had siblings, but both caregivers felt that they were the "logical" choice to take on the caregiving role because they were the only two adults without children of their own. Rose thought that, as a wife, it was "natural" for her to look after Brian and not burden their grown children with that responsibility.

## Individual Differences

All of the caregivers in the study took advantage of some kinds of outside assistance. But in many cases, including Cora's and Simon's, other forms of help were available that they could not or would not utilize because of personal inclination or their family situation. Cora hoped she could carry on without much assistance. Simon's mother resented the possibility of a Home Help, while Simon was uncomfortable with the idea of a support group. A related issue on which caregivers differed, then, was how much help they wanted from outside institutions. Rose began to take full advantage of services soon after Brian's diagnosis. Cora, on the other hand, continued to insist on a minimum of formal help. Simon's case showed how a caregiver's attitude could change over time: Resistant to and rebuffed by certain agencies at the start, he eventually came to feel that people should get all the assistance they could "right at the beginning."

The particular agencies that proved the most valuable varied from person to person. Depending on individual experience, the social workers, doctors, voluntary bodies, and hospital staff were variously praised or condemned. Simon had positive and negative experiences with medical and social service staff. Rose felt she had been well treated by the Department of Social Services and a voluntary agency, but had some qualms about the medical advice and medications she had been offered for her husband. Cora, who made modest use of health services, was especially grateful for the emotional support she had gotten from CHOICE and the Alzheimer's Disease Society.

In a number of cases where a voluntary or statutory agency took the step of first contacting a caregiver to offer assistance, caregivers appreciated the fact that such an initiative had been taken. Cora noted that such a move had been instrumental in getting her into the support group that CHOICE sponsored. In Rose's case, it was a community nurse who first reached out to her after Brian's initial hospitalization. As Rose's experience also suggests, Home Helps were often found to be an especially useful and supportive presence. Friends and family were helpful to some carers but withdrew from contact in other cases. Rose had a helpful daughter, and Cora and Simon had supportive sisters. Cora also had a long-time friend, however, "who stopped coming around" because Laurie's agitation "was too nerve-wracking" for this other woman to be near.

In virtually all the situations studied, the burden of work continued to fall mainly on one person. Respite and relief were seen as crucial in circumstances that could be both relentless and provocative. Rose got some time off each week and had had help from CHOICE the preceding summer in arranging coverage for Brian so that she could go on holiday to see relatives in Ireland. Simon's experiences with respite had been mixed. His mother's resistance to outsiders was a barrier to some forms of relief. Even when his sister Doreen periodically took over as the primary carer, he could not get his mother off his mind or extricate himself psychologically from the caregiving role.

The physical, emotional, and financial costs of their responsibilities took various tolls on people. There were families in which carers had been prompted to violence against an elderly, demented relative, forcing the Department of Social Services to step in and take protective measures. In other instances, such as Simon's, carers said they could understand being pushed to the extreme of abuse (though Simon did not abuse his mother). Family members also frequently cited the monetary and medical "costs" they had paid. Most caregivers, like the three described above, had been forced to give up their jobs to look after a relative. Rose remembered that a well-meaning doctor had once urged her to go back to work, but she could not piece together large enough blocks of time to hold down a job. Many caregivers had also experienced a decline in their own health as a result of meeting this family responsibility. Simon's increased angina attacks were a case in point. A number of people, like Cora, had to fight and reapply for government health and attendance benefits after having their applications turned down by medical or social service authorities. Voluntary agency staff found that a key part of their advocacy role was devoted to helping people secure their legal entitlements.

In summary, these individual differences in the qualities of choice, support, and personal well-being made each caregiver's situation somewhat unique.

## Commonalities

There were also some commonalities in what carers experienced. Emotionally, these included feelings of fulfillment and frustration, anger and anxiety, and guilt and love. While describing their journeys through these emotional states, people consistently presented a self-image that stressed their *family* role—Simon as son, Rose as wife, Cora as sister—rather than emphasize a primary or even distinct identity as a *caregiver*. Being responsible for an elderly, demented relative added great demands to a relationship, but it did not alter the essential way in which caregivers saw themselves. As Rose once expressed it, "I'm a wife who cares, not a carer who just happens to be a wife."

Most of the caregivers interviewed said they had given up their own lives to do this work, and would now no longer expect one of their own relatives to care for them in the same way as they had cared for their loved ones should they themselves become senile. This was usually not expressed by people as a regret for having become a caregiver, but as a cautionary tale for others based upon what they had gone through. Simon's closing admonition to "get all the help *you* can get" was made in this spirit. One of the other family carers in the study, George Trayscott, cited the situation of his senile wife in order to bolster his argument that he would not want a family member to take care of him if he were to become senile:

[I] certainly [do] not want anyone in the family to care for me. Quite honestly, I believe in euthanasia in cases like this. There's no point in living if you're not enjoying it. I would consider suicide, but I'm a coward by nature and haven't got the courage of my convictions . . . [Caring for someone whose] brain is gone . . . feels like a pointless exercise . . . unless there's a glimmer of hope. Unfortunately, with Alzheimer's, there isn't. My wife doesn't really resemble the person she was in any way, really. She's completely different. I can't even think of her as being the same person. It's only when I look at photographs that I remember. She doesn't remind me of herself any more. I don't mean to sound brutal, but a death would be better because at least then you can do your grieving and coping and then get on with a new life. But this goes on and on without an end in sight and no life for yourself.

Those who had finally placed their relative in an institution felt a sense of both relief and failure in that decision, and even some people who had not done so felt compelled to explain their continued choice of home care. Simon, for example, saw justice in what he had done, but he directed the resulting anger he felt toward the government for its cuts in services arguing that these would make the situation of other care-givers even harder than his had been. Rose defended her decision to keep Brian at home for now by suggesting that while an institution might have offered him better medical treatment, giving him home care was "doing no one any harm." A very different note was sounded in the case of Alice Potter, a woman who had nursed her terminally ill father until his death, but who eventually had to put her senile mother in a home. The emotional aftermath of that placement was almost as intense for Alice as what she went through during the caring of her mother, and her sadness at it often gave way to guilt. "It's not what I wanted for my mother's old age," she said. "Having tried so hard, it still feels like some sort of failure. I'd have liked to see it through to the end as I did with my father."

As these various cases suggest, few of the carers looked back on their experience without some doubts about the value of their efforts or the manner in which they had done their work.

## Structural and Perceptual Issues

Within the borough of Islington, there were several structural and perceptual problems that people faced who worked in, or were served by, the voluntary and public sectors. Five of these were of particular significance.

First, many clients and service providers were not well informed about the nature of dementia or the benefits and supports available to elderly people and their families. For example, few of those contacted in the study were aware that Islington employed a nurse who was a specialist in problems of incontinence. Cora had only heard about this person from another caregiver who belonged to her support group. Simon, reflecting on a more general lack of awareness, bemoaned the fact that none of his early professional contacts had advised him about the course that his mother's dementia was likely to take. Her decline would have been easier to handle, he felt, had he been able to anticipate its progress.

Second, most of the agency staff interviewed expressed the hope that families would come to them for help in the early stages of senility, but they found that many caregivers deferred such requests until late in the disease's progress because of their commitment to an ethic of self-sufficiency. While they admired the resilience of people like Cora and Simon, Rose was the kind of client they preferred. A social worker who had handled many such cases explained that she hoped for early referrals because "you get to know the client before the dementia sets in deeply, and then you've got something of that person's history and identity to hold on to . . . But if you only get to meet people after they are far gone, then there is nothing to build on."

Third, cuts in government spending limited what the National Health Service and local authorities could provide for caregivers and the elderly in Islington, and this placed additional demands on the already-burdened voluntary agencies. The borough's Department of Social Services for example, had only one social worker specifically trained to work with the elderly and their carers, which meant that the latter often found more knowledgeable and sympathetic responses from staff in the voluntary sector. Furthermore, Social Services could only offer a limited amount of respite and relief for family carers; therefore, more carers (like Rose) were turning to charitable bodies for Care Attendants or holiday schemes than had done so in the past. Access to medical care was also becoming increasingly problematic. During 1987 and 1988, the National Health Service was planning to close down the major psychogeriatric ward serving Islington as part of a cost-cutting deinstitutionalization process. Consequently, the borough's voluntary agencies found themselves taking a more active advocacy role on behalf of families who would have fewer in-patient hospital options for their demented relatives in the future.

Fourth, the fact that medical and social work responsibility for the borough was divided between two District Health Authorities and 24 Neighbourhood Offices created problems of communication and accountability, as well as an unevenness of services from one locality to another. Rose and her social worker, for example, both felt that she and Brian were fortunate to be living within the catchment area of the District Health Authority with the more effective geriatric services.

Simon, on the other hand, was one of several carers affected by rumors that were circulating about inequities in the level of local support. He had heard (quite correctly, as it turned out) that certain social services that were unavailable at his mother's Neighbourhood Office were being offered to people in other parts of the borough.

Fifth, there were also tensions between the staffs in the health and social service sectors over their respective degrees of competency and appropriate responsibilities for the two client populations of elderly sufferers and their carers. Doctors and social workers often saw one another as the "gatekeepers" or the "linchpins" in the system of care, but neither group would wholeheartedly accept the way these other professionals defined and perceived them. This left carers such as Simon confused about who to turn to for assistance and advocacy, while often being cycled through a sequence of referrals as one person or agency passed them on to another.

### Comparisons

The situation in Islington can be looked at in the light of other studies that have been done on elderly people and their caregivers in Great Britain. This other research has revealed tensions, concerns, and emphases similar to those found in the borough, and seven comparative points can briefly be noted here:

1. Throughout England and Wales, support groups for carers are one of the most widely encountered and effective types of services (Webb, 1987). The positive experiences that Cora and Rose had in such groups illustrate this point.

2. Similarly, Home Helps have been singled out frequently by British caregivers as an especially valued source of assistance because of the relief and personalized attention that they provide (Bowl, 1986, p. 129; Qureshi & Walker, 1986, p. 117). Rose's remarks reflect this kind of assessment.

3. There are widespread disagreements between health and social service personnel in Great Britain over their respective degrees of competency and responsibility for working with the frail elderly and their families (Health Education Council, 1986, p. 112; Mann, 1987; Kohner, 1988). Simon's difficulties indicate how these professional conflicts can have an impact on carers.

4. There is considerable unevenness in the level of services for dependent people and their carers from one locality to another in Great Britain. As

Rose's and Simon's cases show, even within Islington there are differences from one Neighbourhood Office and Health District to the next. Furthermore, in some areas of the country, only voluntary organizations provide significant supports. One reflection of the importance of charitable bodies is that, on a national level, staff from social work and health agencies tend to be better informed about what the voluntary sector offers to carers than they are about one another's services (Webb, 1987).

5. Though voluntary agencies play a significant role in supporting home care providers, voluntarism and the place of the voluntary sector are also issues of controversy in Britain. Labor union concerns have been expressed about the use of volunteers in place of paid personnel (National Union of Public Employees, 1987). In addition, there is a fear on the part of voluntary organizations themselves that they will be used—as one Islington agency director said—"to do the local authority's job on the cheap."

6. Critics of government policy who support the idea of community care argue that its financing is inadequate. They note that official claims about its "cost effectiveness" overlook what family carers actually "pay" in lost freedom, health, family life, and personal wages (Nissel & Bonnerjea, 1982; Henwood & Wicks, 1984; Qureshi & Walker, 1986). The decline in health that Simon suffered, the difficulty Cora faced in getting her benefits, and the loss of work by all three carers featured here, illustrate these hidden costs.[2]

7. Lastly, British observers have noted that family caregiving for the elderly is not only unpaid, but it is also unseen and socially isolating. The "invisibility" of what "informal" carers do has several sources (Levin, Sinclair & Gorbach, 1983; Jones & Vetter, 1984; McGwire, 1988).

   a. Government support and public recognition of the efforts of caregivers are modest at best.

   b. Both neediness and capability can conspire to deprive a carer of support. Agency personnel in Islington noted that the more help a carer needed, the less capable he or she may be of asking for it; the more capably a carer functioned, the less likely it was that others would recognize what she was doing and offer her assistance.

   c. The problems caregivers face in securing help are also derived from their self-image and conception of their role. Specifically, many British carers do not distinguish between their caregiving function and their kin status as spouse, sibling, or child to the demented individual. In the view of some professionals and advocates, the difficulty that people have in defining themselves as carers (and not just as kin) diminishes their chance of securing the help and recognition they require because they do not see this as a legitimate need (Kohner, 1988, pp. 1-2). This, along with the value of independence, contributes to the tendency of many British families to ask for help only as a last resort (Qureshi & Walker, 1986, p. 124). While the roles of kin and carer are often congruent, it is hard to fulfill the demands of the latter without feeling at times that one has compromised the former. It was this ambiguity which lay at the heart of Cora's fear, Rose's doubts, and Simon's sense of failure.[3]

## Conclusion

Carers, and those who supported and served them, were faced with a situation that defied two of the central hopes that medical and social services hold out to people: It was, as one social worker in Islington said, a situation that was only going to get worse, and it was going to continue indefinitely. There was no comfort to be found in a promise of improvement or in the idea that hard times were time limited. Rather, people found their rewards, often quite substantial ones, in a sense of love, duty, or both. Families hoped to fulfill their responsibilities, to get the help they needed, and to endure in an otherwise hopeless situation. Voluntary agencies tried to assist and advocate for carers who were too overburdened to seek help and recognition. People working in the public sector hoped to serve their clients and patients, but they were sometimes unsure of whether the elderly or their carers were the primary consideration. Staff in both public and voluntary agencies hoped that the next round of budget cuts would not imperil their jobs or their ability to perform them.

Hope itself has sometimes been seen as the ultimate delusion of modern times. Camus argued that to live with only knowledge and memories yields "the bleak sterility of a life without illusions. There can be no peace without hope" (1962, p. 253). Kierkegaard felt that while recollection was the illusion of the old, hope was the delusion of the young (1954, pp. 191-192). However, research suggests that for those people who were trying to sustain the elderly and their caregivers, there were also certain cultural factors that could enhance or diminish the quality of hope with which they lived their lives. Hope sometimes foundered on budgets and insensitivity, on professional jealousies and antipathies, or on the incompatible needs and values of the demented, their carers, and those who would help them. Recognizing these problems was a first step towards resolving them. For the demented and their kin, the solutions might not yield the hope of recovery, but they could still offer the recovery of hope.

## Notes

1. Voluntary bodies, labor unions, and political parties have also made comprehensive proposals in recent years to improve the situation among the elderly and their family caregivers (e.g. Age Concern England, 1985; Labour Party, 1987; National Union of Public Employees, 1987).

2. These cases support Gubrium and Lynott's (1987, p. 278) observation that people who care for victims of Alzheimer's are this disease's "second victims."

3. While many people in Islington had found substantial and sympathetic help from medical and human service personnel, there were clearly gaps in the system of care that needed to be considered. Since one of the purposes of this study was to identify weaknesses in the system and suggest policy changes to address them, the full report of the project (Savishinsky, 1989b) contained a number of recommendations. These included the following:

(1) A dialogue should be established in the borough between members of the National Health Service and the Department of Social Services to clarify their respective roles in the system of care. Islington's Joint Consultative Committee, a statutory body comprised of representatives from both of these services, could provide a suitable forum for this process. Its members should consider whether there is one ideal route that all carers should follow to get help, or whether several paths are possible.

(2) Voluntary and public sector agencies should create or designate one staff position in the borough to serve as a central place for caregiving families to turn for information or assistance (see also Webb, 1987; Age Concern England, 1985, p. 91). A simple pamphlet that summarizes the benefits and supports offered in Islington should be prepared for professionals and families.

(3) An annual workshop should be held in the borough to inform service providers about the nature of dementia and the kinds of help available to local families.

(4) Policy-making bodies and advocacy organizations in Islington need to solicit and articulate the needs of caregivers in their work. Voluntary agencies should continue to take an activist role in this regard.

## References

Addison, C. (1986, August). The wish to stay at home. *Social Work Today, 11*, 10-11.

Age Concern England. (1985). *The Age Concern England Handbook*, (2nd ed.). Mitcham, England: Author.

Bowl, R. (1986). Social work with older people. In C. Phillipson & A. Walker (Eds.), *Ageing and social policy: A critical assessment* (pp. 128-145). Aldershot, England: Gower.

Camus, A. (1962). *The plague*. (S. Gilbert, Trans.). New York: Time-Life Books.

Department of Health and Social Services (DHSS). (1981a). *Growing older*. Her Majesty's Stationery Office. Cmnd. 8173.

Department of Health and Social Services (DHSS). (1981b). *Care in the community*. London: Author.

Griffiths, R. (1988). *Community care: An agenda for change*. A Report to the Secretary of State for Social Services. London: Her Majesty's Stationery Office.

Gubrium, J. (1987). Organizational Embeddedness and Family Life. In T. Brubaker (Ed.), *Aging, health and family: Long-term care* (pp. 23-41). Newbury Park, CA: Sage.

Gubrium, J., & Lynott, R. (1987). Measurement and The Interpretation of Burden in The Alzheimer's Disease Experience. *Journal of Aging Studies, 1,* 265-285.

Health Education Council. (1986). *Who cares? Information and support for the carers of confused people*. London: Author.

Henwood, M. & Wicks, M. (1984). *The forgotten army: Family care and elderly people*. London: The Family Policy Studies Centre.

Jones, D. A. & Vetter, N. J. (1984). A Survey of Those Who Care for The Elderly at Home: Their Problems and Their Needs. *Social Science and Medicine, 19,* 511-514.

Kierkegaard, S. (1953). *The sickness unto death* (W. Lowrie, Trans.). Garden City, NY: Doubleday and Co.

Kohner, N. (1988). *Caring at home: A handbook for people looking after someone at home*. London: Health Education Authority.

Labour Party. (1987). *Caring for people: A charter for community care*. London: Author.

Levin, E., Sinclair, I., & Gorbach, P. (1983). *Supporters of confused elderly persons at home*. London: National Institute of Social Work.

Lohr, S. (1988, August 7). British Health Service Faces A Crisis in Funds and Delays. *The New York Times, pp. 1, 12.*

Mann, A. (1987, May). Co-operation Between Health and Social Services in Caring for Elderly People. *Social Work Today, 4,* 10-11.

McGwire, S. (1988). Who Cares for The Carers? *The Guardian,* January 12, 1988, 10.

Means, R. (1986). The Development of Social Services for Elderly People: Historical Perspectives. In C. Phillipson & A. Walker (Eds.), *Ageing and social policy: A critical assessment* (pp. 87-106). Aldershot, England: Gower.

National Union of Public Employees. (1987). *Time for justice: NUPE's report on health care for the elderly*. London: Author.

Nissel, M. & Bonnerjea, L. (1982). *Family care of the handicapped elderly: Who pays?* London: Policy Studies Institute.

Peace, S. (1986). The Forgotten Female: Social Policy and Older Women. In C. Phillipson & A. Walker (Eds.), *Ageing and social policy: A critical assessment* (pp. 61-86). Aldershot, England: Gower.

Qureshi, H. & Walker, A. (1986). Caring for Elderly People: The Family and The State. In C. Phillipson & A. Walker (Eds.), *Ageing and social policy: A critical assessment* (pp.109-127). Aldershot, England: Gower.

Sankar, A. (1988). Home Care: The Issues and The Policy. *Newsletter of the Association for Anthropology and Gerontology, 9*(1), 2-4.

Savishinsky, J. S. (1989a). Families, Dementia Sufferers, and Community Services: An Assessment of Programs in a London Borough. *Newsletter of the Association for Anthropology and Gerontology, 10*(1), 5-7.

Savishinsky, J. S. (1989b). *Dementia sufferers and their carers: A study of family experiences and supportive services in the London Borough of Islington.* Report Prepared for the Working Party on Dementia Sufferers and Their Carers. London: Islington Age Concern.

Shanas, E. (1979). The Family as a Social Support System in Old Age. *The Gerontologist, 19,* 169-174.

Trager, B. (1980). *Home health care and national policy.* New York: Haworth.

Webb, I. (1987). *People who care: A report on carer provision in England and Wales for the Cooperative Women's Guild.* London: The Cooperative Women's Guild.

Willcocks, D., Peace, S., & Kellaher, L. (1987). *Private lives in public places: A research-based critique of residential life in old people's homes.* London: Tavistock.

# PART TWO:

# Patterns of Caregiving

# 5

# *Invisible Caregivers in the Spotlight:*

## *Non-Kin Caregivers of Frail Older Adults*

JUDITH C. BARKER
LINDA S. MITTENESS

The phenomenon of non-kin caregiving, one of the "invisible" ways in which the frail elderly get care, will be examined in this chapter. When talking about the dependent frail elderly, commentators (e.g., Field, 1972; Hendricks & Hendricks, 1986) often see few options between caregiving by family and some form of institutional care:

> Experience points to the fact that when the elderly person is no longer able to care for himself in his own home and does not wish to or cannot share the home of his children, the only recourse open to him is to accept some form of congregate living, often referred to as "institutional care" (Field, 1972, pp. 78-79).

Caregiving by non-kin, however, is a largely unrecognized way by which some frail elderly arrange for care and stave off congregate living. After first presenting sociodemographic information about a sample of non-kin caregivers and their dependents, this chapter will

AUTHORS' NOTE: The research reported in this chapter was supported by an NIA Research Career Development Award (#AG00274) and an NIA Research Grant (#AG03471) awarded to Dr. Mitteness.

The authors wish to acknowledge the valuable contributions of Connie Wolfsen, RN, MS, and Margaret Lynch, MA, to this research project.

investigate how these relationships became established and what tasks and levels of care are involved. Issues relevant to policy will also be discussed.

All I knew for certain as I trudged up the dozen steps toward the front door was that inside this frame house was an elderly woman who had recently received in-home health care. The whens, whys, and wherefores of her use of this kind of health service was what I had come to discover. I had a hint that there was probably a husband present, as a male voice had made the appointment over the telephone. So, I wasn't surprised when the door was opened by a tall, handsome Hispanic man with an infectious smile. But I was not prepared for him to be young. Not a husband, then; a son, perhaps?

Barely had he told me his name, Roberto,[1] and ushered me inside the door when, apologizing, he rushed away to the next room, explaining as he went that he'd left Wilma on the commode. In a rather drab and dim front room, sparsely furnished with a well-worn 1950s-style sofa and chair, I awaited his return. What I could see of the inside of the house was also showing distinct signs of needing a spring-cleaning and minor repairs: An obvious thick layer of dust covered the furniture; in places, the threadbare carpet was stained; the plaster walls had cracks and peeling paint.

Unable to see into the next room, I could hear Roberto talking, explaining, cajoling, saying over and over, "Come on now, Wilma. We have a visitor. Someone's come to talk to you, see how you're doing." At first there was no audible response. Then came a murmur that soon escalated into a loud, tremulous, and reedy voice making querulous complaints about not being able to go back to bed. Complaints that ended abruptly in high-pitched screams followed by unintelligible shouts. Quietly but insistently, Roberto responded, reiterating that they had a visitor and urging her to grasp her walker and go to the kitchen, where he had some of her favorite cookies and a drink of milk for her.

His calm insistence paid off. A few minutes later, they emerged from her bedroom. Wilma proved to be a small, stooped, frail white woman, with a mop of curly white hair and glasses. Dressed in clean slacks, a blouse, and sweater, with slippers on her feet, she shuffled along. Walking backwards in front of her, his hands holding her gnarled and twisted fingers onto the pick-up walker, Roberto slowly maneuvered her, one step at a time. As they went, whenever she could, she swatted him, hitting him on the arm, muttering constantly, screaming occasionally. Eventually Roberto got her seated in the kitchen. While she ate, he returned and told me the story of their relationship.

## Family, "Others," and Caregiving

Roberto is but one of a number of "invisible" caregivers who tend the frail elderly. He is neither husband nor son. He is not even remote kin. He wasn't a friend or neighbor. He is not a paid employee of a professional social service or helping agency. Yet he alone cares for this frail old woman. Roberto is a member of that heterogeneous and largely unknown group of people that the current literature on caregiving and the elderly generally designates as "other". Roberto is a non-kin caregiver.

There is normative support for family involvement in informal caregiving, whereas considerable ambiguity surrounds the role of nonfamily assistance. Sociological theory about the family in modern industrial society argues that spouses and children can be counted on to provide care on a long-term basis to the frail elderly, whereas friends, neighbors, and others outside the (nuclear) family unit provide only supplementary assistance, usually in arenas that do not require intimacy, such as shopping or transportation. Moreover, family theorists assert that because of the lack of formal rights and duties in such optional social relationships, non-kin caregivers cannot cope with disabled individuals on a long-term basis (Croog, Lipson, & Levine, 1972; Litman, 1971; Litwak & Szelenyi, 1969; Parsons & Fox, 1951; Shanas, 1979).

### Prevalence of Non-Kin Caregiving

Investigators of informal caregiving and the elderly have long recognized the existence of a category of caregivers other than relatives, a category composed of friends, neighbors, and unrelated persons. Most authors, however, quickly gloss over non-kin caregiving, assuming it is rare and idiosyncratic. Estimates of the prevalence of non-kin caregiving among the elderly range widely, from 5% or less (Caro & Blank, 1988; Stoller & Pugliesi, 1988; Townsend, 1957) to as high as 24%, depending greatly on the elder's age, sex, number of children, marital status, health, and nationality (Shanas, Townsend, Wedderburn, Friis, Milhoj, & Stehouwer, 1968; Stone, Cafferata, & Sangl, 1987). Shanas's finding (1962, p. 111) that 9.6% ($n$ = 167) of elderly respondents nominated a friend, neighbor or non-relative as the person responsible for their health in a crisis, is mid-range and similar to the proportion of non-kin caregiving reported in many studies (Lawton, Moss, & Kleban, 1984; Stephens & Christianson, 1986; Stoller & Earl, 1983; Townsend & Wedderburn, 1965).

Several factors account for the wide variation in prevalence, the most important probably being the differences in criteria for sample eligibility and selection. Large national or metropolitan probability samples tend to report non-kin caregiving prevalences in the mid-range, around 10%; studies with much smaller or specially selected samples tend to report much higher or lower prevalences. Another factor for the variation is definitional, a common practice being that of including distant kin, such as grandchildren or nieces, in the "other" category along with non-kin. The third factor is that most authors report only household composition or living arrangements, from which the presence of caregiving is inferred.

Despite these methodological difficulties, the available figures suggest that non-kin caregivers are not so much rare as uncommon. Approximately one in ten elderly people receive informal support and assistance from sources outside the immediate family or extended kin group.

### The Study

Roberto and the other caregivers we discuss here were encountered during ethnographic research into how the frail homebound elderly manage their health conditions on a daily basis. Respondents were clients of a large, Medicare-certified, urban, home health care agency, and comprised a random sample of all people aged 65 years or over who had been referred throughout 1987 and 1988. On several occasions during a period of six months, these respondents (or their caregivers, who spoke for those unable to speak for themselves) were intensively interviewed using semistructured protocols. Interviews covered a broad range of topics: sociodemographic factors and informal social support, use of formal services, health history and current medical conditions, health beliefs and management strategies, and daily routines. Standardized measures to assess physical and mental functioning complemented the interview information.

Of the total of 212 elderly respondents interviewed, 29 individuals were discovered to have non-kin caregivers. This is a substantial proportion of the total sample (14%), but is a figure that tallies well with other recent studies. Stephens and Christianson (1986, p. 26), for example, report that 12% of their elderly subjects had unrelated caregivers. Benjamin and colleagues (1989) discovered that between 12% and 15% of their sample of elderly patients discharged from a hospital, either to home care or without, had friends or neighbors as caregivers; and Lawton et al. (1984) discuss three national studies which indicate 11%, 12%, and 18% of elderly respondents respectively,living with people other than a spouse or child.

As used here, a non-kin caregiver is a person who accepts primary responsibility for their dependent's well-being, either at the older person's urging or on their own initiative, and who had no officially recognized family connection to the care recipient at the start of the caregiving arrangement. This definition excludes distant relatives, such as grandchildren, nephews, or cousins, who are so often included elsewhere. It also excludes paid help where the relationship between caregiver and dependent is primarily contractual and monetary (i.e., employees of formal service agencies hired specifically to provide assistance). Moreover, frail old people receiving care in board-and-care or other communal living situations, such as convents, are not included. The one homosexual couple encountered in this study is included because this relationship is not officially recognized by the wider society as familial, as involving the rights and duties usually accorded spouses. Some non-kin caregivers are assisted by paid help or by others, even family members, on either an intermittent or regular schedule, but so long as the caregiver who takes full-time, ultimate responsibility for the elderly recipient's well-being is an unrelated person, then the association is classed as a non-kin arrangement.

All frequencies, percentages, and descriptive material refer to the sample of 29 non-kin caregivers and their elderly dependents.

The total sample in the study was randomly selected and is representative of the older clientele of the agency, but without some external criteria or some prior knowledge of the general characteristics of non-kin caregivers, we do not know if this sample truly represents non-kin caregivers. While this obviously limits the generalizability of the present findings, it does not entirely negate them. This is a sustained exploration of a group of non-kin caregivers that generates some provocative questions. Basically, however, we agree with Lawton et al. (1984, p. 342) that special sampling endeavors are needed to properly delimit and understand this small but nonetheless important group of caregivers to the elderly.

### Who Are the Elderly Dependents and their Non-Kin Caregivers?

Wilma is 84 years old and has lived in this house since her husband built it just after their wedding some 60 years ago. She has been widowed for over 20 years now. Childless, she has become very fond of Roberto, her 33- year-old caregiver. For five years now, he has lived with her and cared for her, 24 hours a day, 7 days a week. Roberto has little knowledge of her early life, family relationships, religious affiliation, education, occupational history, or economic worth.

### Care Recipients

The elderly with non-kin caregivers do not differ from the larger study sample with respect to sociodemographic characteristics, such as age, gender, ethnicity, marital status, or socioeconomic status. The mean age is 79.6 years, ($SD$ 9.4, range 65-96); just over half (56%, $n = 16$) are female; most (76%, $n = 22$) are white; and, a sizable proportion (38%, $n = 11$) have low incomes (less than $15,000 a year).

Respondents vary widely in occupational and educational background, from being successful authors or high-ranking executives in international companies through to small business operators, tradespeople, clerks, secretaries, longshoremen, and janitors. A couple of dependents have postgraduate degrees, but most have simply completed a high-school education, though a few have not finished grade school. All major religious affiliations are represented.

### Marital Status

The majority (55%, $n = 16$) of respondents are widowed.[2] Four (14%) respondents, mainly males, have never married, and three (10%) of the individuals are divorced or separated. Five (17%) care recipients are married.

One spouse is a caregiver who has recently married her dependent. Another is an estranged wife who, after 10 years apart, moved back into her husband's house to care for him after his girlfriend refused to deal with his need for dialysis. The three other spouses, however, are equally or more physically frail or demented than the respondent, so much so, in fact that, the non-kin caregiver is looking after not one but two frail older adults. One such married couple consists of a 66-year-old alcoholic woman with a history of osteoporosis and falls and her 70-year-old bedridden husband, who suffers from very bad emphysema. They are being looked after by the wife's hairdresser whose business is on the same block. Every weekday, for two hours in the early morning and again in the late evening (before and after business hours), the caregiver comes to prepare meals, assist the husband with personal care, and do general housekeeping chores.

## Number of Children

The literature clearly shows that children, especially daughters, are the major caregivers of elderly people (Stone et al., 1987). The pool of potential kin caregivers is restricted for the elderly who do not have children, who have children living out of the area, or who are alienated from their children. Shanas (1962, p. 101) discovered that elderly people without children had a much higher number of "other" caregivers than did people with children. More than half (55%, $n = 16$) of the non-kin dependents in our sample have no living children. In comparison to the total sample and to the people with family caregivers, however, those with non-kin caregivers are not more likely to be without children.

Five (16%) individuals with non-kin caregivers have children who are living out of the area and are thus unavailable for day-to-day caregiving. Usually, however, these children are aware of and supportive of the non-kin caring relationship. Another five (16%) dependents have children from whom they are estranged. None of the respondents elaborated on the reasons for the hostility, anger, or alienation between them and their (adult) children. Only three elderly people (10%) have children (all sons) living in the city and with whom they have a close and caring relationship.

## Caregivers

As expected from the general literature that convincingly demon-strates that caregiving is a female task (Stone et al., 1987), most (66%, $n = 19$) non-kin caregivers are women. It is notable, however, that one-third (34%, $n = 10$) of caregivers are men.

Approximately half (53%, $n = 10$) of the female helpers look after men. The majority (70%, $n = 7$) of male caregivers in this study have female dependents. Irrespective of the sex of caregiver, male depen-dents have caregivers who are significantly (Fisher's Exact $p < .007$) closer to them in age than do female dependents.

Generational distance between non-kin caregivers and their depen-dent charges is large. No non-kin caregiver is older than the care recipient, and only two (7%) caregivers are within 10 years of the age of their care recipients. The majority (93%, $n = 27$) of non-kin care-givers are considerably younger than their charges: 10 (34%) caregivers are between 10 and 30 years younger than their recipients; however, the majority (59%, $n = 17$) of caregivers are more than 30 years younger than their charges.

Two-thirds of the dependent elderly in our study have caregivers from the same ethnic background. Altogether, however, there are nine (31%) cases in which the non-kin caregivers and their dependents are of different ethnic backgrounds. Six (27%) of the 22 white care recip-ients are looked after by non-white women, four Filipinas and two Japanese Americans. Only two (13%) of the 15 white caregivers look after non-white people. Six (40%) white caregivers are of Hispanic origin, all caring for non-Hispanic white individuals. The four black non-kin caregivers all have black dependents.

### Entering the Caregiving Relationship

Roberto was reluctant to provide much detail about how he met Wilma or to tell exactly how the caregiving relationship was estab-lished. Although he grew up in the neighborhood, he did not know Wilma even casually before their caregiving association began 5 years ago. Roberto first met Wilma in the company of her former caregiver, another young man who was leaving to undertake special-ist trade training in another city. Unemployed at the time and recently separated from his wife, Roberto desperately needed a job and some means of getting an income to make child-support payments for his young son, so he volunteered for the job of caring for Wilma.

Quite frank about how at first he saw caring for Wilma as a heaven-sent opportunity, a way of making easy money from a lonely and needy old lady, Roberto says his attitude now is different. He didn't intend to defraud or con Wilma out of her assets; he just thought it would be a quick and easy way for him to make money without really having to do much for it. The reality is very different. Caring for her has not only been long term, but is physically demanding, emotionally draining, and all-encompassing. It has not resulted in many material rewards or cash payments.

With no previous experience of caregiving, he has learned all the necessary skills "on the job" by talking to her doctor, visiting nurses, and hospital staff. Roberto sees this experience as an asset that he could use in the future to care for another old person.

Most studies of informal support and the elderly allude to friends and neighbors as comprising the major component of non-kin caregivers (Caro & Blank, 1988; Stephens & Christianson, 1986; Townsend, 1957; Stoller & Earl, 1983). By the time people become established in a non-kin caregiving arrangement, friendship is the easiest way to explain the association. However, the actual way in which non-kin caregivers commence association with their dependents is much more diverse than the term friend or neighbor implies.

### Initial Contact

Stephens and Christianson (1986, p. 26), for example, found 11.6% ($n = 225$) of their elderly sample were looked after by friends and neighbors, and another seven people (0.4%) were cared for by employees or volunteers who were friends prior to the provision of care. We discovered some very complex and unusual relationships—and some very straightforward and mundane—between non-kin caregiver and dependent.

Seven (24%) caregivers were casual acquaintances, usually living in the same neighborhood as the dependent. Six (21%) people were long-time friends, at least three of whom were formerly, if not currently, lovers. Another six (21%) individuals, being tenants or pupils, had patron-client relationships with their dependent. Four (14%) cases involved housekeepers who graduated to full-time caregiving.

Six (21%) people, however, had less common associations with their charges. One caregiver was the widow of a former junior colleague, while another was the granddaughter of the dependent's conservator. One had simply answered a newspaper advertisement for a companion. Yet another was an ex-wife living in a neighboring apartment, while the fifth was the estranged wife previously mentioned. The sixth caregiver, the recently married wife, has a more complex association with her dependent.

Rosa, now 62 years old, met her physically incapacitated 90-year-old husband, David, when she was hired by an agency several years ago to provide meals and light housekeeping for two hours a day. Very soon thereafter, she voluntarily began to spend more time with him, providing general care. Eventually she quit the agency to care for him full-time. After a number of years during which Rosa resisted David's increasingly insistent requests that they marry, she agreed to do so and they were wed. This made her an heir to his very large estate, to the extreme chagrin of his two daughters, each of whom lived within a 10-minute drive of their father. Neither of the daughters provided care. The marriage did not go unchallenged. In an attempt to salvage an inheritance they saw as theirs by right, the daughters took the issue to court, aided by David's long-time physician and lawyer, both of whom were scandalized by the marriage. They argued that the marriage was not just prima facie evidence of David's mental incompetence, for which he should be institutionalized, but, more importantly, it revealed that Rosa's interest was solely financial. When the case eventually came to trial, the court was not convinced by the daughters'[3] argument. The five-year history of a successful relationship involving very intensive heavy care (by this time, David was bedridden, incontinent, aphasic, and required tube feeding) was more compelling than the kin's outrage.

### Previous Experience

The majority (79%, $n = 23$) of caregivers in the study do not have a background that necessarily equipped them for their caring role. At the beginning of the caregiving association, most caregivers had no previous experience in caregiving, whether it be to children or adults, nor any background in medicine or nursing. Three (10%) caregivers, however, all immigrant women, either have nursing training that is unrecognized in this country or had taken a special training course after coming to the United States that prepared them particularly well for this sort of role.

Three (10%) non-kin caregivers previously cared for other people. One had cared for the deceased wife of the man she currently looks after, while another had cared for her current dependent's sister. The third experienced caregiver, a man in his late 60s, has a history of filling his days by assisting others with such tasks as shopping and banking. Frank, a former janitor, and Barney, a retired taxi driver, live in the same downtown hotel. Barney had hip and knee replacement surgery seven months ago and although he can generally care for himself very well, he is not yet very mobile. He still needs a wheelchair or crutches to ambulate. Every day, Frank goes by Barney's room, picks up a list of groceries or other items that Barney needs, and shops for him. On returning, Frank and Barney sit together and drink beer, chat, and watch sports on TV for an hour or so. Last year, Frank was looking after a now deceased male resident who had cancer; before that, for several years he regularly helped a female resident stricken with arthritis.

## Length of Caregiving Association

Family theory suggests that non-kin caregiving is not only likely to be instrumental rather than personal in nature, but it will not be sustained long term (Croog et al., 1972; Litwak & Szelenyi, 1969; Parsons & Fox, 1951). Stone et al., (1987) discovered that less than 20% of "other" caregiving associations in their large sample had been in existence for under a year, and around 40% had existed between one and four years. In our study, although the majority (59%, $n = 17$) of non-kin caregiving arrangements had been in existence for a year or less, almost one third (31%, $n = 9$) had been in existence much longer; five years or more. Three (10%) other relationships had lasted between two and five years.

Most short-lived caregiving arrangements between non-kin seem to be that way for one of two major reasons: The older adult is only temporarily in need, often because the person (like Barney) is recuperating from surgery or an acute episode of illness, or the care recipient requires mainly light care or instrumental task support (e.g., help in getting groceries, preparing a meal, or doing heavy housework such as cleaning bathrooms or vacuuming floors). Short-term caregiving relationships work well for these types of need where it matters less who exactly performs the task so long as someone does, and where a change in caregiver is rarely a major disruption. Socializing and reciprocal aid is the glue that holds together many short-lived non-kin caregiving relationships.

Matilda, for example, relies on her three young male tenants who live upstairs, none of whom has lived there for more than a year. As she can no longer carry heavy items or walk easily, she gets one of the tenants to take her shopping or drive her to the doctor, bank, or other business appointments. In return, she keeps the rent at a moderate level, takes parcels and messages, bakes cookies for "the boys," jests, jokes, and generally "fusses" over her tenants. Matilda deliberately delays taking a shower until she is certain at least one of the tenants is home "just in case" she should fall. This has not ever happened, but it is a possibility that constantly worries her, and she talks about how reassuring it is to know that reliable help is near.

In most long-term cases (those lasting over five years), what had started as relatively light care has over the years turned slowly but steadily into heavy care situations. Seven (78%) of the nine heavy care cases now involve caring for older adults with severe physical or mental incapacity. These non-kin caregivers have maintained their commitments to their dependents for a long time, even in the face of increasing and severe incapacity.

Take the longest caregiving situation we encountered, for example, a relationship of 12 years duration. Tom, a very frail 91-year-old black man now needs, and receives, maximum assistance from his 65-year-old neighbor who took him into her home. Sally is helped occasionally by her own two sons, and daily by Tom's 60-year-old son, who comes after work for several hours. Tom's social security and occasional small sums from his son provide very welcome financial supplements for Sally, but they do not cover all the costs incurred in caring for him. Far less impaired at the beginning of the relationship, Tom's diabetes has led over time to poor vision, a below-the-knee amputation, and dependence on a wheelchair. He is now also deaf and almost mute, incontinent of urine, and in need of nasogastric tube feeding. Confused, Tom is also becoming highly resistive to care. Sally, however, still insists that the burden of caregiving is not so great that she cannot cope. She's not yet ready to consider having him institutionalized.

**Residential Proximity**

Caro and Blank (1988) report that for their sample of elderly home health care recipients, 29% ($n = 14$) of non-kin (friend) caregivers lived in the same apartment as the care recipient, 43% ($n = 21$) lived in the same building, 12% ($n = 6$) resided in the neighborhood, and 16% ($n = 8$) lived further away. In our study, caregivers lived much nearer to their charges than in the Caro and Blank study.

We found that 16 (55%) of the caregivers share an apartment or house with their dependent. An additional 6 (21%) live in the same building, and 3 (10%) live on the same block. Two caregivers spend the daytime in their dependent's house but return to their own residence at night when another (paid) helper, an agency employee, arrives to take charge.

Unlike family members, non-kin caregivers did not take dependents into their homes but rather moved into the care recipient's dwelling. In almost all cases (88%, $n = 14$) in which the caregivers live with their dependent, the caregivers moved into the apartment or house owned or rented by the care recipient. In only two cases did the dependent move to the caregiver's residence. One such case is Tom, discussed above. The other instance involves a dependent who moved to the city in order to reside with and be cared for by a former junior colleague's widow.

## The Work of Caregiving

Roberto receives no assistance except for occasional visits by home health care nurses. Whenever Wilma has to visit her doctor, the only reason she leaves the house, the man from the store next door helps Roberto carry Wilma in a wheelchair down the front steps.

Only in the last year has she been so immobile, since she fell getting out of bed one night and fractured her hip. Before then, she was quite active, although Roberto did have to keep an eye on her. Wilma used to overflow the tub and flood the bathroom at 2 AM, or leave burners lit on the gas stove, or wander off down the street and get lost. Now the main interruptions to Roberto's sleep come from having to respond to her calls for assistance to the commode several times a night.

Wilma can do little for herself now, so Roberto does it all. He cooks, cleans, and shops. He bathes, dresses, grooms, and toilets her.

Daily, he exercises her limbs, dispenses her medications, and orients her to the world around her. Exacerbated by pain medications, Wilma's lack of mobility leads to a constant battle with constipation. Keeping her well hydrated and as mobile as possible by making her get up and walk several times a day are the strategies Roberto uses to combat this tendency. Sometimes, especially with the damp and chill of winter, her arthritis bothers her so much that she is unable to walk and she is in constant pain. It is this pain as much as her dementia that causes her to scream and to resist care.

Wilma has also had several bouts of intestinal obstruction for which she has been hospitalized three times in the last year. Even this does not give Roberto a break from caregiving as Wilma's disorientation and resistance to care escalate in that unfamiliar environment such that he becomes the only person she recognizes and responds to. So, Roberto spends as much time as possible at the hospital caring for her, thereby earning the gratitude and admiration of the nursing staff.

**Functional Capacity**

Family theory predicts that as the burden and level of caregiving increases, non-kin will opt out of the caregiving situation (Croog et al., 1972; Litwak & Szelenyi, 1969; Parsons & Fox, 1951). The literature implies that elderly dependents of non-kin caregivers will be institutionalized or moved to a higher level of care at an early stage of mental and/or physical deterioration.

Like the elderly people in the total sample, those with non-kin caregivers experienced a wide range and combination of medical problems common among the elderly. Dependents of non-kin caregivers were no more or less impaired than other care recipients, exhibiting the full range of functional impairments.

*Limitations in Function*

Some studies (e.g., Stoller & Earl, 1983; Stephens & Christianson, 1986) demonstrate that neighbors and friends provide considerable daily assistance to impaired older people in the form of shopping, transportation, and so forth. Apparently, it is unusual if that help extends to include such tasks as meal preparation or to personal care, such as toileting or bathing. The non-kin caregivers in our study, however, undertook many caregiving tasks, including such intimate tasks as bathing, toileting, and grooming.

In addition to the 4 people (14%) who were bedridden, 9 (30%) individuals needed transfer assistance in or out of bed, and another 5 (17%) people were chairfast. Eight (28%) elderly respondents were unable to negotiate stairs or ambulate outdoors without being assisted. Special transportation, such as an ambulance or medivan, was needed if 11 (37%) dependents had to leave home.

Altogether, 18 (64%) people were incontinent of urine at least once a week, 8 (26%) respondents experienced bowel incontinence at least once a week, and 1 (3%) person was doubly incontinent. Nine (30%) people did not use the toilet for elimination but were catheterized, diapered, or had a bedside commode.

Severe communication disorders, in the form of aphasia or extreme confusion, afflicted 15 (54%) respondents while 11 (39%) people suffered significant visual or auditory losses. Five (17%) people were resistive or combative, making care very difficult.

Four (15%) individuals needed help eating or were tube-fed; 12 (41%) people were not able to handle medications themselves; 13 (44%) in the sample were unable to handle finances; 19 (67%) people needed help dressing; 19 (67%) care recipients needed help bathing; 23 (81%) cases needed to have meals prepared and cooked for them; 23 (81%) individuals were unable to shop; 23 (81%) dependents did not participate in housekeeping; and 26 (89%) people could not do any laundry.

*Level of Care*

Functional status of the care recipients was evaluated using several functional status scales, including the Katz Index of Activities of Daily Living (ADLs) and the Caro Functioning for Independent Living Scale (see Kane & Kane 1981 for details of these scales). A dependent with light care needs was defined as someone with 0 or 1 impairments of ADLs, as defined by the Katz Index. Intermediate care was needed by those people with 2 to 4 impairments of ADLs and no major dementia. People with heavy care needs had 5 or 6 impairments of ADLs or more than 3 ADL impairments and major dementia.

In our study, 8 (28%) dependents were in need of light care, 10 (34%) required intermediate care, and 11 (38%) needed heavy or skilled care.

In fact, 4 people (14%) presented their caregivers (all women) with very heavy skilled care needs. All four were bedridden and required maximum assistance with personal care, three were catheterized, and two were fed by nasogastric tube. One of these four dependents, a man suffering from ALS (Lou Gehrig's disease), also had a tracheostomy requiring frequent suctioning and respiratory treatment, and was assisted by a long-time friend who quit her job in order to care for him.

Just as occasionally happens with other informal (family) caregivers, despite being willing enough to help, not all non-kin caregivers are capable of providing the level of care required. Most non-kin caregivers approximated well, providing the amount and type of care needed; many learned the necessary skills "on the job." We judged that 2 (7%) male dependents, both over the age of 85, were not receiving the optimal level of care given their functional incapacities. Both these men score highly enough on the functional assessment scales to need skilled care, yet neither one regularly receives other than light care (mainly help with shopping, meal preparation, and housekeeping).

Lawton et al. (1984, p. 342) speculate that people in unusual caregiving arrangements "may be relatively more competent than those living with children," i.e., the elderly being cared for by non-kin caregivers may be in better functional health than those receiving care from family members. In comparison to those in the total sample who had family as primary caregivers, however, people with non-kin caregivers were not significantly different in functional capacity. Our findings, then, suggest this speculation may not be true.

## Gender and Caregiving

Studies of caregiving among the elderly talk a lot about how men, even closely related men such as husbands and sons, tend not to undertake personal care tasks for dependents, but instead provide aid in transportation, financial, and other more instrumental arenas (Treas, 1977; Stephens & Christianson, 1986). Similar trends appear in this sample of non-kin caregivers.

In our study, most women caregivers undertook both instrumental and personal care tasks for their dependents. Women cared for all the very heavy physical care cases, those who were bedridden and/or needed transfer assistance to wheelchairs on which they were dependent for ambulation. Unless they resided with their dependent, male caregivers tended to shy away from personal care tasks, especially those involving intimacy, taking on care recipients requiring mainly instrumental assistance instead.

Not all male caregivers, however, had difficulty providing personal, even intimate, care. Oliver, for example, lives with Josephine, a 75-year-old former neighbor with severe Parkinsonism. She is demented, incontinent, and aggressively combative. Overwhelmed by his mother's condition, Josephine's son is unable to cope with her himself; therefore, for the last 7 years, he has paid Oliver, and a relief person on the weekends, to provide care. Every three hours, day *and* night, Oliver patiently overcomes her resistance to care and changes her diapers, does skin care routines, and makes her comfortable.

In our sample, as the level of care increases, so does the proportion of female caregivers. Women comprise 50% of the people undertaking light care, 60% of those doing intermediate level care, and 73% of those with heavy care burdens. More female than male caregivers live in their dependent's abode. So, as the level of care increases, the proportion of caregivers who live in also increases—25% of those giving light care live with their dependent; 40% of those providing intermediate care live in; and, 82% of those undertaking heavy care duties reside in the dependent's house.

### Rewards of the Relationship

Roberto says that he stays with Wilma because he has grown very fond of her, that she is "a wonderful person." He described her as being "good fun," "full of interesting stories," and a "good companion" in earlier days before her dementia became so florid. Now Roberto is impressed by her indomitability—despite her pain, dementia, and diminished social life, she still enjoys life as much as she can. He marvels at her strong will to live, and says that as long as she's prepared to stick it out, so is he.

Wilma's 80-year-old brother, who lives 100 miles to the north and visits several times a year, is her financial conservator. Roberto gets free room and board, and a small allowance for living expenses for them both, but no formal salary. His only current source of income is the rent received from the garage attached to Wilma's house which he is permitted to keep. Although he has been willed Wilma's house as payment for his years of caregiving, this is only a modest reward.

Given the current real estate market, on Wilma's death, Roberto's assets will increase by the order of around $25,000 per year of caregiving—far less than the annual cost of hiring 24-hour attendant care via a commercial social service agency.

From the dependent's perspective, the rewards of the relationship were pretty straightforward and obvious. Companionship, affection, and socialization were important corollaries to the more instrumental and personal assistance they received.

The non-kin caregivers in our study generally described the rewards of caregiving as intangible, as being in the psychological and emotional realm. Caregivers were relatively inarticulate about why they engage in caregiving and what they get out of it. A few mentioned being moved by the older person's plight and by the fact that no one else seemed to be available to help these "decent," "nice" old people. "Feeling useful" or "good" because they were "doing something worthwhile" was generally as much as the caregivers would comment on the subject of caregiving and their reward for doing so.

We were not able to get all caregivers to tell us if they currently got some material gain from their caregiving or if they expected they would in the future. Of the 22 people who divulged details of their financial and formal legal relationship with their dependent, only two claimed to receive absolutely no material gain in return for caregiving.

Eight people (36%) receive regular payment for their services. For some caregivers, this stipend was formally negotiated and is paid directly from the older person's estate by a bank, lawyer, or conservator. It is usually not a large sum, rarely above $25,000 per year. Often it is accompanied by a regular amount for living expenses for the dependent. For other caregivers, payment is quite modest, consisting only of living expenses from the older person's monthly pension or social security check.

The 16 people who live with their dependents acknowledged that the caregiving association provides them with inexpensive accommodation. For four individuals who get free room and board as direct recompense for caregiving, this is payment in kind rather than cash. One caregiver gets free voice lessons from her charge, a former teacher of music. The exact value of these lessons is doubtful, however, because her dependent is now almost completely deaf.

Seven caregivers (32%) currently receive no money from their care recipients but expect to inherit at least a portion of the dependent's estate. One dependent older man deliberately changed his will to leave his property to one of his tenants and not to the other (his daughter). The unrelated young woman who daily cajoles him into eating, bathing, and dressing, and who assists him run his business, is to inherit—not his daughter who also lives in the building but from whom he is estranged.

Given that so many non-kin caregivers in fact receive some form of current or future recompense, what distinguishes them from people employed by a formal service agency who are paid to provide care to the frail elderly? Paid helpers are hired to do a job for which they are trained. The tasks they perform and the duties they undertake are limited and clearly specified. They work for a set number of hours, and are paid on a regular schedule. Alteration in hours of duty or tasks undertaken requires renegotiation of a formal contract and a change in compensation. In short, paid helpers are professional employees. For non-kin caregivers, in contrast, there are few limits on the kinds of tasks undertaken or the time involved. Many have little preparation or training for this type of work. No formal contract delimits duties, the nature of which can and does change, usually expanding over time. Payment is minimal or deferred, and is unrelated to the extent, duration, or level of technical difficulty of service provided. Non-kin caregivers are committed amateurs.

This amateur status causes problems. A private detailed agreement between non-kin caregiver and care recipient about expectations and recompense does not resolve all issues. Take the example of Fanny. Five years ago when she was mentally competent, this wealthy but childless widow made an agreement with her young neighbor, Kate, that she would inherit Fanny's estate in return for providing all necessary care. At first, Kate lived with Fanny, but after Kate married and had a child she moved out. Every day, however, from 7 AM to around 6 PM, she and her two-year-old son would go to Fanny's house to care for her. Kate has hired a college student to spend the evenings and nights in the house with Fanny, who is now quite demented and becoming resistive of care. Last year, after Fanny's dementia had increased to near its current level, her physician began to insist that institutionalization was necessary. Kate disagreed. Eventually, the physician, aided by an old friend of

Fanny's husband, a lawyer, applied for a conservatorship on the grounds that Fanny had no security of care, that there was no reason to assume Kate would continue to care for Fanny because Kate was not socially obligated to do so and Kate was not family. Kate, however, felt morally obligated and was determined to keep Fanny in her own home as long as possible. Therefore Kate joined in the legal battle. Although gratified that she was awarded conservatorship and had won the right to continue caring for Fanny as long as possible, Kate is bitter. Caring for Fanny is difficult enough, but she believes that to have been forced to fight "the system" for the right to do so was unnecessary and exhausting.

## *The Cultural Image of Non-Kin Caregivers*

Roberto talked of the innuendoes and outright insults that he experienced from friends and family when he took on this commitment to Wilma. His estranged wife was scornful. His friends made salacious comments, insinuating that he is not just a failure but also a gigolo. His father told him to "go and get a *real* man's job." His mother was jealous and wanted to know if Roberto will care for her the same way when she is old. For a Hispanic male, such caregiving is just not macho behavior.

Wilma's neighbors and friends in the community, too, were suspicious. Roberto talked about how when he first moved into Wilma's house to care for her, the neighbors would drop in without warning "to see if I was doing a good enough job or if I was abusing her." Once he had proved himself as a reliable caregiver, their concerns faded and they stopped visiting unexpectedly. But Roberto is still aware of the dangers. When Wilma fell out of bed and fractured her hip, he was worried in case someone—the neighbors, Wilma's brother, the doctors at the hospital—thought he'd done it.

### The Mistrust Of Altruism

The propriety of intimate associations between persons of vastly different ages, between persons of opposite sexes and different ages, and between related and unrelated persons of different ages and sexes is culturally patterned (Vera, Berardo, & Berardo, 1987). There is a fear that non-kin will abuse frail old people either physically, emotionally, or criminally (usually financially).

No matter how erroneous, the "gold-digger" is a common cultural account of the reasons why younger women associate with, or marry, older men (Vera et al., 1987). A probate lawyer summed up the reasons why children want to be conservators of their parent's estate: " The kids wanna make sure that they're [the conservatee] not spending the money on 18-year-old girlfriends" (Dignum, 1982, p. 73). *Girlfriends* is one of the more polite of the many possible terms used to describe such relationships.

Double standards exist. It is acceptable for men to be much older than their wives, but not the reverse (Vera et al., 1987). Thus young men who become attached to older women, especially to widows who are deemed to be particularly vulnerable, are breaking several norms and are especially subject to societal disapproval. These men are frequently categorized as gigolos or con artists.

Not surprisingly, the caregivers of the 29 frail elderly adults in our study are very aware of these cultural images. Recall that the generation gap between dependents and their caregivers is large. Male caregivers to elderly women are particularly sensitive to these social norms. Caregivers have several ways of protecting themselves psychologically from the brunt of these cultural suspicions, and of legitimizing their relationship to the frail older dependent.

All the caregivers said that they liked, admired, and even loved their dependent at some point in time. The commitment to and continuation of caregiving was a way of expressing that affectional link, a link often parlayed into putative kin associations: "At first, you know, she was like a grandmother to me" commented a 35-year-old woman who has cared for an incapacitated, 83-year-old woman, a former neighbor, for the past eight years. Sussman (1985, pp. 424-427) differentiates these "everyday" families from conventional (spouses and children) and discretionary (distant relatives or in-laws) families. Everyday families are composed of fictive kin (peers, friends, or neighbors), interact regularly, exhibit affection and solidarity, and form naturally as a consequence of life-cycle changes or life-course transitions. Hence, non-kin caregivers and their elderly dependents are in a sense unremarkable; they are but one example of "everyday" families.

Assertions of mutual affection and kinship emphasize the importance of past behaviors and feelings in establishing a strong dependent-caregiver bond. They provide meaning to the relationship for both parties and validate it. Society values and trusts kin above others; once established, kin ties have an unquestioned legitimacy that other relationships lack. Thus ex-spouses, estranged spouses, and lovers—relatives at a distance—can be trusted more readily than outsiders. Neighbors, pupils, employees, and tenants first become friends and then family. This construction and presentation of the dependent-caregiver association as having a kin base explains in part why non-kin sustain these physically and emotionally draining relationships in the long term. Fictive kin/everyday family ties emphasize qualities of affection and commitment, and legitimize the relationship.

**Abuse and Exploitation**

The aged as a group do not comprise the largest group of crime victims in general, but they do have a greater risk of becoming victims of certain types of crime (Gubrium, 1984). The elderly are victims of fraud, forgery, and malicious mischief more than other types of crime. Recently, the crime of elder abuse has reached the forefront of public attention. An extension of the societal belief that non-kin are most likely to defraud or harass the aged is the suspicion that non-kin are also most likely to physically or emotionally abuse the elderly. Derived from general family theory, the assumption is often made that the weaker emotional, psychological, and social ties to unrelated elderly dependents will lead to greater and earlier abuse, neglect, or exploitation by non-kin caregivers (Kosberg, 1983).

Unfortunately, the evidence points to abuse of the elderly coming from close kin, spouse or children, not from unrelated others. The prevalence of abuse by non-kin suggests that it is not out of line with the general prevalence of non-kin caregiving in the community, between 10% and 15% of elder abuse cases involving non-kin (Costa, 1984; Kosberg, 1983; U.S. House of Representatives, 1980).

Factors which, jointly and severally, have been shown to operate in elder abuse situations are according to Costa (1984): age (being very old), sex (being female), disability (having severe impairments), residence (living with others), and wealth (being financially dependent). Our findings show that at least some of these factors were present in all the non-kin relationships in our study.

Not surprisingly, all caregivers, either in explicit and lengthy detail or less graphically, deny harming their dependent in any way. The mechanism they use to protect themselves from social pressures—the development of affectional ties to the point of imputing an affectional kin link—also works to protect dependents.

One striking thing about our sample is that the non-kin caregiver generally moved into the dependent's residence. Financial inequality was in the older dependent's favor: He or she had some assets to bring to the relationship. The youngest caregivers generally were not settled into marriages, or careers and were not carrying mortgages. Moreover, they benefited monetarily by virtue of cheap accommodations and a chance to continue seeking occupational or educational benefits before becoming committed to commencing their own families. This, and the construction of these ties as affectional and rewarding might account for the reasons why abuse of elderly non-kin dependents is not as common as theory would lead us to expect.

### Policy Implications

Reasonably enough, family theorists, researchers, policymakers, and service providers responsible for investigating, planning, and delivering services for all elderly people have focused their attention on understanding the caregiving and social support the elderly get from spouses and children since the majority of the elderly receive such assistance. It is time, however, to expand that focus to include the social processes that led to the unusual caregiving arrangements discussed here. These arrangements are undoubtedly worthy of extensive and more refined study.

If the population of those over 65-years of age in the United States today is 28 million, of whom 5% are frail enough to need assistance with some or all aspects of daily life (Siegel & Taeuber, 1986; Cornoni-Huntley, Foley, White, Suzman, Berkman, Evans, & Wallace, 1985),[3] then, assuming that 10% have non-kin caregivers, we can estimate that a minimum of 140,000 frail older people are being cared for by people unrelated to them. This figure might be a relatively small proportion of the dependent elderly, but it is not an insubstantial number. Moreover, it is a number that is likely to rise steadily in the future.

The mood of government now and into the foreseeable future is to expect the family to contribute substantial amounts of uncompensated care for elderly relatives (Doty, 1986). The advent of Medicare diagnostic related groups (DRGs) and prospective payment system (PPS) has already contributed significantly to the acceleration of this in-formalization of care and will continue to do so. Other social forces, however, severely constrain the family's ability (notably the woman's ability in general, especially that of the daughter) to meet the needs of chronically ill elderly on a long-term basis. These other social forces are the decreasing parent-child ratio, the changing nature of the house-hold economy, the movement of older women into the work-force, and the feminization of poverty, especially among elderly women who live alone (Estes, Gerard, & Clarke, 1984). Gaps in the informal care network will be created by such social forces, and they will have to be filled, largely by people unrelated to the care recipient.

Physical proximity is the most important single factor that deter-mines friendship, for the young as well as the aged (Duck & Gilmour, 1981; see also Peters & Kaiser, 1985). Rosow (1967) found that the community-living elderly not only had more or fewer friends depending on the number of elderly in the surrounding neighborhood, the elderly in age-integrated environments rarely made friends with people who were much younger. This latter finding has often been replicated (e.g., Hochschild, 1973). In light of these findings, it is important to discover the circumstances under which elderly people accept, establish, and maintain friendships and caring relationships with younger individuals, and to explore what motivates some younger people to set up and maintain caring commitments to unrelated older individuals. This, however, raises myriad important and thorny policy issues.

Age-segregated housing reduces proximity between older and youn-ger people. In turn, this increases existing barriers to the formation of friendships between generations, thereby reducing the chances for the creation of natural informal helping networks, non-kin caregiving ar-rangements, or "everyday" families.

For some frail elderly people who have few assets other than a home, offering room and board in exchange for caregiving might be a very viable means of staving off institutionalization. Greater support for pro-grams that link up homeowners with tenants (Pritchard, 1983; Struyk & Katsura, 1988) could well be one arena in which policy and govern-ment, be it local, state, or federal, could play a crucial role.

Before such policy could be successfully formulated or implemented, however, many complex and difficult issues would have to be better understood and resolved. The construction of obligation between non-kin and the approbation of such relationships are just two issues. What starts as a relatively contractual association between dependent elder and non-kin caregiver often changes over time into putative kin relationships, with shifting expectations and shifting criteria for evaluation. How to establish policy to deal effectively with such fluctuating and fluid arrangements will be a challenge. Perhaps the greatest challenge, however, will come from society's norms and values. Without further extensive documentation and scrutiny of the ideals and actions of key social actors, the formulation of policy will be impossible. Until we know what the legal, medical, political, and financial gate-keepers of the dependent elderly think about non-kin caregiving relationships, and until we know how they evaluate and act in response to the establishment and maintenance of those relationships, we cannot realistically formulate policy. Until we can delimit the powers and responsibilities of these gatekeepers, non-kin caregivers will continue to face suspicion and harassment from family, society, and its agents. We cannot effectively encourage, support, or sustain non-kin caregiving arrangements until we understand the sacrifices and rewards for non-kin caregivers.

These policy issues are becoming increasingly urgent. In order to address them effectively, it behooves us to begin giving extant non-kin caregiving relationships much more rigorous scrutiny.

## Notes

1. To protect the identity of informants, all names are pseudonyms. In addition, some case material has had minor detail altered or is a composite of two very similar cases.

2. For convenience, we use the term *widow* to refer to a person whose spouse has died, irrespective of the person's sex.

3. Estimates of the proportion of older adults needing assistance vary widely by age, sex, and task considered. Five percent is the minimum estimate for any combination of these factors (Cornoni-Huntley et al., 1985, pp. 352-353). In reality, then, there are more elderly people with non-kin caregivers than this estimate would indicate.

## References

Benjamin, A. E., Feigenbaum, L., Newcomer, R. J., & Fox, P. J. (1989). *Medicare posthospital study: Final report*. Submitted to the Commonwealth Fund Commission on Elderly People Living Alone. San Francisco: Institute for Health and Aging, University of California.

Caro, F. G. & Blank, A. E. (Eds). (1988). Quality impact of home care for the elderly. [Special issue]. *Home Health Care Services Quarterly, 9* (2/3), 1-204.

Cornoni-Huntley, J. C., Foley, D. J., White, L. R., Suzman, R., Berkman, L. F., Evans, D. A. & Wallace, R. B. (1985). Epidemiology of disability in the oldest old: Methodologic issues and preliminary findings. *Milbank Memorial Fund Quarterly/Health and Society, 63,* 350-377.

Costa, J. J. (1984). *Abuse of the elderly.* Lexington, MA: Lexington Books.

Croog, S. H., Lipson, A., & Levine, S. (1972). Help patterns in severe illness: The roles of kin network, non family resources, and institutions. *Journal of Marriage and the Family, 34,* 32-41.

Dignum, K. A. (1982). *Protective services and the elderly: An ethnographic comparison of commitment and probate courts.* Ann Arbor, MI: University Microfilms.

Doty, P. (1986). Family care of the elderly: The role of public policy. *Milbank Memorial Fund Quarterly/Health and Society, 64,* 34-75.

Duck, S. & Gilmour, R. (Eds.). (1981). *Personal relationships. 2: Developing personal relationships.* New York: Academic Press.

Estes, C. L., Gerard, L., & Clarke, A. (1984). Women and the economics of aging. *International Journal of Health Services, 14,* 55-68.

Field, M. (1972). *The aged, the family and the community.* New York: Columbia University Press.

Gubrium, J. F. (1984). Victimization in old age: Available evidence and three hypotheses. In J. J. Costa (Ed.), *Abuse of the Elderly* (pp. 21-31). Lexington, MA: Lexington Books.

Hendricks, J. & Hendricks, C. D. (1986). *Aging in mass society: Myths and realities.* (3rd ed.). Boston: Little, Brown.

Hochschild, A. R. (1973). *The unexpected community: Portrait of an old age subculture.* Berkeley: University of California Press.

Kane, R. A., & Kane, R. L. (1981). *Assessing the elderly: A practical guide to measurement.* Lexington, MA: Lexington Books.

Kosberg, J. I. (Ed.). (1983). *Abuse and maltreatment of the elderly: Causes and interventions.* Boston: John Wright, PSG.

Lawton, M. P., Moss, M., & Kleban, M. H. (1984). Marital status, living arrangements, and the well-being of older people. *Research On Aging, 6,* 323-345.

Litman, T. J. (1971). Health care and the family: A three-generational analysis. *Medical Care, 9,* 67-81.

Litwak, E. & Szelenyi, I. (1969). Primary group structures and their functions: Kin, neighbors, and friends. *American Sociological Review, 34,* 465-481.

Parsons, T. & Fox, R. (1951). Illness, therapy, and the modern American family. *Journal of Social Issues, 8,* 31-34.

Peters, G. R., & Kaiser, M. A. (1985). The role of friends and neighbors in providing social support. In W. J. Sauer & R. Coward (Eds.), *Social support networks and the care of the elderly* (pp. 123-158). New York: Springer.

Pritchard, D. C. (1983). The art of matchmaking: A case study in shared housing. *The Gerontologist, 23,* 174-179.

Rosow, I. (1967). *Social integration of the aged.* New York: Free Press.

Shanas, E. (1962). *The health of older people.* Cambridge, MA: Harvard University Press.

Shanas, E. (1979). The family as a social support system in old age. *The Gerontologist, 19,* 169-174.

Shanas, E., Townsend, P., Wedderburn, D., Friis, H., Milhoj, P., & Stehouwer, J. (1968). *Old people in three industrial societies.* New York: Atherton Press.

Siegel, J. S. & Taeuber, C. M. (1986, Winter). Demographic perspectives on the long-lived society. *Daedalus,* pp. 77-118.

Stephens, S. A., & Christianson, J. B. (1986). *Informal care of the elderly.* Lexington, MA: Lexington Books.

Stoller, E. P. & Earl, L. L. (1983). Help with activities of everyday life: Sources of support for the noninstitutionalized elderly. *The Gerontologist, 23,* 64-70.

Stoller, E. P., & Pugliesi, K. L. (1988). Informal networks of community-based elderly: Changes in composition over time. *Research on Aging, 10,* 499-516.

Stone, R., Cafferata, G. L., & Sangl, J. (1987). Caregivers of the frail elderly: A national profile. *The Gerontologist, 27,* 616-626.

Struyk, R. J., & Katsura, H. M. (1988). *Aging at home: How the elderly adjust their housing without moving.* New York: Haworth.

Sussman, M. B. (1985). The family life of old people. In R. H. Binstock & E. Shanas (Eds.), *Handbook of aging and the social sciences* (2nd ed.). (pp. 415-449). New York: Van Nostrand Reinhold.

Townsend, P. (1957). *The family life of old people.* London: Routledge.

Townsend, P. & Wedderburn, D. (1965). *The aged in the welfare state.* London: G. Bell & Sons.

Treas, J. (1977). Family support systems for the aged: Some social and demographic considerations. *The Gerontologist, 17,* 486-491.

U. S. House of Representatives. Select Committee on Aging. Sub-Committee on Human Services. (1980). *Domestic abuse of the elderly.* (Publication No. 96-259).

Vera, H., Berardo, F. M., & Berardo, D. H. (1987). On gold diggers: Status gain or loss in age heterogamous marriages. *Journal of Aging Studies, 1,* 51-64.

# 6

# Support Systems for the Familyless Elderly:

## Care Without Commitment

LUCY ROSE FISCHER
LEAH ROGNE
NANCY N. EUSTIS

A considerable amount of research has focused on dispelling the "myth" that families "abandon" their elderly relatives (see also, Shanas, 1979). In contrast, there has been little research on familyless elderly, which typically have appeared in the literature as the "only 'X' percent" who lack close family involvement. Unfortunately, the result has been that little in-depth analysis has been done on that minority of elders without close kin. Johnson and Catalano (1981, p. 610) suggested that, "It is even possible that some researchers intentionally downplay the existence of childless aged out of concern that attention focused on them would lend indirect support to the widely held 'social myth' of family abandonment."

The "only 'X' percent" of elderly who either have no close kin or whose kin are unavailable because of geographical and/or emotional

AUTHORS' NOTE: This research was supported by a grant from the All-University Council on Aging/Center for Urban and Regional Affairs, University of Minnesota. We are grateful for the help we received from the staff at "Good Care Hospital," patients, and caregivers who participated in this project.

distance constitute a sizable minority (Stoller & Earl, 1983). Goldberg, Kantrow, Kremen, and Lauter (1986) estimated that perhaps 15 to 20% of older women are both spouseless and childless. In a study of the availability and proximity of kin for a sample of elderly, Hays (1984) reported that 20.6% had no children or siblings within 50 miles, and 54% had no available daughter, the most frequent source of support.

Familyless elderly receive considerably less "informal" care than elderly with close kin and are much more likely to be institutionalized (Shanas, 1979). Various studies have shown that while neighbors and friends can sometimes substitute for family ties, kin are preferred as helpers and neighbors, and friends are more useful in terms of social support and socialization than in the provision of care (see also, Cantor, 1979; Goldberg et al., 1986; Johnson & Catalano, 1981).

Litwak (1985) has theorized that primary groups differ in structure and therefore in function. The essential feature of kinship is long-term commitment. Kin maintain their commitments across geographical distance and time separations. In contrast, ties with neighbors and friends are voluntary and lack "institutional pressures for permanence" (Litwak & Szelenyi, 1969, p.469). In this chapter, we will discuss how care provided to the familyless elderly is *care without commitment.*

### DRGs and the Managerial Family

One of the most important recent changes in health care for the elderly has been the implementation, starting in 1983, of a prospective payment system under Medicare, by which hospitals are reimbursed a preset amount for each patient's care according to the Diagnostic Related Grouping (DRG) of the patient's condition. Prospective payment works to encourage efficiency by providing incentives to hospitals and physicians to limit the use of expensive procedures and to reduce the length of stay. One of the consequences of DRGs is that elderly patients tend to leave hospitals "quicker and sicker."

In Fischer and Eustis (1988, 1990) we examined how changes in hospital structure associated with DRGs affected the role of family caregivers. That research was based on a longitudinal case study before and after the implementation of DRGs (i.e., in 1982 and 1986). In both time periods, in-depth interviews were conducted with hospital staff at

"Good Care Hospital" (fictional name) and with a small sample of elderly patients and family caregivers.

That study, reported that the post-DRG environment has magnified the responsibilities of the "managerial family" such that there has been an increasing need for family caregivers to serve as mediators, supervisors, and planners.

> The health care environment has changed in several ways since the advent of DRGs, and these changes have accentuated the managerial functions of family caregivers. First, the rationing of resources for hospital care has exacerbated the need for patient advocacy and protection. Second, because Medicare patients leave the hospital quicker and sicker, they are much more likely to need post-hospital care. Third, the planning process for post-hospital care has been speeded up so that more managerial responsibility has been placed on family caregivers. Finally, . . . the options for home care services have proliferated. . . .
>
> What has changed in the post-DRG health care environment is the increased importance that patient needs be made salient to maximize the probability of admission and to minimize the possibility of a too early discharge. (Fischer & Eustis, 1988, p. 386)

The findings from that study made us wonder about elderly patients who lack support from family caregivers. If family support is increasingly important, *who is managing the care of the sociomedically needy older person who lacks close family ties?*

### The Study of Familyless Elderly

Our current project entails a qualitative analysis of relationships between familyless elderly patients and their friends and neighbors who serve as caregivers. In-depth interviews were conducted with elderly patients who have no close kin and, where appropriate, with the friends and neighbors who were identified as their helpers. This study parallels the post-DRG study on family care by Fischer and Eustis and was conducted with patients from the same hospital (Good Care Hospital). In order to study actual and not just hypothetical helping relationships, both studies (on family and nonfamily care) have focused on posthospital home care needs.

Good Care Hospital is a 400-bed hospital located in a well-to-do suburb in the Twin Cities. The patients were first contacted by the hospital social workers, who were asked to use the following criteria: The patients were to be 65 years of age or over, in need of posthospital care, able to give informed consent, and had no spouse or other relatives involved in their care.

The sample consisted of 10 cases of familyless elderly patients, with each case consisting of a "patient" and, where available, a "friend"— i.e., a nonfamily caregiver. (For the sake of clarity, we will continue to use the terms *patient* and *friend* even if these terms are not exactly accurate for all contexts.) Interviews were conducted with 9 patients (1 patient was recently deceased) and 8 friends (in two cases, no helper was identified). Eight of the 10 patients were women. One patient was never married; the rest were widowed. The average age of the patients was 80. Three of the friends were neighbors of the patients.

In addition, we interviewed five hospital social workers and one social worker from the hospital-affiliated home health agency. Data on nonfamily caregivers will be compared with data on family caregivers from the parallel project.

### Helping Networks for the Familyless Elderly

Almost all of the familyless elderly in our sample received at least some type of help around the time of their hospitalization, as well as before and after. The most common type of help could be termed *neighboring*. These are task-bound, time-limited services that require proximity. Such services include bringing mail, clothes, food, or other items while the patients were in the hospital; checking on their homes; providing transportation (including, in some cases, taking them to the hospital); and running other errands. The second most common form of care is *social support;* all but 1 of the 10 familyless patients from our cases were visited in the hospital, and many received daily phone calls.

Less common were more intensive types of help. Only three had friends who consulted with their physicians and nurses on their behalf. In contrast, in our research on family care, we have found that virtually all involved family helpers provide a *linkage role*—that is, family members mediate between the patient and the hospital bureaucracy. Family members often are relied on for information when the patient is admitted to the hospital; they routinely discuss the patient's care with physicians and other hospital staff; and they frequently are involved with decisions concerning discharge. When patients are too ill or too disoriented to speak for themselves, the mediating, or linkage role, of family members is particularly important. Furthermore, we have found that in the post-DRG hospital, daughters, sons, and in-laws increasingly have tried to advocate for their elderly parents in order to get them admitted to the hospital and/or to postpone discharge. This type of intercession was largely absent for the familyless patients.

In the familyless sample, one friend had the patient stay in her home after leaving the hospital. Having a patient stay at a home other than their own is much more common for caregiving daughters and sons. The friend who extended the invitation, the patient, and the social worker who discussed this case all regarded this help as extraordinary.

Frail elderly with close family ties tend to rely on one family member, most commonly a spouse, daughter, or daughter-in-law. That person either provides most of the help and/or helps to arrange for and supervise paid and unpaid caregivers. The managerial family role usually is the responsibility of a woman. In contrast, the familyless elderly in our sample rarely had one helper who managed their care. Rather, they relied on a *network of helpers,* each of whom provided one or a small number of services. Their networks included impersonal as well as personal ties. For example, one of the patients in our study called her building manager when she broke her arm; another called a cab to take her to the hospital; another asked the maintenance person in her building to check on her apartment while she was in the hospital. These tasks are all potentially the types of jobs that people who have close personal ties do for one another. In one of these cases, the patient reported that "Edna [her friend] had a fit when she knew that I went to the hospital alone [by cab]."

Most of the familyless elderly in this sample were receiving quite a lot of help from neighbors, friends, and distant kin prior to their hospitalization. For most of these people, it appeared that one or more people checked on them every day. In fact, it was through this daily contact that a number of them made their way to the hospital. One friend, who routinely called the patient several times a day, went to his home when he did not answer his telephone. In another case, neighbors noticed that the patient's light was on all night; they called a friend of his who had a key. Another patient was being picked up by a neighbor to go to an appointment; when the neighbor could not rouse her, her friend with a key was called and she was taken by ambulance to the hospital. These and other cases illustrate the safety network of many familyless elderly; it appears that their support systems are generally adequate to provide help in emergencies.

We found two examples, however, in which familyless elderly lacked a network of support. These patients (both women) had virtually no personal ties to rely on, no close friends or functional kin, and neighbors who were not particularly neighborly. One of these patients complained: "people around this building . . . they're not willing to do anything. John [one neighbor] went down and got my medication. But there's a lot of people in this building—no way." The other patient commented: "Especially for the people who still have a husband. They don't understand what it means."

Hochschild, in her book *The Unexpected Community,* portrays elderly widows who live in a housing project for seniors and who have developed a supportive community. Her study was important in illustrating the vital sense of community that can exist among the elderly, a communal involvement that is "unexpected" given the stereotypes of isolation and loneliness for the elderly. The elderly in our sample are much more dispersed geographically, since they were not all living in one senior housing project, and their helpers were not necessarily elderly. Our findings, however, are similar to those of Hochschild. Most of the familyless elderly in our small sample also seemed to be integrated into a support network. Like Hochschild, we might view the supportive network available to most of the familyless elderly in our study as "unexpected" and as a testimony to the strength of nonfamily support systems.

Even so, it is important to differentiate among the familyless elderly with and without a network support. In our ten cases, there were two examples of familyless elderly who were truly isolated. Given the nature of our sample, it is inappropriate to make statistical inferences about the proportion of isolated elderly. What our data suggest, however, is that the problem of lack of support cannot simply be measured in terms of helping behavior. As we will show below, relationships are framed by social expectations. The distinction between family and nonfamily caregivers is not simply a matter of what they do; it is in their *beliefs* about what they *ought* to do.

## *Obligation, Responsibility and Authority*

Both researchers and journalists have documented the obligation that people feel toward their close kin. Most adult children assume that they should and would help their parents if and when needed. Thus, adult daughters and sons help their elderly parents, at least in some measure, because they believe they *have to*. Moreover, because of a social acceptance of filial responsibility, adult children also assume some degree of authority in their caregiving role—that is, they have a *right* to be involved in decisions about care.

What motivates friends and neighbors to provide care? Are there differences between family and nonfamily caregivers in terms of why and how they help? Several of the nonfamily helpers in our sample accounted for their involvement by referring to friendship. One woman noted:

> I like them [the patient and her sister—both of whom are helped by this friend]. That's all. They're very dear friends, and they're very sweet people . . . I don't do anything anyone else wouldn't do under the circumstances. . . . They don't take advantage. I wouldn't do it otherwise.

We can notice that this helper emphasizes the voluntary nature of her help. She has chosen to help these people because she likes their personal characteristics—they are "sweet"—and because they are not overly demanding ("I wouldn't do it otherwise").

There can be a fine line, however, between voluntary and involuntary relationships. Over time, "dear friends" can be treated almost as if they were part of one's extended family. In our sample, there were two examples in which relationships were described as quasi-kin. In both situations, the friends said that, over the years, they had been inviting the patient for holiday meals. In one of these cases, the friend was a younger neighbor whose mother, now deceased, had been a close friend of the patient. In the other case, the friend noted that the patient is "my children's Aunt Irene." These relationships resemble kinship ties in the following ways: The language of kinship is used; the patient has been incorporated into family gatherings in a fairly stable way; and/or the patient is connected to the friend through their shared ties with other kin.

Altruism is also an underlying theme when the nonfamily caregivers explained their motivations. One man said that he helped because

> He was my neighbor and because I had an old brother in Texas and years ago, without my knowing it, he got bedridden and a couple of women down there very good to him. So, I felt an obligation to repay something there.

A number of the friends in this sample had been offered money for their help. In some cases, there was an on-going struggle, with the patients trying to reciprocate for the help given by paying for the services and the friends refusing or accepting token amounts. One of these friends reported: "She wouldn't let you do anything. She wanted to pay. She was very independent, and, if you did anything, she always wanted to pay you."

Altruism is not really an explanation. It is, rather, a residual category; that is, it is a motivation that surpasses a specific obligation to help. A worker who helps his/her boss is not likely to be doing so out of altruistic motivations; the economic exchange is clear in this relationship. Similarly, help provided by a servant to a master, a husband to a wife, and a lawyer to a client would be unlikely to be defined as altruistic since the help provided would most probably be part of the defined set of obligations and responsibilities in a particular role relationship.

In kinship relationships in our society, the economic component of exchanges often is muted. Even so, there tend to be fairly specific obligations between close kin. There is variability, of course, in family norms, and there are individuals who do not fulfill their familial obligations. However, family relationships are involuntary, and one of the hallmarks of family involvement is that there is at least some measure of obligation. We can identify individuals who have failed to comply with family obligations by the social sanctions that are leveled against them; for example, there are relatives who are labeled the "black sheep" in their families, or there are sons and daughters who accuse each other of "not doing enough for mother."

In our study, the patients, friends, and social workers all pointed to a *lack of obligation* by non-kin. It is in this sense that the motivation for help by non-kin is assumed to be altruism. It is also the lack of obligation that makes care by non-kin be *care without commitment*.

The patients in this sample were aware that they had either no claims or only limited claims on help from their friends. The woman who went to her friend's home after leaving the hospital, for example, accepted her friend's offer because she felt unable to manage on her own; she believed, however, that she was "imposing." A number of the other patients commented that they "don't like to bother" their neighbors and friends, and they indicated that they are often hesitant about requesting help. Some of the patients mentioned that their caregivers had family obligations, which took priority. The friends also made it clear that they are unwilling to assume an unbounded set of responsibilities; a number of the friends stated that they would not want to "do more". Even those friends who had given very time-consuming help insisted on their lack of commitment. One man, for example, once drove his friend to a neighboring state and back; yet he declared during the interview: "I didn't feel I had any responsibility at all."

The attitudes of caregiving daughters and sons are strikingly different. Our previous projects on family care showed that the boundaries around family responsibilities tend to be broad and diffuse (Fischer, 1986; Fischer & Eustis, 1988), which can sometimes lead to problems. Many of the caregiving daughters and sons that we interviewed reported difficulties in balancing their competing commitments to spouses, children, and parents. Even so, it is clear, from our research as well as other studies, that most adult children feel an obligation to care. In fact, their responsibilities tend to far exceed the provision of physical care and services. Sons and, especially, daughters often express a responsibility for the general sense of well-being of their parents. There are usually complex emotional ties (positive and/or negative) between aging parents and their children. Their commitment to the caregiving role emerges from their emotional response to their parents.

The concept of "commitment" relates to attitudes and perceptions, and it should not be confused with the amount of services provided. The situation is analogous to an assessment of the parental role of mothers versus fathers in dual-career families. Even when homemaking and parental tasks are shared, mothers tend to retain "psychic responsibility" for managing their children's care (see Ehrensaft, 1984; Fischer, 1986). In a similar way (in terms of the long-term care needs of the elderly), spouses and adult children often assume "psychic responsibility"—that is, they become the case managers. Our study suggests that nonfamily helpers rarely view themselves as responsible for case management.

Because non-kin are without obligation, there are *problems in the allocation of responsibility and authority* for familyless elderly requiring care. The hospital social workers noted the difficulty of working with familyless clients. As one put it:

> I don't want to be the one making decisions. You feel so responsible anyway. I'd rather have a patient have family, and at least you know somebody to say "yes" or "no" to things besides the patient. Somebody to be following up with them later because we don't have the resources or the time to do much of that.

There are a number of situations in which a patient in a hospital either cannot make his/her own decisions or in which the patient resists the care plan offered by the staff. A family member, for example, might be asked to sign a DNR (Do Not Resuscitate) order or a surgery-permission form for an unconscious patient. Family caregivers also ally with nurses, doctors, and social workers in order to facilitate a patient's care. A spouse or daughter, for instance, might encourage a patient to eat or to comply with a prescribed treatment (Fischer with Hoffman, 1984). In addition, family members sometimes serve as advocates for patients and insist that the patient receive a certain type or amount of care. In our post-DRG study, for example, we found that family members often attempted to influence physician decisions in terms of both admitting patients and delaying discharges (Fischer & Eustis, 1988). With familyless patients, there is no one other than the patient to take responsibility for long-term care needs and who has authority to make decisions about care.

Most of the familyless patients in our sample had a friend, neighbor, or distant relative who was listed on the hospital form and had some contact with the hospital social worker. However, there was only one example of a friend being involved in decisions about posthospital care (this was the friend who invited the patient to her home because she had no adequate help after leaving the hospital). In this case, the friend had gone with flowers to visit the patient in the hospital—only to learn that the patient was being discharged that day. The friend said she felt "overwhelmed" at this news, and after further discussions, she offered to take the patient home with her. This case is the exception that proves the rule; it was through a combination of accident (the friend happening to be there) and altruism that this friend was so involved in the discharge plan. Except for this one situation, we did not find any instances of friends being involved in discharge decision-making. To the contrary, if friends had contact with the hospital social workers, they were merely informed about the plans and were not asked for any input.

Several of the nonfamily caregivers also expressed concern about their authority. For example, one friend was asked to take over the finances or to have power of attorney but refused to do so. Another friend agreed to take power of attorney but would not go to the patient's home alone (and therefore risk being accused of stealing something). Some patients also suggested that their own authority had been inappropriately usurped or challenged; they spoke of helpers (not necessarily the ones interviewed for our study) who "stole" or who made decisions (e.g., sending them to the hospital) that they had "no right" to make.

With adult children, there are occasionally conflicts over authority. More typically, however, adult children make arrangements for post-hospital care; they take care of a parent's finances; and they make de facto decisions about admissions to the hospital or nursing home. When adult children are caregivers, they often portray themselves as protective of their parents. Daughters, especially, talk about a sense of role reversal: "I consider her the child and me the mother now" (Fischer, 1986). The implication is that they have taken on an all-consuming responsibility, which is similar to the parental role. In this study of familyless elderly, none of the caring friends implied that they had an all-consuming responsibility for the long-term care of patients. Conversely, virtually all of the friends made statements revealing that they had neither obligation nor authority in the caregiving role.

### DRGs and the Familyless Elderly

In our project on DRGs and family care (Fischer & Eustis, 1988, p. 389), we noted the increased importance of the "managerial family." We found that almost all of the family caregivers in our post-DRG sample expressed concern about problems in admissions or discharge. Some tried to actively intervene. One son-in-law, for example, camped out in the doctor's office until the physician agreed to postpone the discharge for two days. In the post-DRG family caregiver sample, there were also many caregiving daughters and sons who spoke of their concern about the quality of hospital care. Some of these caregivers were actively involved in supplementing and supervising the in-hospital care—helping to feed parents as they lay in their hospital beds, reminding nurses to answer the call light, and just generally being around if needed. This active family involvement appeared to be much more common in the post-DRG hospital.

These findings made us wonder about the impact of DRGs on the familyless elderly. Because the managerial family role seemed so important, we had anticipated that the implementation of DRGs might be particularly detrimental to familyless elderly. We asked, "Do familyless elderly receive fewer hospital and home care services than the elderly with actively involved family caregivers?" Unfortunately, we cannot entirely answer this question based on our limited research. In this study, we do not have specific measures for in-hospital services. Moreover, we have no comparison of pre- and post-DRG samples for familyless patients.

If expressions of concern were interpreted as indicating problems with in-hospital and posthospital care, we might conclude that there are *fewer* problems for familyless elderly. Whereas almost all of the family caregivers had reported anxiety about problems with admissions or discharges, almost none of the friend-helpers talked of such concerns. In the familyless sample, only one friend noted problems with the timing of the discharge. In two other cases, patients said they felt they were not ready for discharge. We had anticipated that there would be more problems with rapid discharges of familyless patients. How do we interpret this lack of concern about the "quicker and sicker" discharge of familyless patients?

One explanation is that most of the familyless patients went from the hospital to a nursing home and therefore they continued to receive in-patient care. The familyless patients were twice as likely as our sample of patients with close family ties (in our post-DRG family care study) to go to a nursing home after leaving the hospital. Even the patient who went to stay with her friend also spent an additional week in a "rest home." This pattern is not necessarily a consequence of DRGs; familyless elderly have always had a higher risk of institutionalization. In most cases, there was strong evidence that the patients going to nursing homes were either depressed, passive, and/or anxious to get back to their own homes.

A second explanation for the lack of concern about posthospital care for familyless patients is that doctors may postpone discharge for familyless patients. The social workers indicated that, in their opinion, two of the patients in our sample would have gone home earlier if case management had been available.

There is, finally, a third interpretation. The lack of expressed concern about the timing of discharge is consistent with the quality of nonfamily care as caring without commitment. Family caregivers who had an elderly parent coming home "quicker and sicker" were responsible for the patient's care. Non-kin do not necessarily assume any such responsibility.

It is possible that some familyless elderly are sent home inappropriately in the post-DRG health care environment. Perhaps this is more likely to occur in the case of poor patients in inner city hospitals than for patients in the suburban hospital we studied. An examination of such problems was beyond the scope of this research project.

## Summary and Implications

This research project might be viewed as bearing both "good news" and "bad news" about support systems for the familyless elderly. The good news is that many familyless elderly appear to have a wide network of helpers and seem able to get help in emergencies. Thus we might conclude that there are "natural networks" of friends and neighbors and that these networks are largely effective in providing a substantial amount of services to the elderly without close kin. Most familyless elderly probably are *not* isolated and unsupported. Just as gerontologists have dismissed the myth that families in our society tend to abandon their elderly, we might also draw similar conclusions about neighbors and friends. It also appears to be a myth that neighbors and friends are uncaring.

There are, however, two types of bad news that can be inferred from our findings. First, there are some elderly—especially elderly without close kin—who are seriously isolated and who lack even a minimal support network. The fact that most familyless elderly have a network of helpers should not disguise the fact that there is a segment of the elderly population that is exceptionally needy.

The second type of bad news concerns the limitation of the support networks for the familyless elderly—that is, neighbors and friends lack obligation, responsibility, and authority. This is what is meant by "care without commitment." Therefore, although most elderly without family ties are able to obtain help for specific needs, what they lack is a guaranteed support system or backup case manager. Most familyless elderly serve as their own case managers, coordinating, in many cases, complex and fragile support systems. When acute illness impairs the patient's ability to manage that system, the system falls apart.

Our health care system today relies implicitly on assumptions about family care. A prime example is Medicare's DRG policy, the goal of which was to limit expensive hospital stays. When the DRG policy was implemented, there were virtually *no* provisions for posthospital paid care or for case management to follow posthospital recovery. Implicit in this lack of planning is the assumption that someone/somehow (i.e., families!) will be available to provide posthospital care. When hospital social workers are required to do discharge planning for familyless patients, they are in a bind. By training, they are case managers, but their responsibility ends when the patient leaves the hospital. They understand that most of their patients prefer not to go to a nursing home; they dislike making decisions for patients; and they also are aware of the fragility in the support systems for the familyless elderly. Given these conditions, it is not surprising that they prefer to work with patients who have close kin.

There are reasons to suspect that the problems of familyless elderly may increase over time. It is possible that the DRG policy represents just one step in the contraction of governmental supplements for health care services. Moreover, with rising divorce rates and decreasing fertility rates, there will be increasing numbers and proportions of elderly who lack functioning family supports. Therefore, policies that rely on family care will leave large numbers of elderly underserviced.

### References

Cantor, M. H. (1979, December). Neighbors and friends: An overlooked resource in the informal support system, *Research on Aging, 1*(4), 434-463.

Ehrensaft, D. (1984). When women and men mother. In J. Trebilcott (Ed.), *Mothering: Essays in feminist theory*. pp. 41-61. Totowa, NJ: Rowman and Allanheld.

Fischer, L. R. (1986). *Linked lives: Adult daughters and their mothers*. New York: Harper and Row.

Fischer, L. R. & Eustis, N. N. (1988). DRGs and family care for the elderly: A case study. *The Gerontologist, 28,* 383-390.

Fischer, L. R. & Eustis, N. N. (1990). Quicker and sicker: How changes in Medicare affect the elderly and their families. *Journal of Gerontologic Psychiatry, 22*(2), pp. 163-191.

Fischer, L. R. with Hoffman, C. (1984). Who cares for the elderly: The dilemma of family support. In M. Lewis & J. Miller (Eds.), *Social policies and public problems* Vol. III, pp. 612-215. Greenwich, CT: JAI.

Goldberg, G. S., Kantrow, R., Kremen, E., & Lauter, L. (1986, March-April). "Spouseless, childless elderly and their social supports. *Social Work,* 104-112.

Hays, J. A. (1984). Aging and family resources: Availability and proximity of kin. *The Gerontologist, 24*(2), 149-153.

Hochschild, A. R. (1973). *The unexpected community: Portrait of an old age subculture*. Berkeley: University of California Press.

Johnson, C. L. & Catalano, D. J. (1981). The childless elderly and their family supports. *The Gerontologist, 21*(6), 610-618.

Litwak, E. (1985). *Helping the elderly: The complementary roles of informal networks and formal systems*. New York: Guilford.

Litwak, E. & Szelenyi, I. (1969). Primary group structure and their functions: Kin, neighbors and friends. *American Sociological Review, 34,* 465-481.

Shanas, E. (1979). The family as a support system in old age. *The Gerontologist, 19,* 169-174.

Stoller, E. P., & Earl, L. L. (1883). Help with activities of everyday life: Sources of support for the non-institutionalized elderly. *The Gerontologist, 23*(1), 64-70.

# 7

# Personal Care:

## Variation in Network Type, Style and Capacity

### G. CLARE WENGER

In the United Kingdom as elsewhere, the 1980's have witnessed a growing policy emphasis on the role of the family in providing care for elderly people (e.g., DHSS, 1981, 1986; NISW, 1982; Welsh Office, 1985; Cumberledge, 1986; Griffiths, 1988). Implicit in the debate is the assumption that family care will become a more important source of care and that more old people will be cared for at home as the aging of the population progresses.

This chapter is primarily concerned with the different types of support networks available to the elderly in ill health and the significance of variation for the provision of intimate personal care. Not all elderly people are cared for by their families if they need intimate personal care, which in some instances amounts to home nursing. The question of why some families look after elderly relatives at home while others do not is one that has interested social scientists and policymakers for some time. It will be argued here that different types of support networks consist of different configurations of relationships, and it will be shown how the presence or absence of those particular relationships associated

AUTHOR'S NOTE: This chapter draws on data from a study funded by the UK Department of Health and Security (1978–1989) and the UK Economic and Social Research Council, Grant No. G00232334 (1986–1989).

with expectations of personal care determine what happens to the elderly, aged 80 or over, in the face of failing health and growing frailty.

Different types of support networks, it will be argued, have different capacities for caregiving and are associated with different expectations of giving and receiving personal care. For instance, those who have become used to living with or near relatives build up patterns of behavior based on availability and expectation of help, while those who have no close relative (spouse, children, or siblings) or who live distant from their immediate family develop expectations of self-reliance. These patterns continue into old age.

Expectations of care are also associated with the *degree* of relationship. It is expected that spouses will provide personal care unless the spouse is disabled. Personal care from children may be expected if they live near enough, but expectations are greater for care from daughters than from sons, and constraints exist on burdening children when caring becomes long-term. Personal care from siblings or friends is only expected for a short-term illness, but sisters may provide care under special circumstances—when, for example, the dependent sibling is childless (Wenger, 1987a). Different types of networks, reflecting different available relationships and different life-styles, are discussed and illustrated below with case studies.

Most of the literature on the family and personal care for the elderly has focused on the experience of burden by caregivers[1] (see, for example: Finch & Groves, 1980; Gilroy, 1982; Equal Opportunities Commission, 1982a, 1982b; Ungerson, 1987). The emphasis has been on caring by daughters or daughters-in-law, although some attention has focused on caring wives. Male caregivers have typically received less attention (Wenger, 1987b; Arber & Gilbert, 1989). Much of the literature presents an undifferentiated view of caregiving seeing it as a usually negative experience, an unwelcome responsibility, and a financial drain. This chapter attempts to look at variability in caregiving as a function of differences in support network structure and to show that the experience and the provision of care depends on the social environment.

Most of the help provided to elderly people in the community falls short of personal care, which in this chapter is deemed to refer to care of an intimate personalized nature, such as washing, bathing, shaving, doing hair, dressing, toileting, and helping with mobility. Following common UK practice, reference will be made to long-interval needs (needs that usually have to be met less than daily, such as bathing and cutting toenails) and short-interval needs (those that have to be met at least daily and often several times a day, such as dressing, feeding, and toileting). The emphasis in this chapter is on the physical demands of failing health on the caregiving situation and the response of the support network.

Of the 95% of elderly people in the United Kingdom that still live in the community, only a small proportion (approximately 10%) need regular help with at least some aspects of personal care. Help is almost wholly provided by members of the family, usually daughters or spouses, supplemented by professional services for long-interval needs, such as some nursing tasks, bathing, or cutting toenails (Hunt, 1978; Wenger, 1984; Bayley, Seyd, Tennant, & Simons, 1982). Short-interval personal care needs (washing, toileting, etc.) are provided almost exclusively by the family. To those elderly over the age of 80, these needs are present for approximately 5% of that group (Wenger, 1988a). Most formal service provision of all kinds is to those who live alone and have no nearby family members who are able to provide the needed support to those elderly or, whose available relatives do not have the necessary physical capacity or skills.

Various studies have shown that of all relationships, spouses are the most committed to personal care (Bayley et al., 1982; Kendig, 1986; Wenger, 1987a), which is true for both wives and husbands. On the whole, spouses are also less likely than other caregivers to report caring as stressful (Johnson & Catalano, 1981; Wenger, 1987b). Because in most cases one spouse predeceases the other and because others do not marry, less than half of the old people will have a spouse to care for them; therefore, care must come from other sources where expectations of care are more problematic.

A recent study in the Netherlands (Knipscheer, 1989) has demonstrated that in most cases where long-term care for the frail elderly takes place at home, an expectation of caregiving as natural and inevitable exists. This finding reinforces the argument of this chapter which further suggests that such expectations are related to network type.

In the United Kingdom, most elderly people who are not married live alone. One study has found that 5% of those over 75 who live alone received daily personal care. Intimate care was provided in 88% of cases by daughters living nearby and averaged 10½ hours a week. Most of the helpers in this study were around 60 years old (Bayley et al., 1982).

A more recent U.K. study found that 1 adult in 7 was providing some care, and three quarters of the recipients of care were age 65 and over (OPCS, 1988). A significant minority of elderly people in the United Kingdom (Hunt, 1978) lived in shared households with younger relatives; in such a situation, the most likely source of personal care is also a daughter or, in some cases a daughter-in-law or a son, who is usually unmarried.

## Methodology

This chapter is based primarily on an intensive qualitative study, conducted in rural Wales, of 30 old people who were 80 years or older. They were visited two to three times a year from 1983 to 1987. (Several died before 1987.) The study was part of a larger longitudinal study of social support ($n = 534$ in 1979), which included surveys in 1979, 1983, and 1987. Some statistical data from the larger study are also presented in this chapter.

During the intensive phase of study, the respondents, who had already been interviewed in two phases of the longitudinal study, were visited in their own homes. Data collection took the form of guided or structured interviews/discussions that used and built on information received in earlier interviews, emphasizing change and coping behavior. At the end of the study period, surviving respondents were between the ages of 83 and 98.

## Findings

Until 1987, half of those in the intensive study were either managing well without any help with personal care, or had died or entered residential care and required a minimum of only emergency, acute, or short-term help with personal care while in the community. Half of the sample, on the other hand, had received long-term regular help from informal and/or formal sources in regard to intimate personal care. This ranged from regular help with bathing only to total nursing care. Their cases are discussed subsequently in the context of their support networks.

During the course of the intensive study, it became apparent that different patterns or configurations of support could be recognized, from which five different ideal types of support networks (discussed below) were identified (Wenger, 1987c; 1989) on the basis of: proximity to close kin; proportions of family, friends and neighbors involved; levels of interaction between the elderly and their families, friends, neighbors, and community groups.

The five types of support networks were named on the basis of the nature of the old person's relationship to the support network, and they can be summarized as follows:

1. *The local family-dependent support network* has its primary focus on nearby kin ties and close family relationships with few peripheral friends and neighbors. It is often based on a shared household with adult children (usually a daughter), sister(s), or brother(s) or very near separate households. Most commonly, the old person relies primarily on a daughter. Community involvement in religious or voluntary groups is generally low. This type of network tends to be small, and the elderly people are more likely to be widowed, older, and in less-than-good health.

2. *The locally integrated support network* includes close relationships with local family, friends, *and* neighbors. Many friends are also neighbors. Usually based on long-term residence and active community involvement in church and voluntary organizations in the present or recent past, this type of network tends to be larger on the average than others.

3. *The local self-contained support network* typically has armslength relationships or infrequent contact with at least one relative living in the same or adjacent community (usually a sibling, niece, or nephew). Childlessness is common. Reliance is focused on neighbors but respondents with this type of network adopt a household-focused lifestyle; community involvement, if any, tends to be very low key. This type of network tends to be smaller than average.

4. *The wider community-focused support network* is typified by active relationships with distant relatives (usually children), high salience of friends, and few neighbors. The distinction between friends and neighbors is maintained. Respondents with this type of network are generally involved in community or voluntary organizations. This type of network, which is larger than average, is frequently associated with retirement migration and is commonly a middle-class or skilled working-class adaptation. Absence of local kin is common.

5. *The private restricted support network* is frequently associated with the absence of local kin other than a spouse. Contact with neighbors is

minimal. There are few nearby friends and there is a low level of community contact or involvement. Networks are smaller than average.

It will be noted that the first three types are primarily local, inasmuch as they are based on the presence of local kin. The differences between them reflect different interaction patterns with kin and community. The other two types are typically related to the absence of local kin and tend to be associated either with the late-life in-migration or out-migration of younger generations.

Following the identification of network types, it was possible to apply this typology to the survey data from the three phases of the longitudinal study. In this context, it was noted that the distribution of network types remained constant despite attrition in the sample, and this distribution was related to specific community $n = 534$ (1979) and $n = 198$ (1987) $p = .001$); and shifts occurred from one network type to another over time. Attrition of the sample by death or entry into residential care occurred at higher rates in local family dependent networks. Shifts in network type were the most common from locally integrated to local family-dependent or local self-contained types and from wider community focused to private restricted; thus the overall distribution tended to remain stable, Shifts were generally associated with very advanced age and/or decline in health. It is important to stress here, however, that able-bodied elderly persons were present in all network types but, as further discussion will show, not all network types can support those in poor health. The 1979 distribution was as follows: local family dependent, 23%; locally integrated, 34%; local self-contained, 19%; wider community focused, 15%; and private restricted, 10%. This distribution, of course, reflects the general population stability of the region: within the region, wider community focused and private restricted networks were more common in those communities with high levels of retirement migration. In other contexts, localities with high population turnover would be expected to have more of the fourth and fifth types.

**Support Networks and the Receipt of Personal Care**

As noted above, support network types may shift over time, the most common shifts being toward local family-dependent or private restricted networks (Wenger, 1987c; 1988b). Family dependent support networks offer the greatest likelihood of personal care, while private restricted networks offer few opportunities for help from informal sources. As the following discussion based on the intensive study will illustrate, high levels of need for personal care are less likely to be accommodated in networks other than of the local family-dependent type. This means that for other types of networks, unless the network shifts to become a family-dependent one (and only some have the capacity or structure to do this), entry into long-term residential care in the face of chronic illness seems to be inevitable. The case studies that follow are of unequal length, reflecting the fact that caregiving is not only more likely to occur in some types of networks than in others, but that it covers a longer period of time and deals with higher levels of dependency. The case studies of local family dependent and locally integrated support networks are, therefore, more extensive than others. It is important to note that in the 1987 survey of survivors, *all* those requiring help with short-interval personal care tasks had local family-dependent networks. The network types are arranged hierarchically from those that are most likely to accommodate high levels of dependency to those less able to provide personal care.

## Local Family-dependent Support Networks

All six of those identified in the study as having family-dependent support networks (four women and two men) had received a high level of personal care by 1987. Four were cared for by daughters living in the same household; one lived in a granny flat supported by a daughter-in-law; and one lived with a widowed sister.

It is possible to identify two subtypes of family-dependent networks: those that have been family-dependent for many years for reasons unrelated to physical dependency and those networks that have been established to cope with physical dependency. Two of those elderly who lived with daughters had done so for many years and had earlier worked together in family businesses. In the other four cases, shared households had been established to accommodate increasing frailty. Both of those elderly who had lived for long periods with their daughters died at home after long periods of dependency. All of those who had moved in with relatives in the face of dependency entered residential care. Caring daughters who have sisters or brothers and sisters-in-law living nearby appear to receive some help with personal care from these households, but such assistance is likely to be infrequent and may be unreliable.

Since 1979, the stories of progressive decline for all these old people were similar, but there are some important differences in the ways in which families responded. In the two cases where shared households with daughters were long established, the old people and their daughters were accustomed to living together in the easy intimacy of close reciprocal relationships long before the onset of physical dependency. In both of these cases, every effort was made to keep the old parent in his or her own home. This fact was made explicit on more than one occasion.

In the cases of the other four elderly, shared residence was based on dependency and, with the possible exception of one woman in her granny flat, all were living in someone else's home. In each case, space had been made for an elderly relative in an already-established family or household. This sharing of accommodation was not an event that had necessarily been anticipated before the onset of dependency. While the relatives involved helped as much as they were able, they had had to modify previously established life-styles—all felt put-upon to some extent, all worried about coping, and all were relieved when ultimately the parent or, in one case, sister, entered permanent institutional care. In all cases, the elderly people concerned either lived in or moved into the caregiver's household; with advancing frailty, the provision of personal care became concentrated on one female relative.

What is suggested in this analysis is that those with family-dependent networks are likely to receive care from female relatives. Where an expectation of providing personal care exists, together with the established intimacy of long-term joint residence, elderly people are likely to receive a high level of care and have relatives demonstrating a high level of commitment. Where these preconditions are absent, despite the fact that families assume responsibility, caring situations are liable to become stressful for both the relatives (usually daughters), whose established life-styles and expectations are disrupted, and the old people themselves, who fear and resist being a source of strain. In the context of this study, all those where long-term co-residence did not predate dependency entered residential institutions as dependency increased. While caution must be entertained in the context of so few cases, it would appear that in the latter situations, help and support can be provided at lower levels of dependency; however, once regular personal care becomes necessary, with the added likelihood of a need for surveillance, families feel unable to provide the nursing care needed.

The following case studies of Tom Price[2] and Hannah Johnson provide examples of caregiving in local family-dependent networks. The case of Tom Price illustrates the long-established shared household, while that of Hannah Johnson demonstrates the household created to support a dependent parent. Where Tom Price's daughter struggled to take care of her father at home and requested his discharge from the hospital, Mrs. Johnson's daughter was anxious that the hospital discharge her mother. Tom Price and his daughter had always lived together, whereas Hannah Johnson had moved to live with her only daughter as a result of increasing dependency. Both women can be said to have done the very best they could for their parents. Both caregiving situations were stressful, and it would be inappropriate to judge whether either woman could or should have made different decisions. In the intensive study and in the second survey, it can be said that those who formed joint households to accommodate dependency found it easier to relinquish the resident caregiver role.

*Case Study 1*

Tom Price lived on a farm with his unmarried daughter, next door to his son, daughter-in-law, and three grandchildren. (A married childless daughter lived elsewhere.) Mr. Price had been widowed when his unmarried daughter was a baby, and she had kept house for him since she had grown up. He had a reputation in the family for being a bit of a tyrant; although he had a dry sense of humor and appeared to get on well with his unmarried daughter, he and his other daughter and daughter-in-law were estranged.

Mr. Price was 80 when he was first interviewed in 1979. Although he suffered from angina, he claimed that his health was all right for his age and did not limit his activities. He also said that he received no help with personal care. By 1983, his activities were limited by the angina and kidney problems. He still managed to take care of himself, but found taking a bath difficult. However, his son visited every evening to discuss the farm, and Mr. Price remained an active partner in the business, although he claimed to refrain from giving advice.

At the end of 1983, he said he was "peevish, easily vexed and all that," although his daughter insisted he was not too bad. He had been very ill the previous year. His daughter had nursed him through that illness, but he hardly went out anymore. He admitted that he and his daughter disagreed occasionally. His sight was failing, and since he had difficulty reading the papers, his daughter sometimes read them to him. By March 1984, his sight was worse, he could not read at all, and his daughter had to describe to him what was on television.

In November 1984, Mr. Price seemed to be worse again. He now needed help to dress, lost his voice for six months, was almost blind, and had bad hearing. He had fallen twice. His daughter had to call her brother to come and lift him. There were some indications that he was getting confused. He kept losing things, including his pills. His daughter rarely left him alone. However, one evening when she did go out, she returned to find him sitting in his chair with a loaded shotgun; some nights later, he discharged the shotgun into the door. His daughter was increasingly worried about her father. He had started wandering at night. Although he never wet the bed, he had fainted twice and had diarrhea and made a mess. Mr. Price was concerned about the strain his daughter experienced as a result of looking after him, and he felt she should be paid by the state for the care she gave him.

By May 1985, Mr. Price was more frail, his hearing was worse, his sight was very poor, and he was unsteady on his feet. He had been ill twice over the winter (in one instance his son and daughter had had to carry him upstairs). On both occasions, it was feared he would die. He needed help to get up and get dressed, and to get undressed and go to bed. His son sat with him when his daughter went out. His bouts of confusion were more frequent and more severe. Sometimes he did not recognize his daughter.

During 1985, Mr. Price spent two months in the hospital. He had been depressed, afraid to come downstairs because of vertigo, and could not get up one morning. He had had a slight stroke. However, he recovered and, on the insistence of his daughter, returned home. By Christmas he could walk without aids, but his bed had been brought downstairs. He was suffering with angina and took sleeping pills at night.

In 1987, Mr. Price, now 88, claimed his health was only fair and that he never went out. He was interviewed in bed in the living room. Most of the time, he lay flat, sitting up from time to time to make an important point. He said he was not ill, just resting, though he was wearing pajamas. His daughter continued to care for him and run the house with some support from her brother.

Later that year, his daughter was treated for depression. She continued to care for her father until his death in the summer of 1988. After he died, she had difficulties adjusting to his death and again suffered from depression. At the age of 51, she was faced with the need for employment for the first time in her life. Given her experience, the only job she could get was as a care assistant in a residential home for the elderly mentally infirm.

## Case Study 2

Hannah Johnson was living alone in 1979. She had one daughter and one son in the same community. Her daughter and daughter-in-law visited frequently and helped with all the domestic chores and maintenance. She claimed that her health was alright for her age (80), but her activities were limited by her loss of vision. She was therefore, only able to go out with help. Despite these difficulties, she managed her personal care without any help except for the assistance she got with cutting her toenails, assistance she received from her daughter and/or the chiropodist who came to her home. By 1983, she had moved in with her daughter; in addition to her loss of vision she was now limited by the arthritis in her knees. She received twice-weekly visits from the district nurse, although it was not clear for what purpose since her daughter provided help with medication and mobility.

Mrs. Johnson's daughter was feeling the strain of caring for her, not so much because of the demands of personal care, but because of the need to constantly keep an eye on the ailing woman. Consequently, she had to give up her part-time job. Mrs. Johnson was blind, unsteady on her feet, and suffered from dizzy spells. The main source of heating in the home was an open fire. If Mrs. Johnson's daughter went out in the evening, her son-in-law had to stay home to be sure the place was warm enough. Therefore, brother and sister could never go out together.

Mrs. Johnson was in the hospital between August and November 1983. She went in for tests because she was dizzy and vomiting all the time. Her arthritis was also very painful. When she returned home, she used a walker. The district nurse resumed the twice-weekly visits, helping Mrs. Johnson with her bathing and providing treatment for a bedsore.

Mrs. Johnson and her daughter got on very well, but her daughter was disappointed that her brother and his wife did not help more.

Mrs. Johnson went to them for about a fortnight once a year. It was becoming more worrisome to leave Mrs. Johnson alone, even for the short time it took to go shopping, and her daughter was concerned about how she would cope in the future. In the following months, Mrs. Johnson had two falls. The doctor visited only once between her discharge from the hospital in November 1983 and my visit in May 1984, although her condition had not improved.

In July 1984, Mrs. Johnson had shingles and was still suffering pain in December. While she had had shingles, the district nurse came every day and was described as "marvelous" by Mrs. Johnson's daughter, who found her a valuable source of support. The nurse was now coming once a week, but she sometimes popped in between her scheduled visits if she was in the area. Mrs. Johnson had been quite ill and her daughter was tired, but her attendance allowance had been approved. It costs "£18 a week, and they say it costs over a hundred pounds to keep them in hospital for a week. . . . It's no wonder they [the authorities] want them at home, is it?" the nurse commented.

Mrs. Johnson was finding it difficult to sleep because of the pain caused by the arthritis, and sometimes her daughter got up during the night to make her a drink. Mrs. Johnson was feeling a burden: "There is nothing at all that I don't get—in every way. . . . I try to behave. I don't like to give them any work. I try to give them as less (sic) work as possible. I haven't broken any crockery yet. That's what I'm afraid of—breaking things. I haven't made much of a mess yet, I don't think. I've been sick once or twice, but I've had something ready to save the mess. That's what I'm afraid of—causing a lot of washing and things like that."

In 1985, Mrs. Johnson spent more than four months in the geriatric ward of the local cottage hospital. Her dizziness and nausea had been found to be the result of the tablets she was taking for arthritis and were consequently reduced. The arthritis was then very bad in one hip and her knees. She was also very breathless. She went home just before Christmas but was back in the hospital by March after suffering a stroke that affected her right side. She remained in the hospital and was interviewed there in 1987, when she was cheerful but chairbound. Her daughter and son-in-law visited every other evening. Her daughter did not go back to work because "you never know when they might send her home." Mrs. Johnson went home for Christmas, Sundays, and occasional weekends.

In the spring of 1988, she returned home for two months. After suffering a second stroke, however, she was readmitted to the hospital where she remained until she died in December. Her daughter said,

"It seems very strange now not having to visit the hospital after going backwards and forwards for such a long time, but it was well worth the effort and all the time we spent with her." Mrs. Johnson's first grandchild had been born two months before her death, "a great comfort to us all during this sad time."

## Locally Integrated Support Networks

Of the eight old people whose support networks were identified as locally integrated (seven women and one man), few received high levels of regular personal care in the community. Six were living alone, and two were living with daughters with whom they had shared households for many years. At the start of the study in 1979, all were living active lives and were involved in their communities.

The one man in this category was still active and in good health in 1987, relying only on periodic visits from the chiropodist to cut his toenails. Two of the women died after less than two weeks in the hospital. Up to that time, both had received chiropody at home, and one had had help bathing from the district nurse. Otherwise, both women managed without personal care. One other woman also received regular visits from the chiropodist, but received no other personal care until she entered a nursing home.

One woman, who was living with her daughter and son-in-law, managed without any help apart from cutting her toenails until 1986, when she suffered a slight stroke. She made a good recovery, but her daughter helped her with baths after that. She continued to enjoy an active and busy life.

Among those with locally integrated support networks who needed help with personal care, the networks of two women gave indications of shifting to more closely, approximate family-dependent networks in the face of potentially higher levels of dependency. Although both women continued to maintain links with friends and neighbors both had daughters with whom they had lived closely for many years. One died before needing nursing care, and one was still actively involved in the community at the end of the study; in the latter case, it was possible to predict long-term care if the need arose.

It is, of course, impossible to make any generalizations about personal care and locally integrated networks from this small sample, but there are indications that situations in which care is shared between two or more persons are more common. This will be explored further in research planned in the future.

In the cases of Sian Fielding and Glenys Owen (whose case histories are presented below), care was shared by several members of the support network, and high levels of dependency were managed in the community. In Mrs. Fielding's case, she remained in good health until her terminal illness, while Mrs. Owen's death was preceded by several years of severely limited mobility. In the case of one other woman, who had no daughters, help was provided by her daughters-in-law as long as she was able to live alone; once she could no longer do so, she entered residential care. On the basis of available data, it is difficult to explain why shared care was not possible in this woman's case, but a likely factor contributing to her admittance to residential care is the fact that she was suffering from senile dementia. Other data from the same study support this hypothesis, showing that mental illness undermines relationships (Wenger, 1987a).

To summarize, with the caution of generalizing from this small sample, the need for help with personal care among those with locally integrated support networks may result in a shift to family-dependent networks, the development of shared care, or, in some instances that are probably related to senile dementia, to residential care.

*Case Study 3*

Sian Fielding kept house for her unmarried daughter (age 41 in 1979), who worked as a nurse. She had another unmarried daughter and a married son, both of whom lived elsewhere. She had a warm and friendly relationship with her daughters and son and saw those who lived away on a regular basis. Although complaining of arthritis and controlled thyroid trouble, she said her health was good in 1979 and had changed little by 1983, except that the arthritis in her hip "means I can't walk as quickly or as easily as I could." By 1983, she received paid treatment from a chiropodist. However, now in her eightieth year, she still took the dog for walks and enjoyed gardening.

Shortly after Christmas 1983, Mrs. Fielding was admitted to the hospital for tests, was found to have cancer, and subsequently had a colostomy. She was in the hospital for over a month. When she was discharged, one of her granddaughters aged 21, came to stay for a week to look after her while Mrs. Fielding's daughter went to work.

When her granddaughter left, a friend of Mrs. Fielding's who had been a nurse, came for ten days. After that, she managed on her own and seemed well when visited in April.

The district nurse visited Mrs. Fielding once a week to check the colostomy, and a hospital sister (a stoma specialist) came periodically. Mrs. Fielding appeared to be making a good recovery until the end of May, when the unhealed wound became infected. By the middle of June, she was experiencing a lot of discomfort and found it difficult to sit. She was admitted to the hospital, underwent radiotherapy, and was sent home, very ill and unable to get out of bed without help. She could not be left alone.

Mrs. Fielding's other granddaughter, 18, stayed with her for 10 days while her mother was at work. After that Mrs. Fielding's late husband's sister-in-law, who had been a nurse, came every day. By this time, the school holidays arrived; Mrs. Fielding's other unmarried daughter, 37, who was a teacher, came to help her sister care for their mother. Later, Mrs. Fielding's sister-in-law and 18-year-old granddaughter came regularly; between them, they nursed Mrs. Fielding, who was now bedridden, sometimes confused, and eating very little. She cried out a lot at night and was frequently vomiting blood. During the last two weeks of her life, district nurses came three times a day: first thing in the morning, at 2 PM and again at 4 PM. Since Mrs. Fielding could not sleep in her last days, the doctor came to give her injections. She died early in August.

Mrs. Fielding was nursed by her two daughters, sister-in-law, and two granddaughters. Her family found the last two months very hard. One of her daughters and her sister-in-law were trained nurses, and they felt that they coped better because of their experience. The week before Mrs. Fielding died, her young granddaughter was sent away on vacation. In this instance, personal care was needed for a short period of time in an acute situation. While responsibility in most other cases of shared households is focused on one member, care in Mrs. Fielding's case was shared between five female relatives spanning three generations, with additional help and support from friends.

*Case Study 4*

Glenys Owen lived alone in a three-story terraced house. When interviewed in 1979, she said her health was alright for her age (78), despite having recently recovered from surgery to remove a kidney. She managed all personal care tasks without difficulty, but her activities were limited by "rheumatism."

At the time of the 1983 interview, she had just returned home from the hospital, where both knees had been operated on for arthritis. She did not feel the operation made much improvement in her condition, but now claimed her health was good. She was finding it difficult to take a bath, to get up and down steps, and to go out alone. She received help from the chiropodist to cut her toenails. Several friends took her out in their cars.

When reinterviewed at the end of 1983, the arthritis in her knees was causing her a lot of trouble. She had acquired a high-seated armchair but said that getting up was an ordeal. She used a walking stick in the house and walked with a stoop. She received occasional visits from a physiotherapist who had been helpful in providing her with various mobility aids, and a community nurse came once every two weeks to help her bathe.

By the following April (1984), Mrs. Owen's condition had deteriorated. She was virtually chairbound and found it very hard to move around. Earlier in the year, she felt that she was too incapacitated to remain at home and should find herself a place in a private old people's home. However, her closest relative (a second cousin, whom she always referred to as a nephew) and his wife persuaded her to stay at home. They had reorganized her house to make this possible. The bed had been brought downstairs, and Mrs. Owen had a commode to use at night. She had no downstairs bathroom but could use an outside lavatory during the day and wash in the kitchen. Having made this decision, she was now determined to stay home. Her "nephew," his wife and their two school-age daughters, as well as numerous friends and neighbors, came to see her regularly.

The physiotherapist had been very helpful. She had arranged for a walker with a string bag so Mrs. Owens could carry things, a trolley by the chair and within easy reach, a raised seat for the lavatory, and a sloping stool for use at the sink. The district nurse still came once every two weeks and she had a sponge bath by the sink. "I've lost all illusions about modesty," she said. Her main meal was sent in from a local cafe.

Mrs. Owens was concerned about the future. She felt she needed more household help than she had but did not want anybody to live with her. Her next-door neighbor came in every night to make her a hot water bottle, see her into bed, and locked up, thereby locking Mrs. Owens in. Early in the morning, the neighbor returned, unlocked the doors, and opened the curtains. Mrs. Owen got herself up and dressed, although the latter was a struggle. Her household helper came six days a week at 9 AM and made her breakfast. When her helper was away, her relative's wife came.

When visited in July 1984, Mrs. Owen had managed to get more help. She now had two paid helpers, so there was someone who came every day to help her. They arrived at 9 AM and the first job was to empty the commode. Mrs. Owen was looking into the possibility of attendance allowance or domestic care allowance. She was a popular woman and had a constant stream of visitors.

In June 1985, Mrs. Owen suffered her first fall. She became disorientated in the dark and, instead of sitting on the bed, she sat down onto the floor and could not get up. She was very distressed, her heart was pounding, she was sweating, and she thought she might die. She managed to crawl and knock on the wall, and her neighbor's husband came and lifted her up. Her legs were badly bruised, and she was anxious about falling again.

In 1986, she suffered another fall, this time at 1:30 AM She did not know where she was and could not get up. She was on the floor until her neighbor came at 6 AM. "I can't think why I didn't have pneumonia," she said. She was bruised all over and could not walk. She was taken to the hospital for a week and then spent another four weeks in a local authority old people's home. She was desperate to return to her own home, and her "nephew" and his wife supported her in this. They prepared the house for her and acquired a chemical lavatory (commode) so that she no longer had to go outside. She changed her routine and had more help every morning, including the preparation of her main meal, which she then cooked herself.

When interviewed in June 1987, Mrs. Owen was immobile. As well as taking painkillers for arthritic pain, she was also taking a tablet for a lump in her breast, a condition she had not mentioned before. The doctor visited her every three weeks, usually "just for a chat to make sure I'm eating and sleeping." Two community nurses came regularly, one every other day to dress the lump on her breast and the other to help her with a sponge bath every week. The chiropodist still came to cut her toenails. She managed to dress, feed, and toilet herself with difficulty, but was unable to go up or down steps; she could move about the house or go out (rarely) only with help.

A month later, in July, she collapsed when her neighbor was helping her to bed. She was taken to hospital, where she remained for two weeks, but again was determined to return home. When she did so, her next door neighbors felt they could no longer assume the responsibility for her care. They feared coming in one morning and finding her dead. Within days, her doctor persuaded her to enter a private residential home for a week.

I visited her at the home soon after she moved in. She was very appreciative of the care she was receiving and had decided to stay. However, she seemed withdrawn, stayed in her room and did not mix with the other residents. Her "nephew" and his wife visited her every day. She had endured a lot of pain for a long time. For the last two weeks of her life, someone sat with her all the time. She died of breast cancer in September 1987, within a month of entering residential care.

Like Sian Fielding, Glenys Owen's help came from a variety of sources—namely her "nephew" and his wife, her next-door neighbors, paid helpers, and the community nursing service. Mrs. Owen remained in control of her own personal care almost up until the week of her death. Despite her poor health, however, she maintained social contacts, had frequent visitors, and was continually appreciative of the high level of support she received.

## Local Self-contained Support Networks

Five respondents (three women and two men) were identified as having local self-contained support networks. In the absence of a spouse, this type of network was characterized as being dependent largely on neighbor support. All were childless and three had never married. Until 1987, two women managed without any help with personal care with the exception of visits from the chiropodist to cut their toenails. A single woman managed alone until, in the face of failing health and an absence of relatives for whom normative expectations of care existed, she requested admission to a local authority old people's home. Both of the men with self-contained support networks needed intimate care before the end of the study. In one case, a single man moved in with a nearby niece (aged 56) and her husband when he became ill, and the other male respondent was cared for by his wife.

It is impossible to make any generalizations about those with local self-contained support networks because only three of the respondents needed help with personal care. The presence of a female relative living nearby, such as the niece mentioned above, however, may result in a shift to a family-dependent network. The absence of such a relative or the presence of dementia and/or incontinence is likely to result in admission to residential care. The case study below illustrates the importance of spouse support for those elderly with this type of network; without such support, admittance to residential care, in the face of need for personal care, is inevitable. It also illustrates the importance of neighbors.

*Case Study 5*

Wil Hughes lived with his wife. They had no children although he had brothers and sisters who lived in the same area. In 1979, he said his health was good for his age (75) but that his activities were limited. By 1983, he felt his health had deteriorated and was only fair. He needed help from his wife to take a bath, had received bath aids, and the chiropodist came to cut his toenails. He also suffered from confusion, especially at night.

By the end of 1983, Mr. Hughes's confusion was more pronounced, and he suffered from frightening hallucinations every evening and at night. He had irrationally turned against some members of the community, actions that embarrassed his wife. Twice he had gotten lost. His wife never left him alone in the house and felt she could only let him out to go to the shops because he was known in the town. "He's been pretty good for not running away," she said, "but he doesn't get the chance because I'm here with him all the time."

Mr. Hughes had difficulty going upstairs to the bathroom, often needing help from his wife, and the couple hoped to have one installed downstairs. He thought perhaps he had had a slight stroke because he felt very strange at times.

By March 1984, the sense of confusion was worse, and Mr. Hughes had been ill with a bad chest (chronic bronchitis), a condition from which he suffered regularly in the winter. He could not remember what he had done that morning. His eyesight was deteriorating. He kept losing things and tried to return to his childhood home to retrieve them. He tried to talk about his confusion and to explain the nightmare quality of his mental state. His long-term memory was also affected sometimes. He got irrational fixations and went on and on about them for days. He was anxious about the strain on his wife since she had previously been very ill and had had four operations. "I don't want to make bother. I'd rather go to (the local old people's home) and get somebody to look after me. I don't want to be any trouble to no one." He did not want to be a burden and stressed that care attendants get paid for looking after people.

The doctor had prescribed tranquilizers for Mr. Hughes, but Mrs. Hughes did not like giving them to him. They made him drowsy and unsteady on his feet, and she was afraid he might fall, especially on the stairs. She was very tired and complained of dysrhythmia. As I left the house, Mrs. Hughes followed me to the car and told me how hard she was finding caring for her husband. Tearfully, she explained that the worst thing was the loneliness.

As the year progressed, Mr. Hughes' condition became worse and he was described as "living mainly in the past." He could not be left alone. His wife took him out for a walk every day, and sometimes he had a chat with his friends about the old days. In August, he was very ill with pneumonia. Mrs. Hughes, 73 nursed him through this illness, but his confusion and delusions became worse as he recovered and he was shouting all the time. She felt she could not cope, and he was taken to the hospital psychiatric unit. He came home after 10 days.

The couple had applied for a local authority bungalow and moved into one a year later. By then, Mr. Hughes was attending a day center twice a week. This gave Mrs. Hughes time to do her shopping and have some time to herself. He was difficult both at the day center and at home—moving furniture, piling things up, and imagining he was loading a truck. He was very strong and hurt both Mrs. Hughes and the officer in charge of the day center when they tried to restrain him.

Shortly after his 82nd birthday in March 1986, he suffered a stroke. He became bedridden and doubly incontinent. For a week, Mrs. Hughes nursed him at home with the help of a male neighbor (whom Mrs. Hughes had helped when his wife was dying of cancer) and district nurses. Two nurses came in the morning to wash him and change the bed, and one came at night to give him an injection so that he would sleep through until the morning. The neighbor came to help since Mr. Hughes fought the injections. He was catheterized.

Mrs. Hughes did not want her husband to go to the hospital but eventually gave in to pressure from the doctor, nurses, and neighbors. He was in the hospital for 7 weeks and died of pneumonia in June 1986. Mrs. Hughes was not with him when he died. "If I could just held his hand," she said tearfully, "We were together 60 years."

## Wider Community-focused Networks

Six respondents (four women and two men) had wider community-focused networks. All of them had children, who in 1979 lived at least 40 miles away. By definition, respondents with this type of network had independent life- styles that were focused primarily on friends and community groups and activities. One of the women died suddenly while another died within 10 days of a heart attack, during which time she was nursed at home by her daughter and sister-in-law. Neither woman had received any regular long-term help with personal care. By 1987, both men were still managing without regular help with personal care, although neither was in good health. The two other women in this category had much in common: They had both nursed their husbands through terminal illness and demonstrated great determination in maintaining their independence.

What characterizes the old people in this category is the fact that all demonstrated a very independent attitude toward personal care. All managed alone in the face of increasingly restricted mobility, and in some instances, debilitating illness, with the exception of short-term nursing care that was provided by members of the family, who often traveled considerable distances to do so. On the basis of data from the intensive study, it is impossible to say whether such independence results from personality or necessity. However, it is likely that the lack of local family available to help forces, reinforces, or encourages self-reliance in the face of growing impairment as a continuation of established patterns and expectations.

Three of the respondents in this category have died, none of whom received long-term routine personal care help with short-interval needs. It is, of course, impossible to know whether the high levels of independence and determination are the result of adaptation to the absence of available help, but it is significant that none of the respondents entered long-term institutional care, although four of the six spent short periods in the hospital. However, as the following section indicates, in some instances, networks of this type become private, restricted in the face of long-term disability. The following case study is typical of the independence and care from a distance associated with this network type.

*Case Study No. 6*

Caroline Jackson was 81 and already widowed when interviewed in 1979. Although she claimed to be in good health, she suffered from angina (which developed shortly after her husband's death, following several years during which she had cared for him) and arthritis, which limited her mobility. She found getting in and out of the bath difficult and needed chiropody help to cut her toenails. Although she was not receiving help, she always had her private cleaning woman in the house when she took a bath in case she slipped or could not get out of the tub. There was little change in her physical condition during 1983, but she underwent major abdominal surgery in 1984. She was in the hospital for four weeks. After her discharge, one of her daughters-in-law and the wife of one of her grandsons, who was a nurse, stayed with her to take care of her for three weeks. Her household help came as usual. Her many friends were very concerned and attentive, both during her stay in the hospital and afterward. She received postoperative care from the district nurse. She made a good recovery and was back to her preoperative routine by 1987. However, her mobility continued to deteriorate and by 1988, at the age of 90, she received help with bathing from the community nursing service.

### Private Restricted Support Networks

Five respondents (two women and three men) were identified as having private restricted networks. One other, whose network was originally identified as wider community focused, became a private restricted network by 1987. Patterns of needed personal care were less predictable than with other types of networks and demonstrated a wide range of diversity for these six respondents. This group also had the oldest average age. Two of the four men relied wholly on their wives for personal care, although neither required intimate personal care during the study and one of them continued to lead a normal life to the day of his death in 1984. Two of these respondents entered residential care, and the other two remained in the community.

As is the case with those having a wider community-focused support network, people with private restricted networks are determined to maintain their independence, which many in both categories manage to do in spite of high levels of impairment. In terms of receiving help, similar factors apply here as elsewhere. As the following case studies show, where no female relative exists to provide care, the only alternatives are domiciliary services and/or residential care.

### Case Study No. 7

Mr. Hill's decision to enter residential care was made for him. When interviewed in 1979, he was living with his wife in a small seaside resort to which they had moved on retirement, leaving their sons more than 100 miles away. He said that his health was alright for his age (then 79) but was limited by high blood pressure and impaired eyesight. He could not go out without his wife. Sometime between 1979 and 1983, Mrs. Hill, cared for by Mr. Hill, died after more than a year's illness.

By 1983, Mr. Hill was housebound. Walking any distance caused his ankles to swell, and he had suffered one or two falls thought to be due to a heart condition. However, he continued to take care of himself, although his independence was fragile and dependent on home help and Meals on Wheels. His contact with neighbors was minimal, but he was in frequent long-distance telephone contact with his sons, daughters-in-law, other relatives, and friends.

In 1986, Mr. Hill suffered a rectal hemorrhage and was taken to the hospital. After being discharged, he returned home but was anxious about living alone, confiding that he thought his sons were going to "work something out." Less than a week after arriving home, one of his sons drove over and told him that they had arranged for a room in a private residential home near where they all lived. He went there to live permanently the next day and remained there until his sudden death 6 months later.

### Case Study No. 8

Miss Bryant had sisters who were still living in 1979, but for years she had had little contact with them. The only member of the family she saw was a nephew, over retirement age, who came to see her 3 or 4 times a year. At the age of 92 in 1979, she was one of the oldest respondents in the study. At that time, she claimed that her health was alright for her age and that she managed all personal care apart from going to a chiropodist to have her toenails cut. However, she admitted that she could not take a bath and made do with a sponge bath.

By 1983, Miss Bryant's health had deteriorated considerably and she had become housebound. Her nephew rarely visited since his wife had suffered a stroke. Despite a recent cataract operation, Miss Bryant's sight was badly impaired, and mobility within the house was difficult. She complained that she was weak on her left side (due to a stroke?). The only time she left the house was by ambulance to visit the chiropodist, and she relied on the district nurse for personal help. The nurse came every day to wash her, do her hair, and administer eye drops. Shortly after the 1983 interview, Miss Bryant fell in her home and broke her arm, but she refused to stay in the hospital overnight. She returned home, determined to maintain her independence.

By 1987, at the age of 99, Miss Bryant was still living alone, she was blind, and her general health was poor. The district nurse came three times a week to bathe her, and she received home help visits twice a day. The home help assisted her in getting up in the morning, getting dressed, and getting undressed at night. She also helped Miss Bryant with her medication since she could not do it herself due to her blindness, and made sure that Miss Bryant had eaten because she had become very forgetful. She was still alive at the end of the study.

## Conclusions

On the basis of the third survey (Caldock & Wenger, 1988; Wenger, 1988c), it is clear and not unexpected that a deterioration in health and mobility means that more respondents needed help with personal care with the passage of time, although it must be stressed that the majority managed without such help. The findings confirm those of the Department of Health and Social Security (DHSS) study of carers (OPCS, 1988). Most routine help came from spouses or female members of the same household, particularly at high levels of dependency, supplemented by professional help with bathing, cutting of toenails, and specialized nursing tasks. Formal and informal help from outside the household were restricted to long-interval needs. In other words, at high levels of dependency, old people can only remain in the community if someone else in the household or living very nearby can care for them. Of those in the intensive sample of 30, half had received regular help with personal care by 1987 at varying degrees of impairment.

Independent of the type of support network, receipt of long-term informal help with short-interval personal care needs was found to be dependent on the availability of spouses or female relatives. Caring relationships (i.e., situations in which highly dependent old people were cared for at home) worked out well where long-term coresidence or long-term close relationships based on immediate proximity predated dependency and, other than spouses, were limited to daughters or classificatory/surrogate daughters. In cases in which coresidence was established to accommodate dependency, feelings of burden and/or resentment were common. These caring relationships appear to be able to cope only with lower levels of dependency. Admittance to institutional care is more likely in these cases and those in which incontinence or dementia occur. There was also some evidence to suggest that help from other members of the informal network made long-term caring more likely, but this also appears to occur more frequently in long-term relationships. Patterns of formal help provision have also been shown to be related to network type (Wenger & Shahtahmasebi, 1988) complementing the available informal support.

Having said that outcomes are related more to available female relatives and earlier relationships predating dependency rather than network types, it is obvious that these two factors are not unrelated. Availability of proximate kin and expectations of care are directly related to the type of network. Those with local family-dependent and locally integrated support networks are more likely to have potential carers in their networks because of related residential stability and to have built up expectations of both caregiving and receiving over the years. They are more likely to receive informal personal care. In the absence of a spouse, those with local self-contained, wider community-focused, and private restricted networks are less likely to have potential long-term carers in their networks and have thus built up expectations and life-styles based on personal independence. While prepared to provide emergency, short-term help, family members of their networks also have no plans for providing long-term care.

While it is impossible to demonstrate that expectations affect care-seeking or care-accepting behavior on the basis of the data presented here, there are indications that expectations based on a realistic assessment of network potential reinforce behavior designed to maximize independence, even in the face of disabling impairment. It may well be that where informal help is available, old people accept help at a lower level of impairment, while those without available help make other adaptations. In other words, where help is available, *dependency* may occur at a lower level of impairment.

Different types of networks in the community have different capacities for care that are based on the nature of their membership. Because we know that the distribution of network types varies from one community to another as a result of population stability, we can predict that the home care experience is likely to be more common in stable communities. While the different types of networks occur in all social classes, geographical mobility is more common among the middle class; Therefore, so we can also predict that the home care experience based on long-term relationships is likely to be more common and more stable in working-class families.

## Notes

1. While U.S. terminology refers to *caregivers,* the UK equivalent is *carers.*
2. All names are fictitious.

## References

Arber, S. & Gilbert, G. N. (1989). Transitions in caring: Gender, life course and the care of the elderly. In B. Bytheway, T. Keil, P. Allatt, & A. Bryman (Eds.), *Becoming and being old: Sociological approaches to later life,* (pp. 72-92). London: Sage.

Bayley, M., Seyd, R., Tennant, A., Simons, K. (1982). What resources does the informal sector require to fulfill its role? *The Barclay Report: Papers from a consultative day,* Paper No. 15. London: National Institute of Social Work.

Caldock, K. & Wenger, G. C. (1988). *Elderly people and the health and social services (Rural North Wales, 1979-1987),* CSPRD Report to the DHSS and Welsh Office. Bangor, Wales: Centre for Social Policy Research and Development.

Cumberledge Report. (1986). *Neighbourhood nursing - A focus for care: Report of the Community Nursing Review.* London: Her Majesty's Stationery Office.

Department of Health and Social Security. (1981). *Growing older,* Government White Paper. London: Her Majesty's Stationery Office.

Department of Health and Social Security. (1986). *Primary health care: An agenda for discussion,* Government Green Paper. London: Her Majesty's Stationery Office.

Equal Opportunities Commission. (1982a). *Caring for the elderly and handicapped: Community care politics and women's lives.* Research Report, Manchester, England: Author.

Equal Opportunities Commission. (1982b). *Who cares for the carers: Opportunities for those caring for the elderly and handicapped.* Manchester, England: Author.

Finch, J. & Groves, D. (1980, October). Community care and the family: A case for equal opportunities? *Journal of Social Policy, 9*(4), 487-511.

Gilroy, D. (1982). Informal care: Reality behind the rhetoric. *Social Work Service, 30,* 9-19.

Griffiths, R. (1988). *Community care - Agenda for action: A report to the Secretary of State for Social Services* (The Griffiths Report). London, England: Her Majesty's Stationery Office.

Hunt, A. (1978). *The elderly at home.* London: Office of Population Censuses and Surveys.

Johnson, L. C. & Catalano, D. J. (1981). Childless elderly and their family supports. *The Gerontologist, 6,* 610-618.

Kendig, H. L. (1986). Perspectives on ageing and families. In H. L. Kendig (Ed.), *Ageing and families: A support network perspective* (pp. 3-16). Sydney, Australia: Allen and Unwin.

Knipscheer, K. (1989, June 18-23). *The relationship between formal and informal care: Family cultures of caregiving.* Paper presented at the XIV International Congress of Gerontology, Acapulco, Mexico.

Office of Population Censuses and Surveys (OPCS). (1988). *Informal carers: A study carried out on behalf of the Department of Health and Social Security as part of the 1985 General Household Survey,* London, England: Her Majesty's Stationery Office.

Ungerson, C. (1987). *Policy is personal: Sex, gender and informal care.* London: Tavistock.

Welsh Office. (1985). *A good old age: An initiative on the care of the elderly in Wales.* Cardiff: Author.

Wenger, G. C. (1984). *The support network: Coping with old age.* London: George Allen and Unwin.

Wenger, G. C. (1987a). *Relationships in old age - inside support networks.* Report to the Department of Health and Social Security and Welsh Office. Bangor, Wales: Centre for Social Policy Research and Development.

Wenger, G. C. (1987b). Dependence, interdependence and reciprocity after 80. *Journal of Ageing Studies, 1*(4) 355-377.

Wenger, G. C. (1987c). *Support networks - Change and stability.* Report to the Department of Health and Social Security and Welsh Office. Bangor, Wales: Centre for Social Policy Research and Development.

Wenger, G. C. (1988a). *Old people's health and experiences of the caring services: Accounts from rural communities in North Wales.* Occasional Paper 4, Institute of Human Ageing. Liverpool: Liverpool University Press.

Wenger, G. C. (1988b, July 24-30). *Change and adaptation in informal support networks of elderly people in Wales 1979-87.* Paper presented at the International Congress of Anthropological and Ethnological Sciences, Zagreb: Yugoslavia.

Wenger, G. C. (1988c). *Help in old age - Facing up to change.* Centre for Social Policy Research and Development report to the Department of Health and Social Security and Welsh Office. Bangor, Wales: Centre for Social Policy Research and Development.

Wenger, G. C. (1989). Support networks - Constructing a typology. In M. Jefferys (Ed.), *Ageing in the 20th century* (pp. 166-189). London: Routledge.

Wenger, G. C. & Shahtahmasebi, S. (1988, April 16-19). *Variations in support networks: Some social policy implications.* Paper presented at Kinship and Ageing Seminar, Balatonzomardi, Hungary: International Committee for Family Research.

8

# The Dynamics of Long-Term Familial Caregiving

MYRNA SILVERMAN
ELIZABETH HUELSMAN

It is widely recognized that informal caregivers (families, friends, and neighbors) provide considerable amounts of care to impaired older adults. In fact, nearly three quarters of the impaired older adults in the United States are being cared for solely by family and friends (Doty, 1986). These unpaid, relatively untrained, caregivers offer assistance with such personal care as bathing, feeding, and toileting, and with instrumental activities, such as preparing meals, transportation, shopping/errands, and financial management. They may also provide emotional support and assistance with skilled health care, such as injections or catheter care (Tennstedt & McKinlay, 1987, p. 2).

An extensive body of research has provided information on various aspects of the caregiving experience, such as who the caregivers are (Reece, Walz, & Hageboeck, 1983; Horowitz, 1985b; Lee, 1985; Doty, 1986; Stone, Cafferata, & Sangl, 1987); the burdens they experience (Zarit, Reever, & Bach-Peterson, 1980; Cantor, 1983; Soldo & Myllyluoma, 1983; Brody, 1985; Morycz, 1985), and the extent to which

AUTHOR'S NOTE: The research on which this chapter is based was carried out with support from the Howard Heinz Endowment for a randomized prospective evaluation of geriatric assessment units in Allegheny County, Pennsylvania. We recognize the contributions of Pamela Oestreicher, members of the Benedum Geriatric "Think Tank," and Andrea Sankar for their critical comments on this and earlier drafts of this chapter.

173

caregiving is provided solely by one person, designated the *primary caregiver,* or by several people who share in the responsibilities (Shanas, 1979; Cantor, 1983; Johnson, 1983; Soldo & Myllyluoma, 1983; Horowitz, 1985b; Noelker & Wallace, 1985). Detailed studies of the amounts of care provided by specific family members, and the difference among caregivers in terms of the burdens they experience and the functions they perform have complemented the literature on this subject (Horowitz, 1985a; Noelker & Wallace, 1985; Zarit, Todd & Zarit, 1986; Matthews, 1987; Matthews & Rosner, 1988; Gubrium, 1988). The recognition of the persistence and magnitude of services provided by these informal caregivers has stimulated concern about the initiation of public policies to alleviate the stresses associated with this role (Tennstedt & McKinlay, 1987).

Despite the large body of existing research, however, unanswered questions about caregiving remain: Why do caregivers continue to assume these responsibilities, even when they are under extreme duress? What do caregivers experience when the caregiving situation continues for long periods of time? Little is known about the complex strategies families use to keep frail older adults in the community.

Some of the limitations of the research on caregiving stems from the predominance of cross-sectional and statistical studies. Longitudinal studies of family caregiving are needed (Horowitz, 1985a; Tennestedt & McKinlay, 1987). More specifically, studies should describe the characteristics and resources of more "successful" family caregivers rather than simply uncovering the negative consequences of caregiving (Noelker & Wallace, 1985, p. 34). The few longitudinal studies that have been completed (Frankfather, Smith, & Caro, 1981; Johnson & Catalano, 1983) have been limited to a small number of data collection points or emphasize the outcomes of the caregiving experience (Zarit, Todd, & Zarit, 1986). In addition, there has been little information concerning how caregiving systems change as the condition of the older adults or the caregivers change. This information should be useful to policy planners concerned with sustaining this significant body of health care providers without adding costs to the health care system.

This chapter provides a description of the long-term dynamics of the caregiving process in the community, specifically addressing the following questions: How do families divide their caregiving responsibilities? What effect does caregiving have on family relationships? How do past experiences with caregiving affect current care situations? How do religious or family values influence the caregiving experience? Using case histories of frail older adults and primary caregivers, this study provides information on the caregiving experience of a subgroup of families participating in an evaluation of the effectiveness of geriatric assessment units.

Our interpretation of the caregiving experience uses the life-course perspective as set out by Matilda White Riley in 1979. The major premises are that aging is a "life-long process" that spans birth to death; that it is an interactive process involving a combination of biological, psychological, and social processes; that social and environmental changes can affect an individual's life-course pattern; and, that new and different patterns of aging contribute to social change (1979, pp. 4-5).

## Methodology

The 35 families in this analysis varied in several ways although, demographically, they are similar to the national profile of caregivers described by Stone, Cafferata and Sangl (1987). Twenty-six of our families were white, 9 were black. Thirty of the older adults were female and 5 were male. Twenty-seven of the caregivers were female , 8 were male, 2 were spouses of an older adult, and 30 were adult children. The remaining 3 were either siblings or grandchildren. As in most caregiving studies, the majority of adult child caregivers were adult daughters. Only 4 of our caregivers reported having no significant secondary, or backup help. The remainder were involved in varied system of caregiving that included a wide range of family members, neighbors, and paid or formal services.

As part of the research protocol, frail older adults and their primary caregivers were interviewed every 4 months over a period of a year. Older adults were interviewed in their homes using a structured interview to assess mental, social, functional, and physical health status. To collect the environmental, incidental, and interpersonal information that could not be captured by structured interviews alone, case studies were developed for each of the participants and their caregivers. The case studies combined interview data with observations and additional information provided by older adults and their caregivers. A case study was written for each participant after each of the four interviews. These case studies permitted us to capture the more subtle aspects of the older adults' experiences in coping with their disabilities and to learn how they were managing their lives and their relationships with caregivers.

Primary caregivers were designated as the major unpaid helpers with activities of daily living who provide assistance on a regular, ongoing basis. Caregivers were interviewed by telephone, at the same 4-month intervals as older adults in order to assess their reactions to caring for a family member and the level of burden they were experiencing. Case studies for caregivers were developed in the same manner as with the older adults. At the time of the data analysis, there were 35 caregiver/ older adult units that had completed the one-year study period or had completed at least the second round of interviews.

The case studies for caregivers and older adults were combined with open- and closed-ended interview data to develop a collective case history for each family unit. The family case histories reflected changes revealed at each home visit about the conditions of the older adults and caregivers while also providing information about changes in the use of formal and informal services. Not only could we document change over time, but through repeated contact with families, we earned their trust; at each contact, more of the individual intricacies of caregiving and the positive and negative consequences were revealed. The focus of the family case histories, therefore, is the way in which the daily needs of the frail older adults are being met by both family and paid personnel; the reasons why some family members are involved in caregiving and others are not; decision-making regarding the best ways to provide care for the older adults; and the conflicts and adaptations that occur as the needs of caregivers or recipients change.[1]

The case histories were critically reviewed for information relating to the caregiving and caregiving experience. These data were sorted by content as they related to the four research areas: division of caregiving duties, effect of caregiving on family relationships, effects of past experience with caregiving, and the effect of religious and family values on caregiving.

Using the life course perspective as defined by Riley (1979) and interpreted by Silverman (1987) and Schulz and Rau (1985), the case histories were interpreted in relation to three periods of time in the caregiving experience. These are *background,* or experiences or behaviors that occur prior to the current caregiving situation; *emergent* behaviors that develop directly as a result of the caregiving situation; and *prospective* behaviors or experiences resulting from changes in the caregiver or the older adult.

Specific trends are associated with each time frame. When specific patterns of behavior or experiences occurred repeatedly throughout the data, we identified them as trends. A behavior or experience had to be documented in at least four families before it was considered a trend. Many families exhibited more than one trend. All the data were read and analyzed for these trends by both authors working independently. Tabulations were then compared to assess the reliability of the trend categories.

## *Background Trends*

"The life course pattern of any particular person . . . is affected by social and environmental change (or history)," according to Riley, 1979, pp. 4-5). Sometimes this history provides significant information that may enable us to better understand the current caregiving experience. We identified three trends that illustrate this category.

*A. Past family conflict between the frail older adult and other family members influences the backup help available to the caregiver.*

Mary Gold's family illustrates this trend.[2] When her father was dying of cancer, there was a "falling out" between the grandchildren (Mary's sisters) and their paternal grandmother. As a result, Mary's two sisters will take no part in the care of either their grandmother or their great aunt (their grandmother's sister). The burden of their care falls entirely to the youngest grandchild, Mary Gold, even though she has two small children and is currently unemployed. Mary's sisters are caregivers to their mother, who has cancer. Mary has little involvement with her mother, saying "my hands are full." Mary feels that the division of care is fairly equal.

Historical or background information on life-course experiences such as the above enables the researcher to understand the conditions which influenced the choice of primary caregiver and the constraints under which he or she must work.

*B. The past caregiving experiences of caregivers often enable them to better cope with additional caregiving responsibilities.*

Robert Lee is a 65-year-old white male caring for his 90-year-old mother, who lives in her own home not far from him. He helps her with all her physical and instrumental daily care, runs errands, and fixes some meals. Robert receives no backup support except for an aide who helps with bathing and cleaning. He has resigned himself to his role as caregiver and says of his brothers, who live nearby but do not help with their mother's care: "They have their own lives." Since he is single and lives alone, and possibly because he also cared for his father 20 years ago for a year and a half (giving him morphine injections to relieve his pain), he feels comfortable with his role as caregiver.

Previous experience with such life-course events as chronic and debilitating illness in older people may provide the caregiver with the skills to cope with these problems. In addition, when a life-course event is temporally normative, such as when an 80-year-old has a stroke, there is a greater likelihood that the levels of subjective stress and negative health effects associated with the occurrence of this event will be reduced (Schulz & Rau, 1985).

*C. Religious or family values may be used by caregivers to help them accept and deal with the caregiving burden and to moderate it over time despite their continued deprivation.*

Martha Fells is a middle-aged woman who has multiple sclerosis. Her ailing mother lives with her, along with her husband and nine-year-old daughter. Martha receives substantial support from her husband and daughter, who even changes her grandmother's linens when she soils the bed. Martha feels that God plays a significant role and offers her a great deal of emotional strength: "I know the Lord's beside me, 'cause I couldn't do it any other way."

These background trends are useful in explaining what the ground rules are for family caregiving. In Goffman's terms, they "set the stage" for what is to follow (1959). Having family history helps us to understand what life-course experiences the caregivers may have had and why they, rather than others, opted for this responsibility. It allows us to anticipate their potential for resilience and endurance, even under extreme duress, and it provides clues to understanding why some caregiving experiences are more successful than others.

## Emergent Trends

(1) A variety of situations occur during the caregiving process, some of which lead to negative relationships and behaviors in the caregiving system while others lead to positive relationships. We have portrayed these trends as those that generate conflict or family support.

### A. Conflict relationships

When only one person is responsible for the majority of care, that person often angrily resents family members who will not help.

Molly Jones has a sister who never took responsibility for the family when the sisters lived at home and always remained somewhat disassociated, even when their parents were healthy. Molly's mother is quite dependent on her daughter for her care as she experiences confusion and forgetfulness, is a diabetic, and is depressed and apathetic. Molly does all the cooking, house cleaning, and transportation and must occasionally take time from work to perform these activities. Her only relief is a paid aide who comes in two to three days a week. Molly complains that she gets "zero support from her family except from her children." Her sister cannot be relied on to offer any help whatsoever, and Molly resents this refusal.

(2) When two older adults are being cared for by one caregiver, there is often either conflict between the two care recipients or a conflict of time and loyalty felt by the caregiver.

Jane Steel is a 50-year-old unmarried woman who lives with her parents and cares for her mother, who is experiencing confusion diabetes, and some depression, and her father, who seems to be more difficult and burdensome. Jane feels frustrated living with her parents and feels trapped by the situation, although she "can't imagine doing anything else." The caregiving is made more difficult when her parents argue and "scrap" with each other. "Having two to care for is difficult. Dad always did have a temper.

Mom gets agitated with Dad. When she's tearing him down, it's quite hectic."

Conflict resulting from the caregiving situation sometimes causes increased tension between family members or between the family and the frail older adult.

In this case, the caregiver is a granddaughter who cared for both her great aunt and her grandmother, each living in her own home. As her grandmother's dementia worsened, a conflict occurred between the granddaughter and her sister, who wanted to institutionalize their grandmother. Despite the burdens of her own life (unemployment and fighting for custody of young children from a first marriage), she preferred to keep her grandmother at home and continue to provide assistance. Her sister first had the grandmother and then her great aunt placed in a nursing home despite the protests of the caregiver. These events have contributed to the increased depression of the caregiver, who "wanted to avoid a nursing home at all costs." She says, "It's a good home, but I hate seeing them there." Because of this situation, there are continued bad feelings between the sisters.

Many researchers now feel that it isn't only the structure of the support system that contributes to its viability. Its function is equally as important. In support systems in which family members do not agree on their functional roles, conflicts may occur, thereby preventing the development of a harmonious and successful support system.

The positive consequences or benefits to the caregiving experience, such as the pooling of family supports, often tend to be overlooked in the research on caregiving even though these characteristics are extremely important in an assessment of the potential strengths of the family system. Other mechanisms for relieving the burdens of caregiving and fostering a strong support network are described below.

### B. Supportive relationships

(1) Shared caregiving by multiple family members can bring families closer together through better understanding and shared caregiver burdens.

Ellen Jones is separated from her husband. She lives with her two sons and a severely demented father, a situation conducive to considerable stress. Fortunately, Ellen's sister is sensitive to the problem and provides considerable support in the form of respite (the father goes to her home two days each month) and transportation. Ellen's brother also visits in the evenings to provide relief and has begun to help with their father's care. Two paid aides provide care and supervision during the day so that Ellen can go to work. Altogether, the respite provided by siblings and the support provided by the Geriatric Assessment Unit that cares for her father have helped Ellen keep a positive attitude in a difficult situation. It has also produced the additional benefit of bringing family members together in a more unified support system.

(2) Male caregivers seem less likely to experience burden than do females while assuming the role of primary caregiver.

Paul Mann is 77 years old and continues to work part-time while caring for his frail 73-year-old wife. She has arthritis and has been diagnosed as suffering from Alzheimer's disease. According to Mr. Mann, she is beginning to let her appearance go. He has an elaborate set of backup supports, including their daughter, his wife's sister, a cousin, and a paid housekeeper who comes twice weekly. Mr. Mann seems to cope well with this situation. "I don't resent it, it's my obligation," he says, but he is saddened by the situation. As his wife's condition worsened, his support system expanded. Two paid helpers provide assistance in addition to the family. Although Mr. Mann does little of the physical care, he finds himself doing things he had never done before. After caring for his wife for a year, Mr. Mann continued to report no strain on himself as a result of that care. He said that accepting her condition was the most difficult thing for him. "I understand it. I don't like seeing her that way, but why get angry? It's not her fault."

Mr. Mann's ability to utilize available informal supports and seek assistance from formal (paid) supports to supplement the system has enabled him to better cope with his wife's illness. At the same time, doing so has not placed undue stress on his family and friends. Both trends cited above illustrate Schulz and Rau's metaphor of a support system as a "good musical ensemble" in which "there must be some stability in order to achieve high quality performances" (1985, p. 145).

In both cases, illness has triggered the involvement of family in a compatible and positive way.

### Prospective Trends

Over time, both frail older adults and caregivers may experience changes in their physical health and personal lives. These changes can have a significant impact on how the caregiving situation proceeds. In some cases, it may mean that the older adult needs to receive care in a formal setting, such as a nursing home, or have more assistance from formal caregivers, such as home health aides. It may also mean that other family members are willing to provide more resources to sustain both the primary caregiver who is under stress and the older adult whose health is declining. One of the objectives of the study was to assess how caregiving systems change when the frail older adult and/or caregiver experiences some change in the situation. We noted three trends in this area.

A. *The greater the instability of the caregiving situation (because of the caregiver's failing health or inability to cope), the greater the likelihood the caregiving situation will change.*

> Mr. Adams was the primary caregiver for his partially blind, cognitively impaired wife, and he received considerable help from a neighbor with medication and arranging for formal services. The neighbor feared that the minimal educational level of this couple might contribute to their inability to care for themselves. When Mr. Adams had to be institutionalized due to deteriorating health, Mrs. Adam's sister assumed the role of primary caregiver, bringing Mrs. Adams into her home. As a result, the neighbor withdrew completely from the support system.

Family supports change in time of crisis. Relatives or neighbors who have previously contributed only minimal amounts of support may now elect to assume more responsibility. Though their support may be only temporary, it is sufficient to provide respite to an overburdened primary caregiver.

*B. Negative views toward institutionalization voiced by the primary caregiver become less important as the patient's incapacity increases and/or the caregiver's perceived burden increases.*

Despite Jane Mills's strong will to keep her mother at home, she placed her in a nursing home only 3 months after expressing opposition to institutionalization. Her mother's increased confusion and repetitive behavior and her own feelings of stress were cited as reasons for her actions.

Family members often state strong negative feelings concerning the institutionalization of a dependent elder. Extreme confusion and disorientation on the part of the elders, as well as their becoming bedridden seem to precipitate institutionalization despite family values. Nontemporal, nonnormative life-course events, such as when a middle-aged caregiver experiences depression or chronic illness, may alter the caregiver's ability to cope and thus change the course of care. In some cases, changes in the course of care can prove to be beneficial to both the patient and the caregiver.

*C. When the caregiving responsibilities increase and the financial resources are inadequate, the caregivers' feelings of burden are likely to be extremely high.*

Mrs. Smith has her 99-year-old mother living with her in her home. The family's financial strain is severe. Mr. Smith works two jobs, and Mrs. Smith is unable to work, even part-time, because of her responsibility to her mother. She says of her mother, "she's a burden at times, but I love her." Despite decreased leisure and recreation time with less and less time alone with her spouse, Mrs. Smith insists on keeping her mother in her home. The Smiths cannot afford a nurse or other alternate care arrangements and have no other family members who can provide any respite. At the end of the study, Mrs. Smith's mother was extremely debilitated and Mrs. Smith was under severe strain, feeling her mother would be "better off not in this world." Financial strain has exacerbated this family's burden. Perhaps with more funds or more affordable services, the caregiver could have hired companions or home nursing and some of the strain she feels could have been avoided. As she said, "It's all on my shoulders."

There are numerous examples of mitigation of caregiver burden when the caregivers' financial resources allow them to pay for formal care. One caregiver pays for 24-hour home care for his mother, who has Alzheimer's disease. Two other cases (those of Mr. Mann and Mr. Lee) also illustrated this same theme. This may suggest that the negative impact of some life-course events can be mitigated by public policies that provide financial assistance to families experiencing a crisis similar to that of the Smiths.

Overall, these trends highlighted specific features of the caregiving experiences of these families. The data indicate that most families exercise some type of shared caregiving, despite the usual presence of a primary caregiver. The amount of support provided within any family to the primary caregiver ranges from occasional help with transportation to a full division of labor among the constituents. These cases support past research by showing that the division of caregiving tasks reduces the stress and burden to the primary caregiver and draws families together. However, when support is provided primarily by one person and other available family members do not contribute support, additional tension is added to already difficult situations. Both the life-course experiences of the caregiver and those of the care recipient, prior to the caregiving relationship, contribute to the choice of caregiver and the quality of the caregiving situation. Finally, strong value systems lay the groundwork for the existence of enduring caregiver relationships, even at great sacrifice to the caregivers. Religious values in particular seem to function as coping resources and as sources of great emotional strength. Individuals use "God's plan" or "God's will" as an explanatory device and cite biblical references to justify and compassionately accept their caregiving situations.

## Conclusions

These three historical categories (background, emergent and prospective) and their respective trends provide some insights into the process and dynamics of long-term caregiving that have not been fully addressed in earlier studies. Life-course perspectives aid in the interpretation of these data. Using this perspectives, we found the following:

First, history does have an effect on the caregiving experience, often in a positive way. The "practiced" caregiver does it better. Particular persons are chosen for the role of caregiver because of such life-course events as remaining unmarried, being the only adult child living close by, having had a close relationship with a parent in their younger days, having a strong set of religious or familial values, or even because of experiencing family conflict.

Second, families divide their caregiving responsibilities in a number of ways. As Schulz and Rau (1985) note, "the necessary conditions for the occurrence of supportive acts vary systematically with the type of life-course event the individual is experiencing" (1985, p. 144). Our findings support their remark that "A good support system consists of different actors—friends, relatives, colleagues—each of whom has assigned functions and who together cover the full range of support needs" (1985, p. 145). Not all families follow this pattern. Support systems evolve in different ways, with some more harmonious than others. Both personal and financial resources can contribute to the harmony. The absence of one or the other can lead to conflict and/or the perception of caregiving as a burden.

Third, this mode of analysis illustrated that there does not seem to be any ideal model of caregiving. Rather, the model used depends on the context of the caregiving situation and historical events. Gubrium (1988) points out that "people have their own ways of assigning meaning to parts of every day life. They partition and assemble their lives on their own terms, against their past, in ways that might be at odds with the categories we might, as social researchers, use to analyze their contemporary experience" (1988, p. 204). The "principle of substitution" (Shanas, 1979), which suggests a sequential order to the replacement of caregivers, does not reveal what type of caregiving is provided or how the system really works.

Fourth, by assessing the experience of caregiving as it is manifested over time, it is possible to explore the dynamic and changing nature of the caregiving system and to reveal both its benefits and its burdens. These data revealed not only the complexity of the issue of caregiving and its multidimensional nature, but its benefits and the coping measures used by caregivers as well. As others have noted, it is not the level of impairment of the older adult alone that stimulates caregiver burden (George & Gwyther, 1986).

Fifth, a longitudinal study of caregiving that emphasizes life-course perspectives in caregiving provides an opportunity to assess the relationship between informal and formal caregivers and the situations that provoke that linkage. This type of study can, according to Gubrium (1988) reveal "the ebb and flow in family systems as they respond to periods of crisis" (1988, p. 204).

The diversity in family caregiving systems requires the flexible consideration of a variety of services and interventions (Noelker & Wallace, 1985). Therefore, we concluded that in order to understand the dynamics of the caregiving context and its flexibility, and to predict how it will play out over time, a longitudinal study with emphasis on the life-course perspective is necessary. Using this perspective, it is possible to determine why a particular caregiver has been chosen, what conflicts and accommodations are likely to emerge, and possibly, what options are available to a family as the condition of the older adult and/or caregiver deteriorates.

Finally, in public-policy terms, this study provides support for the assumption that what informal caregivers need is the availability of additional formal support services in a manner that is both flexible and timely. There is no longer any doubt that there is a "well established, pervasive and continuing informal system of care" in place in this country (Tennestedt & McKinlay, 1987, p. 24). The concern of health researchers and policy makers should no longer be whether the increased availability of formal services will replace informal services. Instead, it is time for these experts "to conceive, initiate and properly evaluate innovative ways of supporting and perhaps even reimbursing the recognized contribution of informal caregivers. The critical issues are determining the most appropriate type of services and the most effective means of delivery" (Tennestedt and McKinlay, 1987, p. 27). This may enable us to alleviate some of the negative and costly impacts of caregiving, such as the physical and emotional problems experienced by overstressed caregivers, and to enhance positive aspects of this system of care.

Accomplishing this goal of providing an effective family support system that does not place excessive burdens on any one person requires the "cooperation of many, including parents, immediate and extended family members, neighbors, government officials at all levels, and professionals both in the public and private sector" (Sweeney, 1987, p. 53). The question that remains for policy makers is to determine the socially appropriate roles of families, elderly persons, and government in directing the course of family support services.

## Notes

1. Using the case as a "unit of analysis" (Gubrium, 1988, p. 206), it is possible to combine the responses by the caregivers and older adults with the observations of the interviewers, thereby avoiding some of the limits of interviewing only one caregiver.

2. All names of family members used in this chapter are fictitious.

## References

Brody, E. M. (1985). Parent care as normative family stress, *The Gerontologist, 25,* 19-28.

Cantor, M. (1983). Strain among caregivers: A study of experience in the U.S. *The Gerontologist, 23,* 597-604.

Doty, P. (1986). Family care of the elderly: The role of public policy, *Milbank Memorial Fund Quarterly, 164,* 34-75.

Frankfather, D, Smith, M., & Caro, F. (1981). *Family care of the elderly.* Lexington, MA: D. C. Heath.

George, L., & Gwyther, L. (1986). Caregiver well-being: A multidimensional examination of demented adults, *The Gerontologist, 26,* 253-259.

Goffman, E. (1959). *Presentation of self in everyday life.* Garden City, NY: Doubleday.

Gubrium, J. (1988). Family responsibility and caregiving in the qualitative analysis of the Alzheimer's disease experience. *Journal of Marriage and the Family, 50,* 197-207.

Horowitz, A. (1985a). Family caregiving to the frail elderly. In M. P. Lawton & G. Maddox (Eds.), *Annual Review of Gerontology and Geriatrics,* (Vol. 5, pp. 194-246). New York: Springer.

Horowitz, A. (1985b). Sons and daughters as caregivers to older persons: differences in role perspective and consequences. *The Gerontologist, 25,* 612-617.

Johnson, C. (1983). Dynamic family relations and social support. *The Gerontologist, 23,* 377-383.

Johnson, C., & Catalano, D. (1983). A longitudinal study of family support to impaired elderly. *The Gerontologist, 23,* 612-618.

Lee, G. (1985). Kinship and social support of the elderly: The case of the United States. *Aging and Society, 5,* 19-38.

Matthews, S. (1987). Provision of care to old parents: Division of responsibility among adult children. *Research on Aging, 9,* 45-60.

Matthews, S., & Rosner, T. (1988). Shared filial responsibility. The family as the primary caregiver. *Journal of Marriage and the Family, 50,* 185-195.

Morycz, R. K. (1985). Caregiving strain and the desire to institutionalize family members with Alzheimer's disease: Possible predictors and model development. *Research on Aging, 7,* 329-362.

Noelker, L., & Wallace, R. (1985). The organization of family care for impaired elderly. *Journal of Family Issues, 6,* 23-44.

Reece, D., Walz, T., & Hageboeck, H. (1983). Intergenerational care providers of non-institutional frail elderly: Characteristics and consequences. *Journal of Gerontological Social Work, 5,* 21-34.

Riley, M. W. (1979). Introduction. In M. W. Riley (Ed.), *Aging from birth to death: Interdisciplinary perspectives* (pp. 3-13). Boulder, CO: Westview Press.

Schulz, R., & Rau, M. T. (1985). Social support through the life course. In S. Cohen & L. Syme (Eds.), *Social support and health*. New York: Academic Press.

Shanas, E. (1979). Social myth as hypothesis: The case of family relations of old people. *The Gerontologist, 19*, 3-9.

Silverman, P. (Ed.). (1987). *The elderly as modern pioneers*. Bloomington: Indiana University Press.

Soldo, B., & Myllyluoma, J. (1983). Caregivers who live with dependent elderly. *The Gerontologist, 23*, 605-611.

Stone, R., Cafferata, G. L., & Sangl, J. (1987). Caregivers of the frail elderly: A national profile. *The Gerontologist, 27*, 616-626.

Sweeney, S. M. (1987). *Family caregiving: A synthesis evaluation*. A report from the Division of Program Analysis and Evaluation, Office of Policy, Planning and Legislation. Washington, DC: Office of Human Development.

Tennstedt, S., & McKinlay, J. (1987). *Informal care for frail older persons*. Unpublished manuscript.

Zarit, S., Reever, K., & Bach-Peterson, J. (1980). Relatives of the impaired elderly: Correlates of feelings and burden. *The Gerontologist, 20*, 649-655.

Zarit, S., Todd, D., & Zarit, J. (1986). Subjective burden of husband and wife caregivers: A longitudinal study. *The Gerontologist, 26*, 260-266.

## 9

# *Daughters Caring for Elderly Parents*

### EMILY K. ABEL

The relationship between mothers and daughters is a key concern of researchers within the field of women's studies. Feminist psychoanalytic theorists, for example, argue that personality differences between men and women can be attributed to the fact that women are the primary caregivers during their children's early years and that women relate very differently to their sons than they do to their daughters. Mothers identify more closely with their daughters, often failing to perceive them as separate persons. The ambivalence mothers feel about being women in this society colors their behavior toward their daughters. Women are less likely to provide adequate nurture to daughters than to sons or to encourage daughters to achieve autonomy. As a result, these writers contend, daughters have less clearly differentiated ego boundaries. They develop greater relational capabilities, but throughout their lives they also remain preoccupied with issues of separation and individuation, especially in relation to their own mothers (Chodorow, 1978; Flax, 1978).

Although Chodorow and Flax pay less attention to the place of fathers in women's lives, Chodorow argues that women relate far less intensely to their fathers than to their mothers and that fathers remain more distant figures to women (Chodorow, 1978).

Funded by the Alzheimer's Disease and Related Disorders Association and the UCLA Center for the Study of Women and presented at the Annual Scientific Meeting of the Gerontological Society of America, November 1988 in San Francisco.

This theoretical framework has been extremely influential, and it has proved useful in explaining a wide variety of women's relationships. But it also has encountered numerous critics. Some of the harshest attacks come from writers who fault the theory for failing to consider ethnic and racial variations. Black women, for example, charge that this portrait of mother-daughter relationships bears little resemblance to their experiences. Bonds between mothers and daughters in the Black community, they contend, are not characterized by the same ambivalence that feminist psychoanalytic writers describe (see Joseph, 1981).

Another prominent group of critics contend that personality structures are not established immutably during the first years of life. Instead, people develop as they age and respond to new situations. Some researchers have found that older women exhibit less expressiveness and nurturance—traits that the feminist psychoanalytic school attributes most directly to early childhood experiences (see Brubaker, 1985; Gutmann, 1980; Neugarten and Gutmann, 1968). Others have charted the changes that occur in the mother-daughter relationship throughout the life course. According to Fischer, for example, mothers and daughters often achieve a new harmony after the daughters marry and have children themselves (1986).

Even if we accept the insights of the human development school, however, it is still possible that certain events may trigger previously learned responses and revive old patterns of behavior. Rubin (1985) writes:

> Even well into adulthood, we can go "home" and find ourselves behaving in ways we left behind years ago. It's not just the parents who forget that a son or daughter is forty-five; the "child" forgets too. It's not just the parents who want the child to return, even if for just an hour or so; the adult child is not without some ambivalence about the regressive pulls that live inside him or her(p. 27).

Because the gerontological literature on caregiving has grown dramatically during the past few years, we might expect it to shed light on these issues. The great majority of studies on caregivers, however, are based on highly structured interviews that are analyzed statistically. This type of research is more appropriate for examining the discrete tasks of caregiving than for exploring either the human relationships within which those tasks are embedded or the subjective experiences of the caregivers. Although some researchers do focus on the subjective responses of caregivers, we still lack an understanding of the emotional dynamics of caregiving. This chapter represents one attempt to capture this dimension of care. Based on an exploratory study of women caring for frail elderly parents with some form of dementia, it examines the daughters' perceptions of their relationships with their parents. These perceptions constitute an important part of the home care experience.

## Sample and Methods

Respondents were located and recruited through support groups and service agencies. A snowball approach was used to obtain additional names. The sample consisted of 26 women, 16 of whom were married. Their median age was 51. To control for variations by race, only white women were interviewed.

Nineteen women were caring for mothers and seven for fathers. The length of time the women had been providing care ranged from 6 months to 16 years, the median being 4 years. At the time of the interviews, 8 women were living with their parents, and 1 had done so for a period of over a year a few years prior to the interview. Eight women helped their parent with hygiene, 6 assisted with mobility, 8 administered medication, 17 performed household tasks, all 26 shopped and/or assisted with transportation, 25 handled finances, and 5 provided economic help. The intensity of caregiving work was related not just to the level of impairment of the parents. Although these women made little use of community or home-based services provided by formal agencies, 16 hired aides or attendants through ad hoc, informal arrangements.

Three of the 19 women caring for mothers said that their mothers' dementia had progressed so far that meaningful contact was impossible. Because I am particularly interested in how the women experienced relational aspects of caregiving, I emphasize the accounts of the women whose mothers had a mild or moderate dementia.

The interviews in this study consisted of open-ended as well as structured questions. They lasted an average of 1½ hours and were tape recorded and transcribed. Answers were analyzed using standard techniques for the coding and analysis of qualitative data (Taylor & Bogdan, 1984; Glaser & Strauss, 1967).

The usual disavowals are necessary. Obviously, we must be cautious about overgeneralizing from the study. Not only is the sample very small, but it also is biased because it includes a high proportion of women who sought assistance (Gwyther & George, 1986). Also, although the patterns described held true for the great majority of the women interviewed, a few did not conform to these patterns. Future studies should examine the distinguishing characteristics of the women who are most likely to fit the mold delineated in this study.

## Results

Most women in the study focused on the emotional aspects of caring for elderly parents, not the labor involved. They viewed caregiving as a diffuse relationship rather than a series of specific chores. When asked to estimate the number of hours they devoted to parent care, many women responded that it would be impossible to make such a calculation, explaining they remained preoccupied with the well-being of their parents even when not rendering instrumental assistance.

Many women claimed that they found caregiving gratifying, but virtually all also insisted that it was a source of strain. Some problems resulted from the particularities of these women's personalities or their relationships with their parents. Nevertheless, a number of patterns can be discerned.

Very few women anticipated caring for their parents. Some women insisted that if they ever had thought about their parents' old age, they simply had assumed that their parents would die quickly. Those who had considered the possibility that parent care would be part of their lives were shocked by the type of disease that struck.

In addition, many women had little warning that they would be called upon to provide care. Five had lived far from their parents and had not discovered the extent of a parent's impairments until they went to visit. Four women learned about one parent's disability only after the death of the other parent, who had shielded them from the initial stages of the disease. Recent writing has emphasized the need for predictability; we can cope better with events that arrive at scheduled times and for which we have prepared (see Hagestad, 1986). But caregiving obligations often occur precipitately, catching family members by surprise.

These women also felt powerless to terminate caregiving responsibilities. Most had investigated the possibility of institutional placement and had concluded that the quality of available nursing homes was too low to make this a viable option. Several women reported feeling trapped because they realized that caregiving would end only when their parents died.

Most women had little training about how to act. The great majority stated that their parents had not cared for their grandparents. Gunhild Hagestad (1986) remarks, "Family members often face each other in relationships for which there is no historical precedent and therefore minimal guidance on which to rely." Many women in this study complained about being confronted with decisions for which they were unprepared. Some still were pondering decisions they had made months and occasionally years before, and they used the interviews as opportunities to reassess their choices.

Caregiving also competed with paid employment in the lives of many women. Three quit their jobs, at least partly because of caregiving responsibilities; one woman forfeited her chance of a promotion. Other women with paid employment complained that phone calls from their parents frequently interrupted their work and that they took time off from their jobs to care for their parents.

Most women were even less successful when it came to protecting their leisure from the encroachments of parent care. Like most other caregivers (see Horowitz, 1985), the women in this study frequently abandoned vacations and sacrificed social activities. Many stated that preoccupation with their parents put a damper on the leisure activities that they did undertake.

Although these women discussed social and economic disruptions wrought by caregiving, most emphasized interpersonal and intrapsychic factors. Some of these factors were different when women were caring for fathers rather than mothers. I therefore first will examine the experience of caring for mothers. Then, for purposes of comparison, I will discuss the experience of caring for fathers.

## A. Relationships with Mothers

Caregiving brought women into intimate contact with their mothers, often for the first time since they had been adolescents. Issues they assumed had been fully resolved suddenly reemerged. Several women were shocked by the intensity of the feelings this experience provoked. Although a few viewed caregiving as an opportunity to master old conflicts, many stated that they simply slipped back into old patterns.

Jean Barr (a pseudonym), is an extreme example of emotional responses that were common, if less intense, in the study. A 57-year-old single woman, Jean had lived across the country from her parents for many years before moving into their house in 1979 to care for them. She acknowledged, however, that her sense of independent identity was fragile even during the years she lived apart. She nursed her father for six years. When he died in 1985, it was apparent that her mother was suffering from Alzheimer's disease. At the time of the interview, Jean's mother no longer could be left alone, and Jean had been caring for her for two years. Jean did not work, and she had time to herself only during the six hours a week her mother attended a day-care program. She rarely saw friends. Jean described her life this way:

> My struggle is that because I'm sequestered with my mother all the time, I feel that I'm reverting back; I don't feel like an adult. This could be my chance to grow, but in the process I'm regressing. I had overcome an eating problem, and I'm going back to it now—eating a lot at night and then not being able to get up in the morning. Boundaries are hard. Which part is me? And it's hard because Mother always is talking about me as a child.

Because other women in the study had been far more successful in carving out adult identities, prolonged and intense contact with their mothers did not threaten their sense of self as profoundly as the case of Jean Barr. Those who were not living with their mothers were better able to distance themselves emotionally. Most women who shared a residence with their mothers retained at least some links to jobs and other adults. Nevertheless, the majority of women stated that they reestablished old modes of interacting with their mothers and reexperienced feelings that were appropriate to an earlier period. Old resentments suddenly had renewed force. Some women became preoccupied with the ways their mothers had hindered their growth and development or failed to love them adequately when they were children. Many women also acknowledged that they found themselves once again looking to their mothers for approval and striving to please them. A few expected to receive the approbation and affection that previously had been withheld. A 58-year-old woman caring for her mother commented:

"Whatever I do, it's not the right thing. And I keep having the expectation after all this time, that one of these days it's going to be the right thing."

If caregiving reawakened childhood feelings, however, it also compelled these women to acknowledge how much had changed. Many women spoke of the difficulties of watching the deterioration of a person to whom they felt intimately bound. One woman, who had been caring for her mother, a victim of Alzheimer's disease for two years, drew a sharp contrast with child rearing:

> When I brought my mother here I thought it wouldn't be difficult. I thought, I could manage. She acted very much like a three- or four-year old. I had six children, I had ten grandchildren, so I thought I can handle this. But its not the same. Here there is no progress, only a slow deterioration, almost an invisible deterioration, but I know it's there. If you're doing a good job with kids, they move along, they progress, their world expands. But my mother's world is contracting.

Fears of aging and death surfaced. Caregivers whose mothers suffered from Alzheimer's disease worried about inheriting a propensity for the illness. As one caregiver put it:

> Aging never bothered me before. Now I wonder if I will inherit this, if I will do this to my own children. If I forget something, it's not just a funny matter anymore. I wonder if this is how Mama started. It's made me more aware of growing older, and it's not such a wonderful thing anymore.

Alterations of affect and behavior were both painful and confusing to children of mothers with dementia. Many acknowledged anger at their mothers. As the disease progressed, women often felt their mothers' personalities had been ravaged. One woman's comment reveals her frightening sense of loss and abandonment: "My mother was always a very dignified lady. It is sort of like seeing your mother stripped naked when she doesn't care for herself, and her clothes are dirty, and she has a look of total rejection on her face."

Caregiving itself accentuated the sense of loss. The presence of mothers reminded women continually of the former person. One woman, who lived with a mother suffering from Alzheimer's disease, said:

> The person I loved isn't there. It's just a body sitting there. The terrible thing is that she looks like the same person, but she doesn't share my joys or my sorrows or anything. It isn't the same person, but I still have to look at that person that looks like the mother I loved. And it just tears me apart.

In some instances, the level of lucidity exhibited by the mothers fluctuated. When those afflicted with dementia sounded more coherent than usual, hopes were raised that they would recover; the sense of loss thus was recurrent.

In providing care, moreover, daughters must relinquish the illusion that their mothers are omnipotent and still can offer protection.[1] One woman who had been caring for her mother for two years still had not reconciled herself to the impossibility of turning to her mother when she was in need:

> Sometimes I just want my parents. I have my own problems, and I want my mother and she's not in there, and it looks like her but it's not my mother anymore. That's the hardest part, I think, when I just want to be a little girl. Sometimes I try to imagine what it would be like to have parents you can go to and ask help of, and maybe that would be nice, to have a relationship with your parents where they were still your parents and you were still their child. I have friends who still can leave their children with their parents on the weekend or borrow money or ask advice. I can't do those things.

If residues from the past shape the experience of providing care, caregivers also discover that they cannot go home again.

In addition, caregiving demands that women redefine their roles vis-à-vis their mothers. Noddings has commented that "apprehending the other's reality, feeling what he [sic] feels as nearly as possible, is the essential part of caring. . . . Caring involves stepping out of one's own personal frame of reference" (Noddings, 1984). Ideally, then, before a woman cares for her mother, she should be able to view her mother as separate from herself and understand the reality of her life. An article by Gardiner about the school of self-psychology also helps to explain what is called for. Gardiner writes that members of this school "see empathy as an adult process in which one mature self takes the position of the other person. . . . From this perspective, empathy is not the same as but opposite to projective identification in which one person insists that the other is an extension of the first. This self-psychology view of empathy entails no merging, blurring, or loss of self for adults" (Gardiner, 1987). Such empathetic understanding is a critical aspect of caregiving, but it requires that a woman cease viewing herself as a child in relation to her mother. The sense of fusion that many women experience in relation to their mothers is antithetical to the stance women must adopt as caregivers (Chodorow, 1978).

Most of the women I interviewed discussed still other reasons why the shift in responsibilities was difficult. Many were acutely aware that their mothers resented their assertions of authority. These caregivers saw themselves as wounding their mothers further by taking control. One woman viewed caregiving as an aggressive act: "Maybe I'm just getting even with my mother. I have a guilty feeling because I enjoy being in control. It always was a problem that my mother was over-controlling."

Those caregivers who still were seeking to please their mothers and win their approval felt torn between the need to assume responsibility and the desire to accede to their mothers' wishes. Several women stated that, because their mothers were adults, and not children, they were entitled to refuse to surrender control.

In our society, self-determination is viewed as one of the marks of adult status. In order to preserve the dignity of frail elderly persons, caregivers typically seek to respect their autonomy and encourage them to remain in charge of their own lives. Some women defined good daughters as those who respect the wisdom of their parents:

> My difficult problem over the last two years has been trying to get my mother's cooperation in doing the things I have to do to make her life better and that's not been easy. Like when she has to go to the doctor when her foot is sore and she wants to go to the doctor, and then at the last minute, she won't go. I just talk to her till she agrees to go. She has no choice. I yank her out the door and at times she will be very angry and be sputtering at me when I put her in the car, saying she doesn't have to go, and she doesn't understand why, and she can't afford it, and all sorts of strange things that she would not say if she was well. But she is the parent. I have always been trained to respect that role, and so when she says, "get out of my life," she has a right to say that in a sense. You feel that a person in old age should be at the most wise point of their life in a sense, and in your head that means control of every situation.

Although caring demanded that she seize the reins, this woman was loath to dishonor her mother.

But, if women employed the language of rights and obligations, they also used terms that betrayed the sense that they still were operating within the framework of filial relationships. One woman explained her reluctance to wield authority by saying that she couldn't "cross" her mother. Another remarked that she hated being "mean" to her mother. Such words suggest that these women viewed themselves as daughters rebelling against their mothers, not simply as adults responding to the needs of others. When asked how her relationship with her mother had changed since she began rendering care, one woman responded:

> I don't know how to answer that. I suppose it has changed in the sense that I have become bossy and say, "you have to do something my way, and I don't care what you say," which I never would have said before. In a sense, I exert outward kinds of control, and maybe that is a difference. But emotionally the relationship is the same still. I am the child.

A second woman, queried about whether caregiving made her feel more like a child or an adult, answered this way:

> It's a very tricky thing. I think I went between those two. I would feel one and then just the opposite. My mother was a very strong person, and I was a very easygoing person. It was very hard for me to be the strong one. Even in all her dementia I never felt she was that childlike. I felt that underneath, that personality of hers was still there, like I'd help her down the stairs, and she'd pull back.

Preventing mothers from driving, taking control of their financial affairs, and hiring aides and attendants were critical junctures that aroused profound anxiety in the caregivers. Some women initially avoided challenging their mothers' authority, waiting to intervene longer than they later deemed appropriate. One woman confiscated her mother's car keys only after her mother had had three accidents. A second woman hesitated to hire an aide to tend to her mother although she suspected that her mother occasionally lost her way when returning home from shopping. A third refrained from setting up a conservatorship despite her mother's increasing propensity to make serious financial mistakes.

Other types of control were more subtle but equally problematic. One woman gave this account of taking her mother shopping:

> I was always on edge. I lost her four times. They [the times I lost her] were the worst things in my life. So there always was that fear. I wanted to hold her hand, but I didn't want to rob her of her dignity and make her feel she was demented to that extent. I tried always to let her have her self-respect, but always there was a very fine line of where and what to do. So it was very stressful.

To this woman, holding her mother's hand meant crossing a sensitive boundary in parent-child relations.

Women who did manage to assume responsibility over their mothers' lives employed a variety of strategies for doing so. One woman explained that she was able to "edge into" the position of authority because her mother's impairments developed gradually over a period of years. A woman who was thrust abruptly into the caregiving role used her experience as a parent to guide her behavior:

> A couple of years ago, my mother was in the hospital, and she kept climbing out of bed and would fall. It was very difficult. I had to tell them it was O.K. to tie her down. That was so hard for me. I remembered having to make similar decisions when my child was young. Something just has to be done. I immediately went into that mode.

The strategy most commonly adopted, however, was to shield mothers from an awareness of the shift in roles. The few women who helped their mothers financially were careful to conceal their contributions. One woman hid car keys from her mother rather than confront her about her dangerous driving and demand that she stop.

It would be wrong to suggest that caregivers practiced such deceptions solely in order to satisfy their own needs. A central component of caregiving is maintaining the dignity of the care recipient. The great majority of women in this study took as a given that their primary mission should be to protect their mothers' individuality and self-image. Some invoked the advice of experts to support their own definitions of good care and justify their behavior. Books they had read and lectures they had attended counseled them to preserve their mothers' sense of competence and uniqueness as far as possible and to not compel them to confront their growing impairments. Moreover, these women expected others to adhere to their own standards of care. Several expressed fury at relatives and professionals who failed to respect their mothers' worth and humanity.

But, if their own desires meshed with the requirements of good caring, their attempts to preserve their mothers' identity also conflicted with their own needs in two ways. First, they failed to dislodge their mothers from positions of power and instead worked to create the illusion that the original parent-child relationship remained intact. The more they saw their mothers as retaining their former characteristics, the easier it was to lapse into familiar patterns and the more difficult it became to exert their own authority. Second, because they rendered their own work invisible, they were unable to receive the appreciation they craved. When asked if their mothers displayed gratitude, several women responded that their mothers failed even to perceive most of their efforts. There were, of course, other reasons why parents did not show gratitude, including their cognitive impairments. Nevertheless, the daughters were convinced that an important factor was their determination to render assistance as inconspicuously as possible.

In short, although caregiving reactivated feelings of dependency and interrupted activities that promoted a sense of competence and adulthood, it also demanded that women adopt a new stance toward their mothers. The daughters in this study simultaneously revived and reconstructed intergenerational relationships.

Although most caregivers believed that their mothers resisted even essential help, seven women also portrayed their mothers as making impossible demands. Some women complained that their mothers expected them to spend inordinate amounts of time with them. Caregivers also pointed to instances in which their mothers had summoned them for crises that turned out to be imaginary or for trivial reasons. In addition, many women believed that their mothers had boundless expectations about what their daughters could accomplish. Some mothers appeared to hold their daughters accountable for any plans that went awry or any unsatisfactory program or service.

Few daughters, however, perceived the demands placed on them by their mothers as clear-cut. Many mothers rebuffed any assistance offered. Those who asked for a great deal of help often seemed ambivalent about receiving it. For example, some mothers urged their daughters to take charge of certain plans for them but then proceeded to make their own arrangements. Some daughters complained that their mothers gave them overly precise instructions about how chores should be carried out and carefully monitored performance.

Several researchers have argued that elderly women strive to retain their sources of power in the family (Evers, 1985; Fischer, 1986; Lewis & Meredith, 1988; Matthews, 1979). Many women in this study interpreted their mothers' demands as manipulative attempts to remain in control. Many also attributed their mothers requests to personality changes caused by dementia.

In addition, these women frequently stated that they considered their mothers' demands unreasonable. Two contended that their mothers clung to an idealized notion of caregiving relationships in the nineteenth century that was inappropriate to the 1980s. Three complained that the care their mothers expected from them far exceeded what these mothers had provided their daughters when they were young. Still other women felt that their mothers should have been satisfied because the care rendered already had improved their lives dramatically. One woman remarked:

> On Sunday, Mother was very depressed and had nothing to do. This has been going on for months, and she complains bitterly. Sunday is the day with nothing to do. My brother was supposed to take her to dinner, but he had to cancel. This threw my mother into a depression; she was all teary. There was no consoling her. Considering that she spent all her time before she moved out here doing nothing, it seems strange. When she was alone, it never even occurred to her to go out, to look at a tree. And all of a sudden, this woman is frantic because she has nothing to do. And she has the busiest schedule she's had since her children were small. So I'm constantly reading it as, "you don't do enough for me, or you should be taking me someplace on Sunday."

In short, these women believed that their mothers were ambivalent about receiving assistance, perceived their demands to be  unreasonable, and attributed the demands to illness and fears of losing control. Why, then, did these demands exert such a powerful influence over the daughters?

One explanation may lie in the sense of identification daughters had with their mothers, which may have permitted them not just to share their mothers' pain, but also to anticipate their needs and grant them primacy.

In addition, many women interpreted continuing requests as evidence that they had fallen short as caregivers. Chodorow argues that because women fail to differentiate themselves from others, they often have an enormous sense of responsibility, even for events they could not possibly control (Chodorow, 1974). The women in this study embraced a notion of caregiving that required them to improve the overall quality of their mothers' lives. Their mothers typically had experienced irremediable losses and suffered from health problems that could not be repaired. Nevertheless, the daughters held themselves accountable for making their mothers happy. One woman lamented:

> No matter how much help I gave her, I can't seem to give her what she needs, and I can't seem to reconcile it with myself. That's the hardest part. I know I've done a lot of good for her, but she seems so unhappy no matter what I do. I keep wanting to fix it, and I can't, I really can't.

Such attitudes may help to explain why caregiving fails to resolve residual conflicts between mothers and daughters. Had this woman succeeded in her goal of restoring her mother's happiness, she might have demonstrated her worth to her mother and earned the latter's approval. Instead, she felt continually rebuffed. If Chodorow is correct that mothers in this society fail both to nurture their daughters adequately and to encourage their autonomy (Chodorow, 1978) then women who perceive their mothers as simultaneously demanding and ungrateful may feel that they are replaying earlier dynamics.

## B. Establishing Limits

Because this study was cross-sectional rather than longitudinal, it was not possible to trace the evolution of the women's responses to caring for their mothers. Nevertheless, most women who had been providing care for at least a year stated that they experienced the greatest difficulties during the initial stages. Several women pointed with pride to their increased ability to draw boundaries around caregiving responsibilities. They had reduced both the time spent with their mothers and their emotional involvement in their mothers' lives. Some claimed that they no longer responded to each crisis that arose with the same urgency.

Women who had attended support groups or sought individual therapy reported that they had been counseled to establish limits to the obligations they assumed, and they were attempting to follow this advice. Caregivers whose mothers suffered from some form of dementia gained critical distance by learning more about the nature of the impairments. One woman whose mother had Alzheimer's disease stated: "When you understand the disease, you get stronger, you get more confidence, you get clearer, you get less emotional."

Although no woman had extricated herself entirely from the mother/daughter caregiving relationship, many claimed that issues that had consumed them when they first began caring for their mothers persisted only in an attenuated form.

## C. Relationship with Fathers

Seven women in the study were caring for fathers. Although women struggled with issues of authority in relation to fathers as well as to mothers, the experience of caring for fathers differed from that of tending mothers in two important respects. First, caregivers were far less likely to perceive their fathers as making extravagant demands. Although 7 of the 16 women tending mothers with mild or moderate dementia complained about the demands that were placed on them, none of the women caring for fathers reported that the fathers placed impossible demands on them.

Second, caregivers of mothers and fathers responded to personality changes in their parents in very different ways. Women caring for mothers stated that, as the edges of their mothers' personalities eroded, the intensity of their own feelings also waned, and they were better able to extricate themselves from the relationship. One woman was relieved to realize that her mother no longer remembered their arguments; this allowed her to forget them as well. In contrast, women caring for fathers reported that, as their fathers became more vulnerable, they ceased to be objects of awe. As a consequence, the daughters were able to express affection they previously had been afraid to demonstrate and to establish a close connection, often for the first time. One woman discussed her experiences this way:

My father has always been a very difficult person to get along with. I mean, it sounds really perverse like I am glad that he is sick or something, but there has been this period of time where I have a feeling that I can be nice to him and be sweet, and give him kisses and be affectionate in a way that is not at all threatening. It was horrible growing up with him. We were always afraid that he was going to be angry if we had done something wrong. So there is this kind of process of making my peace. When I see my friends whose parents have died suddenly and they have have not made their peace, I realize I am in a way very lucky. I have the perception that he is nicer most of the time, and maybe it's because people can, without any terror, give him more emotional support and attention. Unlike the past, I can laugh with my father and give him little kisses on the cheek, and I can rub his arm or rub his knee and just be affectionate.

A second woman also spoke of forging a closer relationship with her father:

When he got sick, my feelings started changing. I started worrying about him and realizing I really did care about him. I feel closer to him now than when I was a kid. I didn't get it [affection] as a kid, but I'm getting enough now that I feel if he dies I will have felt like I was close to my father. Sometimes if someone's ill or sick, you can give to them more than if they're healthy. If they're healthy, they won't take it, or it's harder. Like before he was real sick, there was that clash of me wanting to give and he not wanting me to. When he's sick, I can give him more. I feel less inhibited.

In short, the personality changes of frail elderly parents enabled caregivers of fathers to develop a greater intimacy and caregivers of mothers to establish critical detachment. This divergence is consistent with theories arguing that women experience relationships with mothers and fathers very differently. According to Chodorow, women remain enmeshed with their mothers but idealize their fathers, viewing them as clearly differentiated from themselves (Chodorow, 1978).

### Conclusion

Parent care involves a constant tension between attachment and loss, pleasing and caring, seeking to preserve an older person's dignity and exerting unaccustomed authority, overcoming resistance to care and fulfilling extravagant demands, and reviving a relationship and transforming it. Some of these contradictions are built into the experience of caring for any person at the end of the life course. When adult children are the caregivers, however, services are rendered within the context of relationships that already are characterized by deep ambivalence.

An analysis of the emotional responses of caregiving has important policy implications. Some policy makers argue that we reinforce traditional values and strengthen intimate bonds by returning care to individual households. The women I spoke to felt overwhelmed by the intensity of the feelings this experience provoked, and a few felt that this sense of being overwhelmed prevented them from rendering what they considered good care. Thus many wanted outside help not only to gain relief from caregiving tasks, but also to achieve the emotional detachment that permitted them to remain involved.

## *Note:*

1. Over 20 years ago, Martha Blenkner coined the phrase *filial crisis* to describe this realization (Blenkner, 1965).

## *References*

Blenkner, M. (1965). Social work and family relationships in later life, In E. Shanas & G. I. Streib (Eds.), *Social structure and the family: Generational relations*. Englewood Cliffs, NJ: Prentice-Hall.

Brubaker, T. (1985). *Later life families*. Beverly Hills: Sage.

Chodorow, N. (1974). Family structure and feminine personality. In M. Z. Rosaldo & L. Lamphere (Eds.), *Woman, culture and society* (pp.43-66). Stanford: Stanford University Press.

Chodorow, N. (1978). *The Reproduction of mothering: Psychoanalysis and the sociology of gender*. Berkeley: University of California Press.

Evers, H. (1985). The frail elderly woman: Emergent questions in ageing and women's health. In E. Lewin & V. Olesen (Eds.), *Women, health and healing*. London: Methuen.

Fisher, L. R. (1986). *Linked lives: Adult daughters and their mothers*. New York: Harper & Row.

Flax, J. (1978). The conflict between nurturance and autonomy in mother-daughter relationships and within feminism. *Feminist Studies, 4,*(2), 171-191.

Gardiner, J. K. (1987). Self psychology as feminist theory. *Signs, 12,*(4), pp. 761-780.

Glaser, B. C., & Strauss, A. L. (1967). *The discovery of grounded theory: Strategies for qualitative research.* Chicago: Aldine.

Gutmann, D. L. (1980). Psychoanalysis and aging: A developmental view. In S. I. Greenspan & G. H. Pollack (Eds.), *The course of life, 11,* Bethesda, MD: NIMH.

Gwyther, L. P., & George, L. K. (1986). Introduction to symposium on caregivers for dementia patients. *The Gerontologist, 26*(3), 245-247.

Hagestad, G. O. (1986). The family: Women and grandparents as kin-keepers. In A. Pifer & L. Bronte (Eds.), *Our aging society: Paradox and promise* (pp. 141-160). New York: W. W. Norton.

Horowitz, A. (1985). Family caregiving to the frail elderly. *Annual Review of Gerontology and Geriatrics, 5,* 194-246.

Joseph, G. I. (1981). Black mothers and daughters: Their roles and functions in American society. In G. I. Joseph & J. Lewis (Eds.), *Common differences: Conflicts in black and white feminist perspectives* (pp. 75-126). Garden City, NY: Doubleday.

Lewis, J. & Meredith, B. (1988). *Daughters who care: Daughters caring for mothers at home.* London: Routledge.

Matthews, S. H. (1979). *The social world of old women.* Beverly Hills: Sage.

Neugarten, B., & Gutmann, D. (1968). Age-sex roles and personality in middle age. In B. Neugarten (Ed.), *Middle age and aging.* Chicago: University of Chicago Press.

Noddings N. (1984). *Caring: A feminine approach to ethics and moral education.* Berkeley: University of California Press.

Rubin, L. (1985). *Just friends: The role of friendship in our lives.* New York: Harper & Row.

Stone, R., Cafferata, G. L., & Sangl, J. (n.d.) Caregivers of the frail elderly: A national profile. Washington, DC: DHHS, U.S. Public Health Service.

Taylor, S. J., & Bogdan, R. (1984). *Introduction to qualitative research methods.* NY: John Wiley.

# PART THREE:

# Service Provision: Defining and Decision-Making

## 10

# Describing Home Care

## Discourse and Image in Involuntary Commitment Proceedings

### JAMES A. HOLSTEIN

Recent efforts to deinstitutionalize mental health care have tried to deemphasize the use of mental hospitals and promote treatment for the mentally ill in the least restrictive settings commensurate with their mental disorders. Over the past 25 years, deinstitutionalization has most profoundly affected those persons diagnosed as chronically mentally ill who might previously have been *involuntarily* hospitalized for care and custody. Today, many of these people live in the community with varying success and comfort, relying upon both formal and informal sources of treatment and supervision. In a sense, then, reformed involuntary commitment legislation and revamped commitment procedures have been the cornerstones of the community mental-health movement (Morrissey, 1982). Indeed, Cameron (1978, pp. 314-15) argues that phasing out institutionalized care would have been impossible without the "ideological thrust" provided by those seeking involuntary commitment reforms. Many mental hospitals closed when new commitment laws took effect, releasing their patients and shifting the burden of long-term care to community-based programs and informal resources.

Under reformed commitment procedures, candidate mental patients[1] may be hospitalized only when they are judged mentally ill and either dangerous to themselves or others, or gravely disabled. In practice, commitment decisions turn on arguments concerning the availability of community living arrangements that can accommodate the special needs of the mentally ill (Holstein, 1984). The discourse of community care and treatment, then, dominates commitment proceedings, with participants comparing and contrasting community placements with institutional treatment. While independent living situations, nursing homes, board and care facilities (which provide limited supervision), and other sheltered living arrangements are routinely considered, the "home care" option is perhaps the most frequently explored alternative to involuntary hospitalization. Participants in commitment proceedings articulate diverse images of home, family, and household as resources for treating and caring for candidate patients, as well as containing the havoc often associated with their psychiatric problems. Depictions of the home care experience may thus be deeply implicated in the commitment decision-making process.

This chapter differs somewhat from others in this volume in its approach to the home care experience; its topic is the *discourse* of home care. The chapter focuses on the *articulation* of images of home care during involuntary commitment proceedings, analyzing home care in terms of *descriptive practice*—that is, the context-sensitive procedures through which the meaningful realities of "home" and "care" are produced. This interpretive perspective suggests that social reality is interactively constructed and sustained (Garfinkel, 1967). Interaction in general and talk and language-use in particular, do not merely convey meaning, but rather, are ways of "doing things with words" to "create" meaningful realities. From this perspective, the orderly and recognizable features of social circumstances are "talked into being" (Heritage, 1984, p. 290). Descriptions—like those of home care that are formulated in involuntary commitment proceeding—are not disembodied commentaries on ostensibly real state of affairs. Rather they are reality *projects*—acts of constructing the world for the practical purposes at hand. This chapter demonstrates how descriptions of home care provide interpretive foundations for understanding and evaluating the viability of alternate community placements for the mentally ill. The analysis considers the *rhetorical* use of home care imagery as participants in involuntary commitment proceedings advocate particular understandings of commitment cases and argue the pros and cons of hospitalization versus release.

## Background and Settings

Data for this chapter are drawn from ethnographic fieldwork in several mental health and legal settings. I observed and interviewed extensively in Metropolitan Court in California and less extensively in four other communities across the United States (see Holstein, 1984, 1987a, 1987b, 1988a, 1988b, in press; Gubrium & Holstein, 1990), focusing on involuntary commitment issues. Commitment proceedings involve a variety of participants. Community mental-health professionals frequently consider hospitalizing their clients and routinely assist in making arrangements for commitment or release. During formal commitment hearings, legal counsel—nearly always a public defender (PD)—represents the candidate patient, while the district attorney's office (DA) argues for commitment. Hearings, typically conducted by a judge in a public courtroom (although several hearings I observed were closed to the public, and a few were conducted informally in non-courtroom settings), vary in length, and typically include testimony from a psychiatrist[2] and the candidate patient, both of whom may be cross-examined. Other witnesses rarely appear. Judges interact freely with witnesses and attorneys, eliciting the information they need to decide a case.[3]

Reformed mental health legislation guides civil commitment proceedings in all the study sites. Laws varied somewhat in their wording, but were quite similar in application. California's Lanterman-Petris-Short Act (LPS) allows commitment based on a diagnosis of severe mental illness and danger to self or others, or grave disability.[4] Two other jurisdictions have basically the same commitment requirements, but the terminology, *grave disability* is not employed. Grave disability is not recognized as grounds for commitment in the other jurisdictions; danger to self or others is the only criterion. In practice, however, someone seen as unable to obtain necessary food, clothing, shelter, or medical care due to mental illness would be considered dangerous to him- or herself. Consequently, these communities hospitalize persons based on *de facto* grave disability provisions as well.

Most involuntary commitments result from judgments of "grave disability" or informal versions there of (Holstein, 1984; Warren, 1977, 1982). Whether or not this criterion is written into law, parties to commitment decisions routinely consider whether or not the candidate patient can establish viable living arrangements outside the hospital that can contain the havoc, both internal and to the community, associated with mental illness (Holstein, 1984). Diagnosis of psychiatric disorder is necessary, but not sufficient, for civil commitment; the pragmatic assessments of the judges regarding the *tenability* of the proposed community living situations of the candidate patients are equally important. This tenability is negotiated in light of the following factors: (1) the person's ability to provide for, gain access to, and properly utilize life's basic necessities (i.e., food, clothing, and shelter); (2) the willing presence of someone who will serve as a competent "caretaker" and look after the released candidate patient; and (3) the candidate patient's cooperation with a community-based treatment and/or custody plan. In the conspicuous absence of any of these factors, social and psychiatric disturbances are considered inevitable and commitment is likely (Holstein, 1984).

Tenability, however, is not established solely by reference to features of a living situation. Rather, it is constituted by formulating an appropriate *match* between a particular candidate patient and a living situation's ability to accommodate that person (Holstein 1987a). A living situation's viability partly depends on "what kind" of person it is asked to accommodate. To establish a living situation's viability, then, hearing participants must argue that the arrangement's *accommodations* are responsive to the candidate patient's particular *needs* and *demands*. The adequacy of the accommodations of the living situations thus depend upon both their rhetorical depiction and portrayals of demands to which they must respond.

The discourse of commitment proceedings displays the logic of a matching procedure whereby a candidate patient and his or her proposed community living environment are aligned and the person-situation fit is assessed. This understanding, however, overlooks the negotiated character of matches between persons and environments (Holstein, 1987a, in press). Descriptions of candidate patients—including their problems, needs, and demands—and environmental accommodations are situationally assembled; the match between them is also a situated production, the result of description and persuasion. So while the decision-making process superficially resembles a search for, and contingent discovery of, a match between person and living situation, that match or mismatch is better construed as a *rhetorical accomplishment*—the product of purposive description, persuasion, and argumentation.

Not surprisingly, participants in commitment proceedings routinely mobilize images of the home care experience as they explore matches between candidate patients and proposed living arrangements. While it is typically just one of many placement alternatives, and nothing mandates the consideration of the home care option, its possibility is clearly the most frequently investigated. Participants, it seems, are eager to argue the home's ability to provide candidate patients with their basic needs, caretakers, and assistance with treatment regimes. These discussions *make* the home care experience relevant to the commitment decision-making process. By articulating the various facets of the home care experience—its potential advantages and drawbacks—with the particulars of a candidate patient's case, participants descriptively advocate or discount home care as a resolution to the problem of "placing insanity" (Holstein, 1984). The following section considers the use of home care imagery during tenability assessments, exploring its diverse interpretive possibilities.

### Images of Home Care and Tenability Assessments

Nearly all commitment proceedings orient to a constellation of material, social, and relational features of a candidate patient's proposed living situations as participants argue how to best use commitment laws to manage the troubles associated with mental illness. Judges are most likely to consider release if they are convinced that a benevolent, caring form of "community custody" (Holstein, 1987b) awaits candidate patients outside the hospital. Care in the candidate patient's home, especially a family home, is routinely and sometimes passionately argued to be the best, most healthful of all possible living situations. Consider, for example, how the public defender representing Leon Mason[5] articulated the possibilities for home care against the special problems and demands that Mason presented.

We're proposing that Mr. Mason go home and work out his problems in surroundings that are more conducive to some kind of recovery. Dr. Lester [the testifying psychiatrist] said that his medication level has been adjusted, and it's not clear what more Muni [the mental hospital] can do for him. On the other hand, getting him back home has a lot to offer. First, it's clear that his family wants him home. His wife and kids miss him, and he misses them. That alone gives him a sense of security and reduces his anxiety level, and it seems that he's most likely to have problems when he gets anxious. There's something to be said for home cooking and sleeping in your own bed. . . . People at home love him, care about him. That's got to count for something. . . . We know Mr. Mason has gotten out of control in the past, but with his sister living at home now, there'll be someone there to watch out for him all the time, someone always around who he knows, cares about him. . . . I think we can even expect Mr. Mason to be more cooperative if he's at home. He says he just feels more comfortable there, and he's less agitated. He says he'll take his meds if his wife reminds him, and I think trusting her means he's more likely to follow through and not go off the program again.

This description of home care not only enumerated the advantages of home care over the mental hospital, but it also spoke directly to the court's tenability concerns. The PD suggested, both directly and tacitly, how home placement ensured Mason's basic needs and supervision, and how it represented a sort of home-based therapeutic regimen, complete with medication plan and affectional treatment. Note also how the PD matched features of the home environment with Mason's specific problems and demands. The "fit" between person and living situation was *descriptively constructed* so that the appropriateness of Mason's release was apparent.

The previous extract is an exemplary use of home care imagery to argue in favor of placing a candidate in a deinstitutionalized setting. However, reference to the home care option may also supply the background against which the accommodative inadequacies of a community placement are displayed. This practice is clear in the following account by a Metropolitan Court judge, who decided to commit Victor Ruiz.

I appreciate Victor's willingness to get into a [CMHC out-patient] program, but I'm very skeptical about this plan to move across town to take an apartment. [Spoken in the general direction of the PD:] Do we know anything more about this roommate? It really doesn't matter. I'd be more comfortable if we were talking about familiar surroundings, some kind of home life. [Directed at Ruiz:] But what you're proposing is to start from scratch, and I'm not sure you're up to it. . . . If I was sending you home, it might be different, but they won't have you and, as well-meaning as your friend may be, these things usually don't work out. At home you'd have someone to take care of you, someone who'd be there for the duration. I don't feel like we can count on that right now. I'm concerned that something might happen to Mr. Ruiz, and there would be no one around to keep him from getting hurt.

Here, the home was explicitly offered as a standard against which the candidate living situation of Mr. Ruiz could be compared. Criteria for establishing tenability were implicitly articulated in the discourse of home care; the proposed living arrangement was then compared with established criteria, this time unfavorably, thereby providing substantial warrant for a decision to commit. Comparing and contrasting descriptions of the case at hand with images of the idealized home care experience was an essential rhetorical feature of the judge's account. Indeed, the practice was commonly used by all participants in the commitment process.

Tenability assessments focus participants in commitment proceedings on three primary dimensions of concern regarding the personal characteristics of candidate patients: vulnerability, manageability, and remedial prospects (Holstein, 1987a, in press). Therefore, the features of home care that are routinely mentioned in discussions of placement options are likely to address these concerns. Recall, for instance, how the home care argument for Leon Mason's release spoke directly of how family members could adequately manage Mason's behavior and keep him on a medication program. Similarly, the judge in the Ruiz case was implicitly concerned about Ruiz's vulnerability as he voiced his preference for commitment. He highlighted the inadequacies of Ruiz's proposed living situation by noting its failure to supply the sort of care and security one might find "at home" for a particularly vulnerable person. Home care, then, may be a common referent in commitment proceedings because of its versatility in speaking to these focal concerns. As an exemplar of reliable, salutary accommodations or as a standard for violation, home care offers an extensive collection of images that are diversely available for rhetorical, descriptive practice.

## Contests and Negotiations

Because the "realities" of commitment cases are interpretively assembled, the arguments of participants are best conceived as rhetorical *versions* of the case at hand. Therefore, with the "facts" of a case always *in production,* claims relating to the characteristics and features of the living situations of candidate patients are always subject to challenge. Images of the home care option are no exception. Depictions of home situations as viable community placements are routinely disputed; indeed, what one participant may claim to be a salubrious home environment may be considered "no home at all" by another. This occurred, for example, as a public defender tried to argue for Marsha Martin's release:

*PD:*   Her husband says he will be more attentive. He's got his own problems under control, and he'll be able to look after her, see that she gets the things she needs. Being at home is important, your Honor. She really thinks that she'll be able to manage on her own, get all the care she needs at home.

*Judge:*   You've made your point, Ms. Owens [the PD], but I've got to disagree with you about Mrs. Martin's home life, if you can call it that. The man's an alcoholic [Martin's husband]. There's good reason to believe that her problems are something of a reaction to the way he's treated her. He's not around all that much, and when he is, he hasn't been good for her in the past. Quite frankly, I can't see any caring in this home at all. This is no home; it's a nightmare.

Clearly, the judge dismissed the PD's version of Mrs. Martin's home environment, focusing instead on past occurrences as a framework for understanding Mr. Martin's claims of sobriety and willingness to care for his wife. In effect, the judge rejected the Martin residence as a "home"—that is, an adequate source of care and concern. The PD, however, refused to acquiesce to the judge's interpretations:

*PD:*   But there's more to it than that. She'll be back in her own house, sleeping in her own bed. She won't be surrounded by strangers. I mean, look at how upset she gets when she's on the open ward. She's not going to have to go through that at home. There's good reason to believe that she's going to settle down once she feels at home. Her husband's on a program, and having her home is going to do him good, too. They can help each other.

This response shifted the grounds of the interpretive context from concerns regarding the husband-as-caretaker to other ameliorative aspects of the home atmosphere. Initially, the PD had portrayed the home as a source of concerned care, but the judge's response rendered that version untenable. The PD then turned to the home's therapeutic contributions, apart from the husband's care, as warrant for Mrs. Martin's release. She realigned the dispute, changing its topic from the husband's capabilities to the remedial qualities of a familiar environment. The tactic apparently struck a responsive chord, because the judge's adversarial stance softened:

*Judge:*    But who's going to look out for her? Even if it is important to have familiar surroundings, that still doesn't answer my question of who's gonna be the responsible one. How's she going to take advantage of all this if there's no one there we can count on?

While upholding his skepticism regarding the husband, the judge acknowledged the familiarity of the Martin residence, a tacit concession of its homelike quality. And perhaps more importantly, the judge's questions opened the possibility for *negotiating* a practical understanding of home care. In the following exchange, note the transformation from opposing versions of the Martin "home" into what appeared, for practical purposes, to be a reconciliation of the divergent interpretations into a working understanding of a potentially tenable, if somewhat tenuous, home life:

*PD:*    Things have changed with her husband. He's got his program, and they're gonna be checking up on him, keep an eye on how he's doing with Marsha, too. And she's got the neighbors. Her sister lives in the same building.

*Judge:*    How's the sister feel about this? What's she gonna do for her?

*PD:*    She wants Marsha to come home. It's a family matter, and she wants to do her part.

*Judge:* So what you're telling me is that if I let her go home, both the sister and the husband can be counted on.

*PD:* I think so.

*Judge:* Now I can understand how going home is gonna help Marsha calm down a little, how she'll feel more comfortable and all. But why should we think that this is gonna make her problems disappear?

*PD:* It won't, your Honor, but staying at home is a way of giving her enough care and supervision so she'll have a chance to get herself, her life, more under control.

*Judge:* Well, I can see that, but I need more. I'm going to deny the writ [extend the commitment] for now, with the stipulation that you put the hospital in touch with Mrs. Martin's sister and iron out how she's gonna pitch in. I have to be convinced that there's really a decent home to send her to before I'll take that chance.

The judge's decision to consider Mrs. Martin's release thus hinged on his evolving understanding of the home situation, an understanding the PD diligently cultivated. The meaning of home care was shaped by sometimes countervailing concerns for the Martin home's supervisory and therapeutic capacities. Those services the home could provide— indeed, the very things that constituted the Martin residence as a home—were as much products of negotiation as they were objective features of the home setting itself. What the home care experience would be, for the practical purposes at hand, was established rhetorically; it was an interactional accomplishment.

### Constituting Home Care Imagery

Because the images of home care used in involuntary commitment proceedings are formulated in response to particular situations and circumstances, they resist general typologies or categorization. Similarly, their effects on commitment decisions are essentially indeterminate, depending upon how the home care option is depicted and employed in commitment arguments. It is therefore impossible to specify a shared understanding of precisely what home care means to various participants in commitment proceedings, or the circumstances under which reference to the home care option will be more or less compelling. The meaning of home care for the mentally ill is realized only through descriptive *practice*—that is, in the articulation of home care imagery with actual cases.

While participants in commitment proceedings regularly portray the material advantages of home care—for example, adequate food, clothing, and shelter—they are apt to use home care discourse to address a constellation of less tangible aspects of the mental health care experience. To speak of caring for an ex-mental patient "at home" typically suggests more than simply the availability of adequate lodging. Images of home care conflate the caregiving site and the caregiver to provide a more encompassing sense in which the patient will be afforded a comprehensive range of material, therapeutic, and emotional necessities and comforts. The home is, at times, anthropomorphized, with abilities and capacities associated with volitional, personal caregiving. At other times, it is equated with "family" to even more emphatically convey the compassionate, affectional, nurturant character of enduring familial relations (Gubrium & Holstein,1990; Holstein, 1988b). "Home care" is thus used to denote "real" caring, not merely instrumental custodianship. It conveys deep concern for, and commitment to, sensitive, responsive relations between caregiver and patient. To argue, for example, that a candidate patient would benefit from "home cooking" offers far more than the assurance of adequate nutrition. And recall from the case of Victor Ruiz how home care was linked to long-term obligation—being there "for the duration"—to underscore caregiver commitment to the patient.

But such meanings are not automatically attached to all instances of home care usage. Participants must secure them. The range of home care depictions and their uses that was encountered in the author's fieldwork is too extensive to document here, and it was virtually impossible to predict beforehand if or how home care images might be articulated in any particular case. Home care was diversely associated or equated with the emotional security, autonomy, self-control, and dignity of candidate patients, for example—meanings that were generally understood even if they were not considered persuasive or relevant to the case at hand. Articulating the advantages of the home care option, then, is a rhetorical maneuver that relies upon generally shared notions of what a "home" is like—collective representations in Durkheim's (1961) vocabulary—to underpin, but not determine, its specific applications. Artful descriptive practice renders home care depictions persuasive. But as we saw in Marsha Martin's case above, the mere suggestion of a particular home care advantage, as well stated as it might be, does not necessarily address the most situationally salient concerns, nor is it unquestionably persuasive.

Up to this point, I have discussed the uses of home care imagery as a way of depicting and advocating "in-home" placements for released candidate mental patients. We can see how descriptive practice is even further implicated in the production of case-relevant "realities" when we examine the ways in which hearing participants descriptively constitute a wide range of living arrangements as "homes." In the course of commitment proceedings, participants routinely attach the significance of home care to a variety of living situations—everything from family residences to privately operated board and care facilities to the mental hospital itself. Consider, for example, what a PD accomplished in the following description of the board and care facility he proposed as the future residence of a client, John Becker, whose release he was seeking: "Valley View has agreed that John can return once he's back on his medication program. This is the perfect place for him. They know him there, they take good care of him, and he wants to go back. It's been like home to him, certainly more of a home than he had living with his parents."

By rhetorically converting the board and care facility into a "home" for Mr. Becker—indeed more of a "home" than the house in which he was raised—the PD tried to secure a broad range of understandings about the quality of life, especially its affective and therapeutic aspects, that Becker would experience at Valley View. Calling the "facility" a "home" was more than a mere exchange of labels; it fundamentally transformed its meanings. Such transformations resemble those that advertisements for nursing and board and care facilities hope to achieve when they proclaim their "home-like atmosphere," "warm, home-like environment," "home-cooked meals," and their pledge to "make you feel right at home" (Wisconsin Bell Yellow Pages, 1988-1989). Significantly, these establishments announce themselves as board and care *homes* and nursing *homes,* rather than "facilities." Such characterizations convey a distinctive set of possibilities for caregiving. Similarly, in commitment proceedings, reference to any dwelling as a "home" insinuates a set of meanings and potentials that speak poignantly to caregiving and tenability concerns, as well as to the abilities of living situations to satisfy them. Therefore, for example, when a DA arguing for commitment claimed that the mental hospital "has become his home," he was attempting to infuse hospitalization with a special meaning for a particular candidate patient; he was implicitly describing the hospital's domestic, salutary character.

Finally, home care imagery can be used to establish contrasts that underscore the *unsuitability* of various accommodations for candidate mental patients. While alternate community sites are sometimes compared unfavorably to the home, this usage is more often reserved for arguments against institutional treatment. Such was the case as a mental health social worker for the Northwoods County Department of Social Services discussed one of his clients—Harriet Baker—with a psychiatrist who had examined her in preparation for Baker's impending involuntary commitment hearing. The social worker was convinced that hospitalization would be counterproductive:

> I'm afraid of what might happen to her if you send her to Milford [the mental hospital]. How familiar are you with the place? It's up to code and all that, but it's not, it won't be, the kind of loving home that Harriet needs. She's real involved with her family; it's about all she has. Milford's great and all, but it can't give her what she needs emotionally. It's just not home.

Here, the social worker twice indicated that the hospital was "not home" to demonstrate that it could not adequately provide for a troubled person with special needs. He implied the "emotional" benefits of home care as a way of underscoring the mental hospital's deficiencies. Those arguing against commitment routinely use home care depictions as foils to display the inhospitable or situationally inappropriate climate of institutional settings. Contrasts between home and hospital highlight each site's distinctive characteristics; the advantages of home care are accentuated by comparison.

## The Descriptive Culture of Deinstitutionalization

Discussions of home care in involuntary commitment proceedings convey a constellation of understandings about community treatment and care for the mentally ill. Participants routinely offer the home care experience as an alternative to in-patient treatment. They argue that, in a sense, home care offers a prototype for deinstitutionalized care, one that provides superior services without depersonalization or deprivation. "Home care" is used to epitomize concerned treatment and care without stigma or restriction. The discourse of home care thus provides a way of interpreting and conveying the ideals of community mental health care; the range of its meanings and uses constitutes a *descriptive culture* of deinstitutionalization.

As a stock of descriptive responses to claims regarding the needs and demands of candidate patients, the discourse of home care speaks to the central issues of involuntary commitment proceedings. Commitment decisions orient to the ability of living situations of candidate patients to nourish, shelter, manage, protect, and heal their occupants. Moreover, decision-makers consider the ways in which care is delivered and are concerned, for example, about affective tone, devotion, intimacy, and responsibility. Taken together, these interests coalesce into a *configuration of concern* (Gubrium & Holstein, 1990) regarding community custody. The configuration of concern represents and expresses what "home care" means to participants in commitment proceedings, drawing together ideas, sentiments, and experience regarding both demands for care and the way it is provided. As a form of collective representation (Durkheim, 1961)—a shared pattern of understanding— the configuration encourages us to attach its diverse components to one another, summoning one as we invoke any of the others. Thus common and tacit assumptions about home care are consolidated in its descriptive usage so that general, commonsense understandings about the nature of home care are conveyed without specifying individual features. To say that a candidate patient would benefit from being placed "in the home" thus imparts assurances of security, familiarity, and devotion, without specifically mentioning each characteristic by name. Consequently, the discourse of home care is rhetorically compelling because it so clearly expresses the ideals of deinstitutionalization.

The configuration of concern, however, must be realized in *practice*. As a collective representation, it provides only a general outline of a domain of interest; descriptive practice must specify its concrete connections to actual experience. As this chapter shows, the application of home care imagery is rhetorical activity that is continuously shaped by the context and practical exigencies of description; the discourse of home care is thus *organizationally embedded* (Gubrium, 1987; Holstein, 1988b)—that is, conditioned by the socially organized circumstances of its use. Recall, for example, Marsha Martin's case discussed earlier. In the negotiations regarding the tenability of Mrs. Martin's home placement, the judge and PD engaged somewhat divergent discourses of home care. Not surprisingly, their opinions of the viability of the home care option differed. The judge's judicial responsibilities supplied him with a pressing interest in controlling the trouble that usually accompanies severe mental illness. Consequently, he articulated home care in terms of its custodial, supervisory capacities. For him, home care was completely lacking in this instance; indeed, there was "no home" at all because the domestic circumstances of the Martin's household seemed completely incapable of supervising and controlling Mrs. Martin. The PD, however, expressed concern for Mrs. Martin's emotional well-being, translating these concerns into a home care discourse focused on the compassionate, salutary qualities of the home. From this perspective, Mrs. Martin could "get all the care she needs at home." Organizational and professional interests and affiliations provided the judge and the PD with distinctive practical agendas and divergent interpretive frameworks. Their conceptualizations of home care—embedded as they were in *local* cultures (Gubrium & Holstein, 1990) of deinstitutionalized mental health care, and orienting to diverse configurations of concern—differed accordingly.

## Discussion

Involuntary commitment proceedings furnish myriad occasions for participants to articulate the interpretive connections between images of home care and the notion of deinstitutionalization. Commitment decisions explicitly and conspicuously are oriented to the proposed community living situations of candidate patients, and, as this chapter shows, "home care" is routinely submitted both as an alternative to mental hospitalization and as a standard against which other options are compared. As the discourse of home care permeates and, indeed sometimes dominates—commitment discussions, it offers an array of *commonsense theories* of deinstitutionalization. As participants in commitment proceedings articulate home care options for community placement, they implicitly suggest paradigms of out-patient mental health care, theorizing the needs of patients and modeling practical versions of deinstitutionalized care. In a sense, then, "home care" has been descriptively integrated into the community mental health movement as a commonsense ideal for deinstitutionalization.

Commitment proceedings explicitly consider both the psychiatric conditions and possible community placements of candidate patients, yet an imbalance clearly exists in the emphasis placed on formally and systematically assessing the two. Persons may be involuntarily detained in order that psychiatric evaluations be conducted, and psychiatric testimony is methodically delivered, in elaborate detail, at all commitment hearings. In contrast, assessments of proposed community living situations of the candidate patients—evaluations of the home care option, in many cases—are typically made on the basis of "hearsay," or secondhand knowledge. Or, more precisely, they are based on rhetorical secondhand accounts. If the goal of involuntary commitment proceedings is to secure adequate shelter, nourishment, and care for the mentally ill in the least restrictive available setting, then further systematic attention might be devoted to assessing home and community care options. Some jurisdictions currently employ professional personnel to assess candidate living situations, assessments that provide an environmental counterpart to psychiatric diagnoses. My fieldwork in those settings suggests that these "court liaisons" or "mental health social workers" provide less "partisan" descriptions of the situations in question, descriptions that judges appear to find more useful than the arguments of attorneys and claims of candidate patients.

Of course, even nonpartisan evaluations are unavoidably contextualized (Garfinkel, 1967). No assessment can be isolated from background knowledge, organizational location, professional training, or cultural assumptions. Involuntary commitment proceedings offer competing discourses and alternate interpretations, not objective facts. Each depiction of the home care experience presented in commitment hearings, then, will be unavoidably rhetorical as its author *advocates,* as much as describes, a version of reality.

### Notes

1. All persons whose commitment is being considered in the proceedings studied here are called candidate patients, although their status in California *habeas corpus* proceed-

ings is technically that of petitioner because they have been hospitalized and are now seeking their release through legal review.

2. For convenience, I will refer to all expert psychiatric witnesses as *psychiatrists,* even though doing so is not always technically correct. On occasion, clinical psychologists and nonpsychiatric MDs also provided testimony in all of the jurisdictions studied.

3. Invariably, the psychiatrist testifies that the candidate patient is mentally ill. This diagnosis is seldom challenged, although candidate patients may try to refute this opinion with other expert testimony. Thus, the assumption that candidate patients are mentally ill is an invariant background feature in all commitment hearings (Holstein, 1984, 1987b).

4. Formally, a person is gravely disabled if he or she is unable to provide for basic personal needs of food, clothing, and shelter as a result of mental disorder. One is dangerous to the self if one threatened or attempted to take one's life prior to or during the initial commitment, and who presents an imminent threat of taking one's own life. A person who has threatened, attempted, or inflicted physical harm on another person either before or during the initial commitment, and who presents an imminent threat of substantial physical harm as a result of mental disorder is a danger to others.

5. All names of persons and places are fictitious.

## References

Cameron, J. M. (1978). Ideology and policy termination: Restructuring California's mental health system. In J. V. May & A. B. Widavsky (Eds.), *The policy circle* (pp. 301-328). Beverly Hills: Sage.

Durkheim, E. (1961). *The elementary forms of the religious life.* New York: Collier-Macmillan.

Garfinkel, H. (1967). *Studies in ethnomethodology.* Englewood Cliffs, NJ: Prentice-Hall.

Gubrium, J. F. (1987). Organizational embeddedness and family life. In T. Brubaker (Ed.), *Aging, health, and family: Long term care* (pp. 23-41). Newbury Park, CA: Sage.

Gubrium, J. F., & Holstein, J. A. (1990). *What is family?* Mountain View, CA: Mayfield.

Heritage, J. (1984). *Garfinkel and ethnomethodology.* Cambridge, England: Polity Press.

Holstein, J. A. (1984). The placement of insanity: Assessments of grave disability and involuntary commitment decisions. *Urban Life, 13,* 35-62.

Holstein, J. A. (1987a). Producing gender effects on involuntary mental hospitalization. *Social Problems, 34,* 141-155.

Holstein, J. A. (1987b). Mental illness assumptions in civil commitment proceedings. *Journal of Contemporary Ethnography, 16,* 147-175.

Holstein, J. A. (1988a). Court ordered incompetence: Conversational organization in involuntary commitment hearings. *Social Problems, 35,* 458-473.

Holstein, J. A. (1988b). Studying "family usage": Family image and discourse in mental hospitalization decisions. *Journal of Contemporary Ethnography, 17,* 261-284.

Holstein, J. A. (In press). The discourse of aging in involuntary commitment proceedings. *Journal of Aging Studies.*

Morrissey, J. M. (1982). Deinstitutionalizing the mentally ill: Process, outcomes, and new directions. In W. Gove. (Ed.), *Deviance and mental illness* (pp. 147-176). Beverly Hills: Sage.

Warren, C. A. B. (1977). Involuntary commitment for mental disorder: The application of California's Lanterman-Petris-Short Act. *Law and Society Review, 11*, 629-649.

Warren, C. A. B. (1982). *The court of last resort*. Chicago: University of Chicago Press.

*Wisconsin Bell Yellow Pages.*(1988-1989).

*11*

# Transformations of Home

## The Formal and Informal Process of
## Home Care Planning

ANN E. P. DILL

When older persons become clients of home care services, their lives at home become evaluated in terms of their implications for service delivery. Through this evaluation, formal care providers construct the representations of clients' homes that are essential for their agencies' work.

This chapter examines the care planning process and analyzes ways in which service providers interpret the *homelives* (the experiential and symbolic dimensions of life at home) of clients. In addition to formal assessment and referral procedures, service providers use an informal system of care planning based on perspectives derived from clinical judgments as well as the logistics of service delivery. Formal and informal processes of care planning yield representations of clients' homelives that differ in significant ways from one another; *home* becomes different things within these interpretations.

AUTHOR'S NOTE: Financial support of the research on which this chapter is based came in part from a National Research Service Award from the National Institute of Mental Health. An earlier version was presented at the 41st Annual Meeting of the Gerontological Society of America, San Francisco, November 21, 1988. I am grateful to Phil Brown, Jeanne Leffers, Betty Wolder Levin, and David A. Rochefort for their careful reading of previous drafts and their comments.

Following a description of the study on which this chapter is based, current analyses of the definition of home will be used to identify aspects of the homelives of older persons that become important in the delivery of home care. The chapter then describes how homelives became interpreted in the course of formal and informal care planning in one particular program.

It will be seen that through these interpretations the process of care planning expands the boundaries of home beyond the domain of client action and control; the characteristics, goals, and social relations of service providers become as influential as those of clients. Better understanding of the consequences of this process can contribute to the future development of policy and practice regarding services for the elderly.

## Research Site and Methods

The research on which this analysis is based was an ethnographic study of a project that provided case management of home care services to elderly individuals. Operational from 1980 to 1984, "the Project" (as it will be termed) was part of a social service agency devoted to programs for older persons. It had a caseload of 250 clients drawn from one district of a major metropolitan area.

Clients came to the Project primarily as a result of referral by other social service agencies. Individuals aged 60 and over who were "homebound" by physical impairment were eligible for Project services; the actual clientele were, on the average, in their 70s, and more than half were sufficiently impaired to be at risk of nursing home placement.

The project had two subunits funded through separate auspices. The first was one of several research and demonstration programs authorized through federal legislation that waived Medicare requirements for community-based services. Termed here the "waivered component," this program provided clients with homemaker services, transportation to medical care and payment for prescription drugs. The other part of the Project, termed the "nonwaivered component," provided no direct services other than case management; it served mainly referral and advocacy functions for its clients.

The staff of each part of the Project included a case management team of one nurse and one social worker who were supervised by a project coordinator. Except for case management and the waivered services, the

Project itself did not provide care directly to clients, nor did it have the authority to authorize services or payments thereof. It depended instead on referrals to other agencies and on the case managers' ability to take clients through the process of obtaining, for example, entitlements, public housing, or nursing home placement.

The methodology of the study consisted of participant observation research conducted over 18 months of the project's operation. This included informal interviews with case managers regarding their activities, views of clients, working relations with other agencies, and other factors. It also involved the observation of their daily routine in the office as well as interactions with clients. Case material presented here represents an accurate account of events transpiring during the study, as recorded through fieldnotes. Names and clearly identifying personal attributes have, however, been altered to preserve the confidentiality of research subjects.

### Homes and Homelives

Scientific research and lay wisdom attest to the axiom that a home is more than a place of residence. "A complex entity that defines and is defined by cultural, sociodemographic, psychological, political, and economic factors" (Lawrence, 1987, p. 155), a home reflects and sustains the social world of its inhabitants. Physical, interpersonal, and symbolic dimensions govern the ways a home is experienced in everyday life as well as affect lives in material ways (Willcock, Peace, & Kellaher, 1987). Each dimension has particular implications for an older person.

Physically, a home consists of the dwelling and the environment surrounding it. Home decor and arrangements, in addition to the allocation of space for different activities, reflect cultural rules adapted to individual needs and preferences (Rubinstein, 1989). Physical features of home environments that particularly affect the functioning of older persons include its location relative to needed goods and services, the presence of geographic or architectural barriers, and the layout of space and furnishings (Stegman, 1985).

The interpersonal dimension of home involves social interaction within and across its physical boundaries. Home in this sense provides a "setting for the development and maintenance of interpersonal relationships" (Werner, 1987, p. 170). It also constitutes a base from which to engage in social exchange that can either enhance or diminish personal power and control (Willcocks et al., 1987). These dimensions of home assume heightened importance as life course changes, such as retirement and widowhood, alter the interpersonal relations of older persons. For those whose mobility is impaired, home may become the sole arena for the elaboration of social ties.

Meanings and values attached to physical and social features are one source of the symbolic dimension of home. More generally, concepts of privacy and familiarity are intrinsically part of what home means: a haven and place of order, "insideness" and belonging (Dovey, 1985; Korsec-Serfaty, 1985). In addition, homes both reflect and embody the social status of their residents (Amaturo, Costagliola, & Ragone, 1987). Temporal qualities must also be recognized here since homes are imbued with culturally derived values regarding the appropriate timing and sequencing of events taking place in and around their boundaries (Werner, 1987). For older persons, the control over space, time, and personal identity that homes provide may become keys to a sense of personal competency (Rowles, 1987).

While physical, social, and symbolic dimensions define the concept of home, specific homes are created by the individuals occupying them. This process of creation involves the everyday manipulation and activation of a home environment, the subjective experience of daily life in a particular setting, and the attribution of personal meanings to household space and objects (Rubenstein, 1989; Faletti, 1984). The term *homelife* is used here to encompass daily routines and experience within the home, as well as the interpretation of the home environment by individual residents. The product of complex transactions among individuals, culture, and environment, homelives are defining elements of personal identities (Rubinstein, 1989).

### Interpretations of Home in the Care Planning Process

When service providers plan an older person's care at home, they must develop an understanding of the capacities of the home environment and the capabilities of the client. Both the home, particularly its physical and social dimensions, and the client's homelife are thus subjected to assessment and interpretation. This takes place through procedures dictated by the design, operation, and objectives of service programs. While specific to the site studied, the structure, instrumentation, and content of the Project's care planning procedures were equivalent to those of similar demonstration programs and comparable to those in general use by social service agencies (Austin, & Seidl, 1981; Huttman, 1985).

**Formal Care Planning**

As part of its care planning process, the Project used a battery of standardized instruments to measure a client's cognitive functioning, independent activities of daily living, available social supports, and conditions of the residence and neighborhood. These forms were used to assess client status at the time of admission to the Project and every six months thereafter.

The interpretation of homelife through such formwork defined and codified the information about clients routinely obtained by case managers. This set of data was used in reporting to funding agents and superordinate agencies; it served as the basis for evaluations of the Project's outcomes. It did not, however, inform day-to-day decisions of the staff regarding what they did or planned to do for specific clients. To understand why this was so, it is necessary to describe the ways in which case managers perceived and implemented the formal assessment process.

The case managers recognized the formwork as an essential part of their jobs, but not one that translated meaningfully into their relationships with clients. To them, having to describe a client's life in terms of standardized questions and response categories was a distortion. This reaction is illustrated below by the interaction that took place during the reassessment of "CB," an 83-year-old woman living alone.

The nurse (N) conducts her assessment by looking at the form in her lap and covering the questions in each category. At first, she sticks fairly closely to the form's phrasing; as the assessment continues, she paraphrases more loosely. The social worker (SW), fairly recent to the job, stays close to the question phrasing. (The exchanges below are presented in the sequence in which they occurred; asterisks between sections indicate intervening conversation.)

* * *

*N:*   Do you have any trouble falling asleep or staying asleep? [The question calls for a yes/no answer to be followed by questions asking if the client feels anxious or disturbed at night.]

*CB:*   Lately I've been up. I couldn't breathe.

*N:*   What caused it?

*CB:*   My mother had it. It gets better in the summer. . . .

* * *

*N:*   What was your husband's job before he retired?

*CB:*   I married a man who was a swindler; he had somebody else. I wanted a coupla children so I wouldn't be alone, but he wouldn't give them to me. I had bad luck. I wanted to leave the first year, but he wouldn't give me back the money [she had saved and he had taken].

*N:*   Do your teeth hurt you?

*CB:*   I have no teeth. My life is not going to be so long now.

*N:*   Why do you say that?

*CB:*   Because I'm old. . . .

* * *

*SW:*   Can you tell me your address?

*CB:*   [gives correct street address]

*SW:*   And the town?

*CB:*   [Looks at the nurse, then starts repeating the story about her husband.]

* * *

*SW:* [hands CB a card with categories from "very satisfied" to "very dissatisfied" printed on it and asks her to respond in those terms.] How satisfied are you with this neighborhood as a place to live?

*CB:* It's terrible, no more good here.

*SW:* [to herself:] I guess that's very dissatisfied. And how satisfied are you with your home as a place to live?

*CB:* Well, I live here for so long, so I think I die here.

*SW:* How satisfied are you with your life as a whole today?

*CB:* Well, I cry every week because they [someone in the neighborhood] broke the big glass [window in the front of her house]. I want to stay here in my house [a statement she repeats frequently during the interview]. When the time comes for questions about the condition of the house, an extended set of ratings regarding the condition of the lights, toilets, and other fixtures, the social worker asks the homemaker, who has been standing nearby.

* * *

In assessing clients like CB, the case managers had to improvise both the questions and responses that would be entered on the forms. These improvisations were essential if the case managers were to complete the assessment process, in and of itself a major Project objective. The case managers recognized and treated the assessment process as an artificiality.

This was apparent not only in the way they conducted individual assessments, but also in the way they processed the assessment forms. They felt it more efficient to see two clients in the field in one day, working up the forms later, than to spend a full day on one client's assessment. The case managers in the nonwaivered component also liked to have an informal visit with the client before introducing the formalities of the assessment. Technically, their forms were supposed to be sent immediately to the agencies from which they sought services in order to provide a common set of referral information on the client. In reality, the forms were sent as an afterthought to the referral process, which took place over the phone after the initial home visit. Again, the main function of the forms became one of official communication rather than care planning.

As this account suggests, understanding the care planning process requires an examination at the level of informal activity rather than formal procedures. In making judgments about client needs and decisions regarding their care, case managers were guided by two sets of interpretations: those derived from clinical perspectives and those engendered by the logistics of service delivery. The ways these interpretations were fashioned are examined below.

## Informal Care Planning: Clinical Perspectives

The Project's case managers were professionally trained nurses and social workers. As such, they brought to their jobs the knowledge and skills of their disciplines, as well as norms favoring an individualistic, holistic, and autonomous approach to casework. This clinical framework guided the interpretation of the client's homelife on a day-to-day level, providing a perspective different in form and substance than that of the formal assessment procedures.

There were certain predictable variations in the perspectives of the nurses and social workers. The nurses focused more on the physical functioning and medical conditions of the clients, while the social workers were more concerned with family relationships and socioemotional functioning of clients. In conferences (the Project's equivalent to medical rounds) with the project coordinator (C), the contrast between nursing and social work orientations could become jarringly apparent:

*C:*   What about Mrs. D.?

*N:*   She has had Parkinson's and can't even hold on to the stair rail. Her daughter's still living there [because the client needs so much help].

*SW:*   Her main problem is that she has to show her children that she's failing. She hates to be a burden to them.

*C:*   Mrs. M.?

*N:*   She's getting eight hours a week of [homemaker] service. She has a pacemaker and a colostomy.

*SW:*   She's resourceful, has lots of interests. She enjoys her home and knits and reads.

*C:*   The Cs [a couple]?

*SW:*   They're terrific, wonderful, very supportive of each other.

*N:*   He has poor mental status [due to] CVA's [cerebrovascular accidents; strokes]. He's incontinent, needs a lot of care. Mrs. C won't take more than eight hours [of homemaker service] . . . She says, "I have to keep busy."

While their different professional orientations could yield variable reports of clients' situations, the perspectives of the nurses and social workers were often indistinguishable. This was in part a function of shared prior experience in social service agencies and their current work together in teams. A central element in this mutual clinical perspective was that both classified the home situations according to their pathological implications.

At one end of such classifications were those situations, be they physical, social, or experiential that indicated there was no problem; and the situation was adequate for client needs. Such circumstances were noticed and reported in the shorthand manner indicated by the social worker's comments on Mrs. M and the Cs, as well as her report on another client's home: "It's clean and in order. There's a Bates [good quality brand] spread on her bed." By singling out pieces of homelives in this way, case managers were able to communicate their sense that clients were doing as well as could be expected and their judgment that the services provided by the project were sufficient.

At the other extreme were situations that the case managers perceived as indicative of underlying pathology or some form of endangerment to clients. Physical features of homes were a major focus of such concern for many clients, such as those described by the nurse in a case conference:

The Ks are a couple [sic: they are sisters; the younger one is the Project's client, but they are generally referred to together], both close to 90. Their house is about 100, a three-story that they maybe will have a problem heating. We can't get them to move, even downstairs; one of them is scared to do that. I think we'll get some help with the heat [paying the heating bill] from another agency.

There are mice, and they go at their nightgowns, pjs, and bathrobes. Everything's dusty and creepy. They'll die there, that's the way they want it. They're ashamed of the way the place looks, hadn't changed the bed linens in weeks [until the Project's homemaker did so]. They won't let anyone go up there. They have mice poison down but can't find the holes. They are in bed all day—one has an upset stomach, the other just doesn't feel well.

In this presentation, the identity of the Project's client is fused with that of her sister, which in turn is fused with the physical condition of their surroundings. Descriptions of person and house are symmetrical: the sisters' ages and the house's age, their intractable life-style, and the material conditions needing remedy.

Like the physical features of home environments, the social relations of clients could form the focus of clinical judgments. Here, there could be an expansion of the definition of "the case" to incorporate family members whose problems were seen as making problems for the client. An illustration comes from the Gs, a married couple both of whom were clients. At the time of the following descriptions, a program that provided an escort to take Mr. G shopping was considering terminating its service.

*Nurse:*   The person taking Mr. G shopping thinks he doesn't need the service. He does okay by himself and doesn't buy much when they're out, so he must be doing his own shopping. But there are many family problems, and they need emotional support as much as the shopping. . . . They moved from upstate, where they had many services for [Mrs. G], at the request of their daughter, who has a history of depending on her mother for emotional support. Consequently, her mother has high blood pressure—she's in the wheelchair with MS, and this means there's not much she can do for her family, which makes more frustration and leads to her high blood pressure.

Their grandson has been on drugs and is now working for his stepfather. He just got his license and bought a car and had an accident over the weekend. He and his stepfather had a fight in McDonalds. . . . [Mrs. G told the nurse] They waited for me to leave [on her last home visit] before they explained the fight fully so they could dump it on [Mrs. G]. Her blood pressure reflects the family mood.

The Project had been trying for over a year to get the couple moved to a wheelchair-accessible public housing project. The coordinator noted that the move was intended in part to enable the couple to engage in social activities "so they don't sit home with nothing to do but bicker with each other" about their family problems. Physical and social aspects of home are merged in the service provider perspectives on this couple. Problems with family members are seen as translating directly into physical problems; the solution is seen as a move to a physically and socially more supportive environment.

In the two cases just described, physical and social qualities of homes are interpreted as putting the client at risk. Symbolic and experiential dimensions of homelives were also subjected to evaluation for their potential pathology, as the following vignette illustrates:

DS is an "oldie"—a client in the Project since its beginning. She has a history of high blood pressure and has been diagnosed as having Organic Brain Syndrome. A singer on the stage in her youth, she lives alone in an apartment surrounded by records and books she treasures.

She enjoys a daily ride on local public transportation and does her banking in the transit terminal. In the process, she reportedly shows people her money and talks about how much she has. She has been mugged several times after such episodes. The Project has tried unsuccessfully to convince her to have a volunteer service do her banking for her. The Project also referred her to Meals on Wheels, but the service was discontinued after she said she had flushed the meals down the toilet.

The plan at that point became, as a case manager described it, to "put her in a nursing home because she's unsafe." She reportedly agreed with this description of herself and agreed to be put on the waiting list for one of the homes the staff took her to visit, but then balked at going to be interviewed there. The staff then arranged an appointment for her at a geriatric counseling service at which she was "known" (that is, she had been a client there before) in order for the staff there "to talk to her about going to a nursing home." When the nurse arrived to take her to the appointment, she refused to go. The nurse called the service to reschedule the appointment. When DS stated she still would not go, the nurse called again, canceling the appointment and saying the client had a cold. Shortly before the rescheduled time, DS herself called the service and said she was ready to go, and it was the nurse who didn't feel well.

The interpretation of DS is cast in classic symbolism surrounding the concept of home. The haven she enjoys inside her home, surrounded by the symbols of a past and better time, is insufficient protection against the evils of the material world outside. She is interpreted as a woman living in a fantasy world, unsafe in the real one. The agencies who "know" her are united in their mission to remove her to a more protected environment. In her attempt to rebuff these efforts (as well as previous endeavors to change her life at home), she displays behavior that is taken as further evidence of her distortion of reality. She has accepted, at least in part, this view of herself and is moving along the course planned for her, albeit with as much resistance as she can muster.

These cases demonstrate the transformation of various dimensions of homelives that occurred as the Project's case managers applied their clinical training and experience. Other facets of these interpretations are also apparent in the case descriptions: They are tailored to individual cases, involve multidimensional views of clients, sometimes incorporate other players into the very definition of the case, and require ad hoc responses by service providers.

These attributes stand in explicit contrast to the standardized routines prescribed by formal assessment procedures and are essential benchmarks of professional activity (Freidson, 1970). By interpreting a client's homelife through these criteria, case managers asserted not only their view of a client, but also their view of themselves as active professionals. The arena in which they were active—that of delivering services to clients—provided a third source of interpretations of the homelives of the clients.

## Service Logistics and Perspectives of Homelives

As seen from previous descriptions, the work of the Project involved a process of assessing clients and connecting them with services. This work consumed the majority of the case managers' time and attention, and completing service arrangements became an objective of their activity that was independent of the specific goals of care plans. The homelives of clients thus became interpreted according to the ease with which clients could be taken through assessment and referral processes.

The majority of the Project's clients presented no major processing difficulties: They were amenable to assessment procedures, had service needs that were relatively straightforward, and cooperated with the services to which the Project connected them. When this degree of fit existed between the Project's processing objectives and the client's behavior, the client's homelife was also seen, and treated, as unproblematic. This is illustrated by the case of Mrs. A; the description below was drawn from a reassessment home visit.

The social worker describes Mrs. A as a "fairly average case with no tremendous problems but frailer than most" due to chronic heart failure and strokes. In her early 80s, Mrs. A has lived for over 15 years in a house with a daughter and the daughter's husband; another daughter and two grandsons live in separate sections of the house. The social worker describes the homemaker assistance Mrs. A receives as being geared primarily towards giving the daughter who cares for her "some time to herself."

The house where Mrs. A lives is in a 1960s era suburban development. It is modest in size, and the furniture is arranged against walls to allow Mrs. A to move through in a walker or wheelchair, which she uses when she tires at night. Everything in the house is tidy and visibly clean.

During the visit Mrs. A sits in a rocker next to large windows at the front of the house, a typical location for her during the day as she enjoys watching the children when they come home from school. She wears a neat pink robe and pink lap throw, and she has a pink crocheted afghan, made by her daughter, over the back of her chair. Mrs. A's daughter stands nearby during the reassessment procedures, often answering the case managers' questions but is responsive when they tell her they need her mother's answer.

At the beginning of the visit, the nurse tells Mrs. A that we had come "to ask her some questions again." During the administration of the assessment instrument, the nurse says, "See, I told you, some of these questions are silly," after asking if Mrs. A smokes. Mrs. A's responses to the questions are generally phrased colloquially, but she gives a categorical rating when the nurse probes. Asked, for example, to describe her appetite, she says, "I'm not that hungry, but I eat." The nurse responds, "So would you say it's good, fair . . ." Of her health, Mrs. A says, "It's not that good at my age," a response the nurse translates into "poor" on the form.

A few times, mother and daughter answer the same question with mild contrasts between their responses. Asked if she has trouble reading (because of her eyesight), Mrs. A says, "I don't read like I used to," while her daughter states that "she reads every day." When asked about Mrs. A's social contacts, her daughter responds, "She has the family." Mrs. A reports, "I had friends where I lived before, but not here; but I have my family."

About the neighborhood, Mrs. A says, "I don't bother." Of her life, she reports, "Thank God, I'm able to get around. You gotta be satisfied." She states that she goes out in a car less than once a month. At home, she listens to the radio when her grandchildren turn it on and watches *Family Feud* nightly.

Both Mrs. A and her daughter say they are very satisfied with the homemaker currently assigned to them. The daughter sees the homemaker as essential: "We never could do it all if we didn't have [her]." "It all" includes the daughter's employment a few mornings a week, a schedule shortened from the full-time job she left to care for her mother.

After the assessment, the case managers talk with Mrs. A's daughter about the service options available once the Project ends. Mrs. A chats with me, asking if I have children. When I respond, "not yet," she says, "Take your time; when you have children your troubles begin."

The entire visit takes roughly an hour and a half. As we leave the house, the nurse remarks that she "had forgotten how sweet [Mrs. A] is." We all wave up at her, still sitting at the front window. My fieldnotes, drafted during the visit and expanded that evening, indicate puzzlement over Mrs. A's remarks about children and trouble, given the obvious support provided by her family. I write that "I felt frustrated that I couldn't get more than a glimpse of what she is really like."

What Mrs. A was "really like" for the Project was a "sweet," "frail" lady with a supportive family, clean house, and "no tremendous problems." Her remarks during the visit provided occasional glimpses of a person who has "gotta be satisfied" with the current situation because no alternatives exist. They hint as well of a family situation more real—that is, with its own set of feuds and troubles—than the neat pink image we saw.

On the way to see Mrs. A, the social worker had remarked that she enjoyed home visits because they "let you make a connection with a client on a personal level." Contrasted with the formwork and telephone calls that made up her work in the office, this remark made sense. As long as Mrs. A remains "fairly average" as a client and easily processed, this type of visit, the Project, is as personal as it needed to get.

The case of CB described above illustrated a situation in which client processing was more problematic for the project. CB's responses did not collapse as easily as those of Mrs. A's into the categories required by the formal assessment instrument; furthermore, CB was unable or unwilling to respond directly to those categories. Beyond those difficulties, CB was reluctant to have the homemaker do anything in her home. Other cases as well exemplified the "treatment resistant" client who can torment service providers, particularly those whose service consists of getting clients to receive services (Bachrach, Talbott, & Meyerson, 1987). One such client is described below.

During one winter of the Project's operation, Mr. V was being pressured to pay an overdue heating bill. The bill was high, in part, because heating the house was complicated by a hole in the roof. The Project had gotten an agreement from his union to cover the cost of repairing the roof, but Mr. V rejected the money, saying the union should increase his pension instead.

The Project's next strategy was to get Mr. V an application for public assistance with the heating bills. Though unable to write, he balked at having the case managers complete the form for him, saying he'd "let them know" if he wanted their help. In the meantime, a nurse at the medical group he used tried to persuade him to enter a nursing home, a move favored by his sister, who went so far as to contact several homes about placing him. While the nurse reported to the Project that he seemed willing to consider these arrangements, Mr. V himself denied this and bitterly criticized the nurse to the Project staff. He said his main reason for remaining in his house was his son, who for years had been in a mental institution. Though he acknowledged that he never expected his son to come out, he stated, "but this is still his home."

Mr. V's determination to maintain his home, as well as his efforts to control the services he would receive and the terms on which he would receive them, constituted logistic dilemmas for the Project. The response of the case managers was a pragmatic one of trying to redress the situation piece by piece. Given that they lacked the authority to authorize services for clients, as well as sanctions with which to compel clients to accept them, the case managers were often understandably frustrated and adopted an attitude of resignation. As the nurse stated at one point regarding the hole in Mr. V's roof, "At least it's in his dining room. He doesn't go in there much."

Between clients who could be handled as easily as Mrs. A and those, like Mr. V, whose situation seemed futile were the majority of clients who had needs warranting particular services that were more difficult to obtain but acceptable to the clients. Perspectives on these cases were shaped by the need to match client attributes to the eligibility requirements, service specifications, and reimbursement mechanisms of provider agencies. In the process, the physical and social dimensions of the clients' lives were separated into discrete elements and then repackaged to make the best fit with an optimal number and type of services. An illustration of this process is evident in the case of Mrs. T.

> In her 70s and terminally ill with cancer, Mrs. T also has heart and pulmonary disease. Currently living with her daughter, she realizes her condition is deteriorating and wishes to enter a nursing home. Neither she nor her daughter can pay for this, however. Mrs. T never obtained a legal separation from the husband she left years ago; until she does so, her ability to claim Medicaid coverage will be limited by her husband's financial status. Her husband is unwilling to provide money for her care, but is also unwilling to cooperate with separation proceedings. The Project social worker plans to contact a Legal Aid lawyer who specializes in cases involving older people; she will try to get him to expedite the case. In the meantime, the case managers are trying to find home care services (and payment for them) since Mrs. T's daughter has gotten a part-time job that will require leaving her mother alone a few hours a day. The Project has arranged for the local branch of the Cancer Society to provide a homemaker for a few weeks. The social worker is also checking on the possibility of receiving payment for home care from a union to which Mrs. T's husband belongs.

In the course of the gymnastics the Project went through to piece together sufficient care for Mrs. T, the set of roles the client occupied becomes apparent: She was a mother, a cancer patient, a legal supplicant, a pensioner's wife, and (potentially) an unmarried woman. The case managers chose the roles to activate; then, according to the likelihood that such activation would yield the desired result, they devised a service package.

Developing such service packages was further complicated by the fact that attributes that made a client eligible for one service could be irrelevant or even disqualify eligibility for others. Additional complications were that intake workers at other agencies had variable degrees of discretion in making decisions about which clients to accept, and even the most standardized criteria were more flexible in the hands of some workers than others. The challenge for case managers thus became to selectively emphasize, and coach clients also to self-present, the "right" attributes to the "right" workers at the "right" agencies. Attempts by one of the social workers to secure a nursing home bed illustrate the use of these presentational strategies:

> The social worker called the nursing home office to assure them that the client would appear the next day for an intake interview. She stated that the client was "very eager" to enter the home and informed them that he was a "very together" person who had already made his funeral arrangements as well as plans to obtain Medicaid coverage, attributes she felt would increase his chances of getting a bed. She then called the client, who had previously canceled plans to enter a different home and expressed reservations about entering this one. She reminded him to be on time for the interview and to wear the one good suit he owned, saying "these are the orders from the nursing home. You could lose the bed if you don't do things the way they want. . . . I don't want you to lose out this time—this is the best thing that ever happened to you."

The negotiation of clients' identities between case managers and staff at other organizations did not end once services were "in place." The programs most involved with Project clients were also in social service agencies, however, and their professional staff tended to share the clinical perspectives of the case managers. Further, the service domain of the Project had been carefully designed to ensure that it was not competitive with other agencies for clients or other resources; this kept to a minimum the potential for conflictual perspectives on client needs (Dill, 1983; see also Warren, Rose, & Bergunder, 1974).

When views among programs did differ, they were generally resolved through conversations between case managers and other frontline staff. These interactions centered on the establishment of a consistent perspective on the client in order to achieve a clear sense about the division of labor of the agencies. In the process, client preferences could become secondary to logistic imperatives. The case of Mrs. R illustrates these processes.

> A widow living alone, Mrs. R had multiple sclerosis and had been hospitalized following a sudden decline in physical functioning. The case managers had been informed by a nurse at the home care agency contracted to the Project that the hospital was planning to discharge Mrs. R at her request to her home. The case managers were opposed to this decision and felt, as one stated, that the hospital staff "did not understand Mrs. R's living conditions." In her current state, Mrs. R would need to use a wheelchair on an indefinite basis; her bedroom was, however, too small to accommodate the chair. Furthermore, doctors informed the home care provider that she would need 24-hour attendance and medical supervision, which the agency's workers would not be able to provide. After the case managers discussed this with the hospital discharge planners, the decision was made to start working on nursing home placement.

In this case, the involved agencies reached a conclusion that was phrased in terms of the clients best interests but was actually framed by the negotiation of perspectives on her life at home. The Project's success in carrying out placement plans would depend on service logistics as well as the reaction of the client. Mrs. R could reject the plan, leaving the case managers powerless to enforce it other than through persuasion. But the outcome of the plan also would hinge on such factors as how much pressure the hospital staff felt to discharge Mrs. R, the availability of nursing home beds, and the source of payment for the bed. Organizational and economic contingencies such as these lead increasingly to the discharge of patients with inadequate arrangements at home (Sankar, Newcomer, & Wood, 1986) and create the need for service planners to get as much "lead-time" as possible on a nursing home placement; hence, the willingness of case managers to proceed despite likely opposition by the client.

A final case illustrates the situation in which perceptions of the client's homelife led to a different type need to activate care plan as soon and consistently as possible. In the process, the service providers ended up intentionally excluding the client from their deliberations.

Mrs. F was a client in her 60s with a history of chronic obstructive pulmonary disease and several strokes. She lived in a two-bedroom apartment with her two sons and the wife and baby of the younger son. A long-time client of the Project, she also received a number of services from different agencies, including the Visiting Nurse Service (VNS) and a homemaker from Medicaid.

Over time, a number of questions about the case troubled the Project and other agencies, all the more so because there seemed to be no clear answers. One of the most persistent concerned the possibility that Mrs. F was being abused by one of her sons. At different times, she would state to a service provider that she had been hit or otherwise abused; subsequently, she would recant her story, or an investigation would prove her account erroneous. Another puzzling aspect was that Mrs. F would seem initially to go along with care plans and then reject or fail to follow through with them.

Both reflecting and contributing to this confusion, the agencies serving Mrs. F had developed variant interpretations of her case. For example, at one point, Mrs. F owed the electric company over $1,700 in unpaid bills. Her sons had told her that she could not turn on her oxygen machine and the air conditioner at the same time. The VNS nurse interpreted this as cruel treatment. The Project staff felt that the whole family might be manipulating the electric company, knowing that it would not turn off the electricity of someone dependent on an oxygen machine. They also felt that the action the sons had taken was a rational response to the situation of indebtedness.

A number of such incidents that caused confusion among the service providers occurred during one summer. As the Project Coordinator put it, the case reached the point where the "pieces [didn't] fit together," and it was not clear to the staff whether the client was "manipulating the situation," or "seeking attention" by playing one agency against another, or whether she herself was really confused.

When Mrs. F was hospitalized with injuries suggestive of physical abuse, the Project Coordinator contacted officials regarding possible court intervention under the Protective Services Act. In this consultation, it was decided that the facts were not clear enough to initiate such action and that the involved agencies should meet to discuss the case.

By the time of the meeting, Mrs. F had been diagnosed as having a disorder that caused seizures; abuse was ruled out in this instance. Discussions at the meeting then led to the conclusion that the case did not seem to fit the criteria for Protective Services; there was also skepticism that Mrs. F would cooperate with such a plan. The agencies agreed that they would pool their information in the future and not respond to Mrs. F's statements or requests until they could check with one another. They also agreed that the Project should resume efforts to obtain public housing for her and shared ideas about how to expedite that process.

The outcome of the meeting between the service agencies was the assertion of formal organizational control over the case. In the future, they would listen first to one another's interpretations of Mrs. F's homelife, secondarily to hers. This case was in some ways extreme. Protective Services was viewed and used as a last resort for clients whose welfare was seen as endangered. This was also the only case observed during the Project's operation where supervisory-level representatives from different agencies had to meet to resolve service logistic dilemmas. Nonetheless, the case illustrates how those dilemmas are grounded in the service providers' perspectives of clients.

The case also demonstrates the need of service agencies to have a shared perspective in order for each to proceed toward the achievement of its own objectives. When the creation of this shared perspective is blocked by a client's actions or attributes, the outcome, as with Mrs. F, can be to interpret the client as introducing "noise" into the communication system and to take steps to eliminate that noise.

Like the versions of homelives created through clinical interpretations, the representations developed in the course of service delivery were tailor-made to individual clients. They also involved decisions made by service providers acting autonomously in that they exercised some discretion in the enforcement of official rules and procedures.

Service logistic interpretations were unlike clinical ones, however, in the extent to which a holistic perspective on homelives could be maintained. First, information completely independent of the client had to be responded to: the characteristics, preferences, and objectives of other organizations became as critical as those of clients. Second, to be effective within that organizational environment meant having to break apart the description of the client, fitting the pieces to the categories of assessment instruments or service eligibility requirements. Reshaping the client into the form of a case then required presentational strategies that further distanced the image of homelife from a holistic view.

While the case managers were aware that the logistics of service provision influenced their perceptions of clients, they applied their own criteria in judging the outcomes of this process. A home visit thus was seen as more personal than office work, regardless of how close the "personal" contact really was. Discussions with other service providers became a way to discern how much the client was manipulating the presentation of her case. The need to keep clients moving through assessment and referral procedures meant that clinical perspectives, as well as the formal rules governing those procedures, would be attended to on a discretionary basis.

## Summary and Discussion

Formal and informal care planning processes involve different transformations of homelives of the clients. Formal assessment measures turn the social and physical aspects of homelives into standardized descriptions that can be separated from the home context and compared across clients and programs. The creation of this "documentary reality" (Smith, 1974) involves treating all homes and all clients as equivalent units; by standardizing the performance of persons doing the measuring, it also treats them as equivalent units (Diamond, 1986).

Clinical perspectives, in contrast, yield holistic, individualized representations made by professionals acting with autonomy and discretion. Dimensions by which homelives are judged derive from the knowledge and values specific to those professions.

The logistics of service provision separate the "facts" of homelives from their context in an nonroutinized, nonstandardized manner responsive to organizational constraints and contingencies. As organizational needs introduce new information into the case, the client may be pressured to conform to a particular representation of her- or himself.

Although documentary, clinical, and service logistic perspectives can lead to contrasting views of clients' lives, they are not logical alternatives. Instead, they serve different functions for care providers, who can communicate different, yet equally true, messages through them to different audiences (see Gubrium & Buckholdt, 1982). Documentary perspectives provide the basis for formal discourse with other agencies, particularly superordinate ones. Clinically based viewpoints allow service providers to formulate among themselves an interpretation of client needs that matches their own needs for clinical autonomy and that can be translated into care plans. Putting those plans into action means reformulating the description of clients to communicate views to other agencies that will enhance the likelihood that clients will receive services.

The Project described is a specific example of an organizational setting in which professionals deliver bureaucratically determined services through direct contact with clients. A seminal analysis of such "street-level bureaucrats" (Lipsky, 1980) notes that their work is oriented toward maximizing the amount of autonomy and individual discretion they exercise. It is grounded as well in the competing demands of concerns for clients and organizational objectives.

A primary aim of the worker in this situation is that of processing the client as expeditiously and autonomously as possible. In the course of such processing, formal organizational rules and client-centered goals can become subverted. The operation of formal and informal care planning processes in the study Project confirm the relevance of this analysis.

Viewing social policy as activated at this "street level" has implications for future planning of home care services for the elderly. First, since documentary, clinical, and service logistic perspectives are situationally specific, their content, structure, and relative importance are likely to vary among programs, providers, cases, and over time. How then, can the reliability and validity of home care provider judgments be assumed or assured?

Other research (Austin & Seidl, 1981) confirms that this is indeed problematic. The study found an extremely low level of reliability in the judgments of home care case managers regarding the risk of their elderly clients for institutionalization. Case managers tended to see their clients as more at risk than did an expert panel, a finding the authors ascribed to pressure on the case management program to recruit high-risk clientele. The evaluations of the case managers were also barely correlated with data obtained from the assessment instruments they themselves used. Here again, the documentary, clinical, and service logistic frames of reference produced separate versions of clients' lives.

Based on this work, the authors recommended the development of assessment measures within diverse organizational settings so that practice context effects could be identified. They also advocated that case management be located independent of other services to decrease the adverse impact of organizational pressure on the validity of professional judgments.

Because professionals work in and with organizations—and because all acts of description are subject to the conditions under which they are performed (Gubrium & Buckholdt, 1982)—it may never be possible to remove the effects of organizational pressures from professional judgments. Still, the above recommendations could go far toward specifying and controlling the extent of that influence.

The research reported here also suggests that the evaluation of specific programs providing home care should include qualitative analysis of the ways in which providers evaluate the homelives of elderly clients. This assessment would take issues of reliability and validity to a deeper level by specifying the social process through which such judgments are constructed and communicated (Gubrium & Buckholdt, 1982). Better understanding of the informal dynamics of service programs for the elderly could also identify reasons why they succeed or fail to achieve formal objectives. Given current controversy regarding the effectiveness of home care and other community-based services (Austin, 1989; Callahan, 1989a, 1989b; Lawton, Brody, & Saperstein, 1989), such knowledge is critically required.

Finally, while the focus of this chapter has been on the perceptions and perspectives of service providers, much of the case material illustrates situations in which interaction between clients and service providers was based on different and even conflictual interpretations of home. At the least, this can lead to communication difficulties; more dangerously, the autonomy of clients can be undermined when their voices are not understood or other voices are attended to more. The challenge for research and practice is to identify these situations and find ways of resolving them.

This analysis suggests that client perspectives must be incorporated before the definition of home is transformed by service delivery, as well as during that process. Current efforts toward this end involve restructuring local care delivery systems to provide more choice by and options for elderly clients (Austin, 1989). Research can help by clarifying the framework of values underlying policy on community-based care (Callahan, 1989b) and by illuminating the value preferences of different groups interacting in the policy process.

The planning of home care requires setting goals that are realistically grounded in an understanding of homelives and the ways services can support or undermine them. Given the meaning of home, efforts to achieve that understanding are essentially significant to the futures of older people.

## References

Amaturo, E., Costagliola, S., & Ragone, G. (1987). Furnishings and status attributes: A sociological study of the living room. *Environment and behavior, 19*(2), 228-249.

Austin, C. D. (1989). He can't get no satisfaction. [Letter to the editor]. *The Gerontologist, 29*(3), 412.

Austin, C. D., & Seidl, F.W. (1981). Validating professional judgment in a home care agency. *Health and Social Work, 6*(1), 50-56.

Bachrach, L. L., Talbott, J. A., & Meyerson, A. T. (1987). The chronic psychiatric patient as a "difficult" patient: A conceptual analysis." In A. T. Meyerson (Ed.), *Barriers to treating the chronic mentally ill: New directions for mental health services,* No. 33 (pp. 35-50). San Francisco: Jossey-Bass.

Callahan, J. J., Jr. (1989a). Play it again Sam—There is no impact. *The Gerontologist, 29*(1), 5-6.

Callahan, J. J., Jr. (1989b). Callahan replies. [Letter to the editor]. *The Gerontologist, 29*(3), 413-414.

Diamond, T. (1986). Social policy and everyday life in nursing homes: A critical ethnography. *Social Science and Medicine, 23*(12), 1287-1295.

Dill, A. P. (1983, November). *Coordinating care for the elderly: A study of inter-organizational negotiation.* Paper presented at the 82nd annual meeting of the American Anthropological Association, Chicago.

Dovey, K. (1985). Home and homelessness. In I. Altman & C. M. Werner (Eds.), *Home environments: Human behavior and environment,* Vol. 8 (pp. 33-64). New York: Plenum.

Faletti, M. V. (1984). Human factors research and functional environments for the aged. In I. Altman, M. P. Lawton, & J. F. Wohlwill (Eds.), *Elderly people and the environment: Human behavior and environment,* Vol. 7 (pp. 191-237). New York: Plenum.

Freidson, E. (1970). *Profession of medicine: A study of the sociology of applied knowledge.* New York: Harper & Row.

Gubrium, J. F., & Buckholdt, D. R. (1982). *Describing care.* Cambridge, MA: Oelge-schlager, Gunn & Hain.

Huttman, E. D. (1985). *Social services for the elderly.* New York: Free Press.

Korsec-Serfaty, P. (1985). Experience and use of the dwelling. In I. Altman & C. M. Werner (Eds.), *Home environments: Human behavior and environment,* Vol. 8 (pp. 65-86). New York: Plenum.

Lawrence, R. J. (1987). What makes a house a home? *Environment and behavior, 19*(2), 154-168.

Lawton, M. P., Brody, E. M., & Saperstein, A. R. Let them eat cake. [Letter to the Editor]. *The Gerontologist, 29*(3), 413.

Lipsky, M. (1980). *Street-level bureaucracy.* New York: Russell Sage.

Rowles, G. D. (1987). A place to call home. In L. L. Carstensen & B. A. Edelstein (Eds.), *Handbook of clinical gerontology* (pp. 335-353). New York: Pergamon.

Rubinstein, R. L. (1989). The home environments of older people: A description of the psychosocial processes linking person to place. *Journal of Gerontology: Social Sciences, 44*(2), S45-S53.

Sankar, A., Newcomer, R., & Wood, J. (1986). Prospective payment: Systemic effects on the provision of community care for the elderly. *Home Health Care Services Quarterly, 7*(2), 93-117.

Smith, D. E. (1974). The social construction of documentary reality. *Sociological Inquiry, 44*(3), 257-267.

Stegman, M. A. (1985). Housing and the elderly. In H. T. Phillips & S. A. Gaylord (Eds.), *Aging and public health* (pp. 147-179). New York: Springer.

Warren, R. L., Rose, S. M., & Bergunder, A. F. (1974). *The structure of urban reform.* Lexington, MA: Lexington Books.

Werner, C. M. (1987). Home interiors: A time and place for interpersonal relationships. *Environment and Behavior, 19*(2), 169-179.

Willcocks, D., Peace, S. & Kellaher, L. (1987). *Private lives in public places.* New York: Tavistock.

## 12

# Policing the Family?

## Health Visiting and the Public Surveillance of Private Behavior

ROBERT DINGWALL
KATHLEEN M. ROBINSON

The rise and decline of health visiting in the United Kingdom will be examined in this chapter. Health visitors are public health nurses whose main work has traditionally been the unsolicited routine visiting of all families with young children for the purposes of health screening and health education. The history of their occupation provides a case study in the conditions under which the surveillance of domestic behavior in a liberal democracy becomes possible, of the working practices that sustain it and of the ideological movements that can destroy it. If home care is to be shaped by the felt needs of the carers and the cared, it will be argued that such a proactive system of population surveillance is essential. The search for need must be an overriding objective of social policies and organizational designs.

This objective was a major influence on the development of health visiting in Britain from the 1880s to the 1980s. It never gained wide acceptance in the United States, as illustrated by the failure of the attempt to provide a coherent system for child health and welfare through the Sheppard-Towner Act in the 1920s (Rothman, 1981; Halpern, 1988). The opposition remains as fierce as ever. In 1975, for example, there was a celebrated exchange in *Pediatrics*. The journal had published a commentary article by C. Henry Kempe, the leading pediatrician and researcher on child abuse, advocating health visiting on the British model as the key to effective child protection. It was the way to discover need in those too young to articulate it for themselves and whose caretakers might have a vested interest in denying its existence. Kempe anticipated the obvious objections:

> Visits by the health visitor do not deprive the members of the family of their civil rights but do guarantee that the civil rights of the child will be recognized and protected . . . [they] do not significantly infringe on the parent's right to privacy but demonstrate that society has the obligation to ensure access to the child during the first years of his life rather than waiting until he enters school. . . . If the plan is made equalitarian and universal, it would obviate the concern that it is a repressive program for those who are poor or from minority groups. (Kempe, 1975, pp. 693-694)

This article brought such fierce responses that the editors and publishers felt obliged to print a defense of the principle of free debate in professional journals. The views of Dr. Herbert Rubinstein from New York are typical:

> It is despicable that the Academy would be party in the propagation of such totalitarian-egalitarian views. . . . Those who feel they can, because of their own inclinations, subjugate others should become dictators, not healers. Those who feel they want to force changes in child-rearing should become social workers, not scientists. Those who feel parents must be forced to raise their children in a preconceived beneficial manner should become terrorists, not educators. (Rubinstein, 1976, p. 577)

Similar voices were heard in Britain at the beginning of the twentieth century when health visiting acquired state sponsorship. Why did they fail?

### Policing the Home[1]

In preindustrial Britain, home visiting was an important aspect of the traditional relationship between women of different classes. The social obligations of the better-off included the provision of personal charity and instruction to the poor. These relationships were disrupted by the process of industrialization and urbanization. The result was perceived to be the weakening of a significant moral force in society at a time when social discipline was becoming more important. The new production technologies required continuous operation and a more sober attitude to work. The concentration and growth of population in towns increased the potential scale of any form of disorder. Rapid population growth also meant that there was a high proportion of children and young people, a population that stretched the capacity of the community to control and socialize its new members.

Home visiting was reestablished by middle- and upper-class women during the 1830s as one response to these concerns. Rather than be a matter of personal initiative, it now took a more organized form through voluntary associations. As French social historian Jacques Donzelot (1980) has pointed out, such philanthropic activities addressed some of the grievances of working-class women in exchange for their acceptance of a role in the transmission of social discipline. While the lady visitors saw themselves as missionaries for Christian virtue, temperance, and domestic economy, they were, in effect, generalizing the workplace control they imposed on their own domestic servants. The ideologies held by the ladies concerning domesticity and motherhood were intended to influence the conduct of poor men through their wives. The price these men would have to pay for the benefits of family life in a patriarchal society was their commitment to the economic and social behavior necessary to sustain it.

In the wake of the cholera epidemics of 1832 and 1848, the model of the home missionary was adapted to the transmission of a secular gospel of health. This adaptation took two forms. In one version, committees of lady volunteers employed working-class women to visit in their own neighborhoods in order to advise other poor women about domestic hygiene, family budgeting, and child care. The other version relied on the ladies themselves as home visitors. The former schemes were generally considered to have been more effective because of the difficulties of organizing and controlling voluntary workers. During the 1870s, some of the workers began to receive financial and organizational support from local government, whose own public health responsibilities were increasing. By the beginning of the twentieth century, paid visitors could be found in most of the major industrial areas of Great Britain. The following decade (1910) saw the term *health visitor* generally adopted as a label for these employees; by 1918, all local public health departments were obliged to provide this service. In the process, however, the original working-class women had been largely replaced by educated middle-class women, who were entering the labor market during this period.

The state-sponsored growth and professionalization of health visiting was driven by quite specific concerns for the fitness of the working class. The UK birthrate had been falling steadily since 1880, and middle-class women had shown themselves increasingly reluctant to bear the numbers of children thought necessary to the interests of a modern economy and great empire. The resulting gap between the labor demands of industry and the military and the supply of healthy, educated, and compliant volunteers led to a policy concern for the quality of the children produced by working-class women. This process was given a particular impetus by the military setbacks of the Boer War (1899-1902) and the economic recession of the 1890s, which fueled nationalist concern about the ability to compete with Germany and its growing welfare state.

The problem for policymakers, however, was to devise a means of influencing domestic behavior that could be reconciled with the peculiar status of the family in the liberal state. The privacy of the family is seen as an important check on state power (Donzelot, 1980). Liberty is defined at least partly in terms of the legal barriers preventing uninvited entry by other citizens or state agents (Stinchcombe, 1963). At the same time, the family's role in the reproduction of the social order means that its internal workings are of considerable public importance. Classically, liberalism views social order as the product of a series of free contracts between individuals. However, as economists have forgotten since Adam Smith and sociologists have reiterated since Emile Durkheim, free contracts depend not merely on a legal structure, which the state can provide, but also on a moral environment that restrains their abuse. The law can only intervene after a breach in contract has taken place; the confidence that makes the contract possible derives from the more complex social institution of trust. The moral socialization of children plays a key part in the process of persuading people to regulate their own actions in order that the social order can survive. However, much of this socialization occurs in the family which, as we have seen, is constituted as a private zone. The liberal state cannot avoid concern for child care, but its fundamental principles restrict its ability to police parental behavior.[2]

Up to the crisis of the Boer War, the problem of policing family life had been addressed largely by being left in the hands of philanthropists. As Donzelot (1980) points out, one of the virtues of the philanthropic solution was that it could achieve state objectives while remaining at a distance from the exercise of state power. The fiction of a voluntary intervention in the family could be maintained. However, as we have seen, this solution is relatively inefficient. Its effectiveness is also questionable since philanthropy depends mainly on rewarding the recipients of charity for compliant behavior, which is difficult to monitor, and has few available sanctions.

There had been private sector attempts to remedy this, notably in the work of the Charity Organisation Society (COS). As its name suggests, this organization hoped to unify the efforts of the patchwork of private charities operating in any particular area. Its program of scientific casework involved trained middle-class visitors who responded to requests for financial or material help with a rigorous investigation of the applicant's circumstances, an exact measurement of their needs, and continuing visits to monitor the extent to which the applicant followed the caseworker's prescriptions for behavior intended to avoid distress in the future. This moral work was expected to have an indirect influence on children, who would see their parents benefiting from thrift, sobriety, and self-restraint. The main sanction was that those applicants whose requests were rejected would be forced to rely on the Poor Law, material aid provided by the state under conditions were designed to punish or humiliate the recipient. Families were often split up so that children could be insulated from the bad examples of their parents; in turn they were exposed to the supposed benefits of workhouse discipline, learning the hard fate that awaited those who failed to lead a respectable life. The COS opposed most attempts to mitigate the harshness of the Poor Law in order to protect the space in which it operated.

In practical terms, the COS was comparatively unsuccessful: Although influential patrons made it a formidable pressure group and its casework techniques were widely copied, the numerous vested interests of private charity prevented it from achieving its grand goal of a unified response to the problems of the poor. Many of those whose applications for help were rejected preferred to go without than turn to the Poor Law; The COS criteria for giving aid were widely criticized for their insensitivity to the extent to which the old and the sick could be held responsible for their own misfortunes. Moreover, the Society's reactive casework failed to deal with the problem that occupied the political agenda of the late nineteenth and early twentieth century, namely what to do about the vast mass of working-class families on the margins of poverty who rarely exposed themselves to social intervention by applying for relief. A third tier of intervention was required that could deal with incipient problems and was focused on the improvement of the respectable but ignorant working-class rather than the correction of its rougher elements. An intervention on this scale could only be contemplated by a state agency.

The ideological basis for this third tier came from two sources. One was the public health movement, whose experience of managing mass problems like epidemics had shown that a medicalized intervention would be accepted where a more obviously social one was not. The universal character of diseases like cholera dictated universalist responses, which did not stigmatize the recipients in the same way as applications for material assistance, whether from charities or the state. The other was the theory of "practicable socialism" developed by defectors from the COS line in response to growing working-class demands for the redistribution of wealth. This theory proposed that the state should recognize the real problems faced by the working class in making adequate provision from their own resources for sickness, unemployment, and old age. Those workers who had led respectable lives should be rewarded by positive entitlements to assistance in times of need rather than be dependent on a grudging charity.

Health visiting was one of the practical expressions of this ideological shift. It medicalized the problems of domestic life and child care, circumventing the barriers around the family with the construction of what Donzelot (1980, pp. 82-95) has called a "tutelary relationship" between visitors and mothers.[3] In the words of one leading public health physician: The health visitor "is not an inspector in any sense of the word. Her functions are rather those of a friend of the household to which she gains access" (Newman, 1906, pp. 263-264).

Under a tutelary relationship, home visits are occasions when the respectable poor can display their good moral character and receive a public validation for it. The refusal to participate in this exercise, by denying entry to the state's representative, is treated as, in itself, evidence of a lack of respectability that may legitimate some more authoritarian corrective intervention. In interactional terms, the essence of a tutelary relationship is the acceptance by the surveyor of the self-presentation of the surveyed. Dingwall, Eekelaar, and Murray (1983) have described this as the "rule of optimism," an expectation that the most favorable gloss will be placed on any observations of behavior or moral character. It stands in contrast to the investigative behavior of the COS caseworker or the Poor Law relieving officer, that assumes that all self-presentations are calculated to deceive.

We shall examine tutelage as an interactional form in more detail below. For the present, we need only sketch the evolution of health visiting since 1914. It was given additional impetus as an instrument of state policy by the perceived need to replace the manpower losses of World War I, and its reach was gradually extended to middle-class families during the 1920s.[4] This strengthened the universalistic aspects of health visiting, while also becoming more firmly medicalized with the restriction of recruitment to registered nurses and its increasing identification as a nursing specialty. These features were largely unaffected by the establishment of the National Health Service, and its basic ideological justification remained unchanged. Indeed, one of the last acts of the Council for Education and Training of Health Visitors (CETHV), the accrediting body for training programs before its absorption in 1980 by a new council regulating all branches of nursing, was to reassert the primacy of the search for unmet need through the home visit in terms used almost a century before:

> Our original employers sent health visitors into communities which had obvious and desperate health needs. It was left to the individual worker to search for and identify the health needs of individual families. Without this painstaking and time-consuming search, the identification of individual need could not have been made with any precision, nor appropriate remedies applied. . . . As health needs have become less overt, search was and is even more importantly now, the source of all health visiting. . . . There is no other group in the health or the social services with the tradition of visiting people in their own homes so that health needs may be identified before health problems develop. (CETHV, 1977, pp. 26, 29)

What does this search look like in practice? How is it distinguished from the sort of investigation that might be conducted by a police officer, social security official, or social worker from child protective services? How is it actually possible for state agents to enter the private domain of the family?

## The Home Visit

The data presented here are taken from a sample of 28 transcripts of *primary visits*—that is, home visits made on or about the tenth day after the birth of a new baby.[5] The family will have been visited daily by a midwife up to this time as part of the clinical follow-up to the actual delivery, whether the birth took place in a hospital or at home. This is the first postnatal contact with a health visitor.[6] Fifteen health visitors participated in the study, recording their own work with equipment supplied by the researcher in order to minimize observer effects. The community in which they were working was generally affluent, but the families in the sample range from relatively poor agricultural workers to professionals who commuted to jobs in London.

Ever since the 1908 work of Georg Simmel (translated in Wolff, 1950), analysts of social interaction have recognized a broad distinction between two party and multiparty encounters (dyads and triads, as Simmel called them). With the benefit of modern recording technology, Sacks, Schegloff, and Jefferson, (1974) were able to show that two-party interaction depended upon a set of tacit conventions that formed the basis for the consensual regulation of talking and listening so that both parties remained focused on the encounter and it proceeded in a relatively orderly way from beginning to end. Atkinson (1977) and Atkinson and Drew (1979) pointed out, however, that this system was inadequate for the regulation of multiparty settings. Dingwall (1980) elaborated this in proposing two broad types of management systems, one rule based, as in the courts described by Atkinson, and one role based, as in college tutorials where the tutor allocated turns to talk and listen, maintained a topical focus, and organized openings and closings.

Dingwall questioned, however, whether the choice of management system was solely a function of the number of parties involved. Some professional-client encounters, for example, seem to use role-based systems, where one party orchestrates both the structure and the process of the interaction.[7] Dingwall argued, then, that the concern of conversation analysts for the description of systems for the management of interactional structures needed to be linked to a broader interest in context and content. He suggested that this might be done through Goffman's concept of framing. This refers to the set of working assumptions established by the parties to an encounter, which provide for the allocation of moral identities, for the definition of legitimate and illegitimate behavior, and for the ways in which macro-features of the parties and the context can influence the interaction.[8] The nature of the frame defines the possibilities for subsequent behavior by either party.

If the health visitor were indeed purely a "friend of the family," we would expect to find the interaction during her visits to approximate the form of a conversation, with both parties introducing topics and sharing responsibility for movement through the encounter. On the other hand, if the health visitor were an inspector, we would expect to find her tending to monopolize the encounter management, probably with long chains of questions as in other kinds of investigation. In practice, however, we find neither.

The health visitor's entry to the house is a key point for analysis. In a liberal state, unannounced official agents do not have the power to force entry. However, the theory of tutelage provides that a refusal of access to the health visitor may cause the family to be treated as disreputable and consequently referred to other agencies, like the police or child protective services, who do have access to such powers. As the health visitor secures an invitation to enter, however, she creates a frame for the subsequent encounter.

Visit openings have a distinctive form, that is somewhat different from the greetings sequences classically described by conversation analysis. The visit proper cannot begin until the mother is identified and established as the second party for interactional purposes. If the door is answered by someone other than the mother of the new baby or the mother is not known to the health visitor, the first turn normally takes the form of a summons rather than a greeting. Summoning describes a particular method of opening an encounter:

> Whereas greetings can be polite ceremonies in the "ritual organization" of sociability, wherein the greeter need not necessarily "want something" from the one greeted, summoning builds on a different structure of expectations about the act. To call someone into one's presence or to locate them or to catch their attention in a very strong way has nothing of the ceremonial about it. Rather, it is a different mode of communication altogether—one that is based on *urgent communication,* one might say. The urgency is precisely understood in terms of needs or reasons for calling another in this manner. (Speier, 1969, pp. 208-209)

The summons below is a simple device based on the caller's identity as a health visitor:

*HV:* Sarah Dawson, the health visitor. Hello. It's Mrs. Jones. I'm Dr. Arthur's health visitor. Shall I go up?

If the person at the door is hesitant, the identity might be repeated but not elaborated:

*HV:* Hello there, I'm Erica Tate, the health visitor. . . . Is your wife in? Erica Tate, the health visitor.

Sometimes, even the label of health visitor (HV) is unnecessary.

*HV:*   Hello, how are you? Is Sue in or is she busy or . . . ?

These summonses have two notable features in this context. One is their cursory character. Although the health visitors do not enter without an invitation from the person who opens the door, there is no attempt to "sell" the visit. They do not attempt to explain their presence or to justify their entry. Indeed, their behavior implies an expectation of entry, even an entitlement. Tutelage presupposes the legitimacy of inspection and the illegitimacy of its refusal. The other feature is the establishment of the mother as the appropriate interactional partner. If she was not the person who opened the door, the respondent would produce her or account for her absence.

*Father:*   Maria is just about to come down with the baby.

*Grandmother:*   Now let me see where we are. If you'd just like to come up.

The framing pairs "health visitor" and "mother" as membership categories (Sacks, 1972a). Indeed, this pairing is so strongly defined that other possible co-participants would normally take themselves off the scene. Whatever health visiting is about, it is women's business.[9]

Once the mother was available as a co-participant, the health visitor began the visit proper with a starting utterance, typically some variant on, "Hello, how are you?" The length of the visits varied from less than 20 to up to 70 minutes. In the instances for which data are available, the closure was also initiated by the health visitor (compare Schegloff & Sacks, 1973).[10] The closings themselves varied in length from 12 minutes to 33 seconds, because movement out of the sequence occurred on a number of occasions, but there was no evidence of mothers seriously challenging this move or initiating closures themselves. Such monopolization of openings and closures is characteristic of orchestrated encounters.

What did the health visitors actually *do* with their role as orchestrators? This is where the data, at least superficially, are most surprising. There is no apparent evidence of any grand scheme or purpose, unlike say an encounter on the doorstep with a Jehovah's Witness or a double-glazing salesman. Much of the interaction has a somewhat desultory character. This is best seen through an examination of the movement from one topic to another in the course of the interaction.

Sacks (1972b) has summarized the way in which topic organization works in ordinary conversation:

> A general feature . . . is movement from topic to topic, not by topic close followed by a topic beginning but by a stepwise move, which involves linking up whatever is being introduced to what has just been talked about, such that, as far as anybody knows, a new topic has not been started, though we're far from wherever we began. (pp. 15-16)

With this system, the actual content represents the preferred outcome of the parties. this does not mean, however, that the content was designed in advance but, rather, that at each decision point (at every turn), continuation was organized to the parties' satisfaction by a selection from the range of options seeming to be legitimately available. By definition, then, a conversation cannot *pursue* an agenda. An agenda *may* be covered in the course of a conversation, if it goes on long enough or the agenda is brief, but it is more likely that one of the parties will have to breach the convention of stepwise transition and indicate a specific subject as a preferred topic. This would involve special procedures to block opportunities for stepwise movement. Orchestrated encounters use these procedures with some frequency in order to maintain the participants' joint focus of attention on some particular task.

There are many examples of such procedures in these encounters. One set relates to the organization of direct information exchange. The health visitors frequently ask the mother for an account of her health or the recent birth, although they may well have information on this from other sources and, indeed, sometimes contradict or enhance the mother's version from their records. This is an example, where the request is for information:[11]

*HV:*   Yes, now. Any family history of deafness?
(1.0)

*M:*   Don't think so not [on my side

*F:*                                [Pardon
((Laughter))

*F:*   No

*HV:*   I wondered if you'd do that.
((Laughter 3.0))

*HV:*   Um, diabetes?

*M:*   No=

*F:*   =No

rapidly develops into a monologue from the health visitor:

*HV:*   Lovely. Then you didn't have any drugs, aren't you beautifully normal. This is lovely. And she was forty-one weeks, which is super, and her birthweight was very good, and you didn't have a prolonged or difficult labor, and she breathed immediately? Yes, she did because I've got a thing ((3.0 Sound of rustling papers)). Marvellous.

The intensity of such compliments is a recurrent feature of health visitor/client interaction. It may be linked to the way tutelary surveillance normalizes its recipients. These continuous tokens of approval derive from the rule of optimism as assurances that the intrinsic moral character of the client has not been compromised either by some confession of failure or, indeed, by being the object of the visit.

But there is little evidence in this sample of topic change being orchestrated in support of a positive agenda. The health visitors seemed to be concentrating on the maintenance of the encounter as an end in itself with, at most, the negative objective of preventing their attempt to mimic a conversational form and a "friend of the family" relationship from overly diluting the thematic orientation to childbirth and mother-hood with general conversational topics. Agenda-oriented talk was rare and generally occurred as a justification for a breach of stepwise transition, anticipating the questions, "Why this, why now?" Several examples refer to the completion of paperwork:

*HV:*  Can I just fill in some paperwork?

*HV:*  Now I've brought the card and all the bits and pieces.

*HV:*  I must fill in my card.

The absence of work on content, however, is most apparent at the points where the interaction lapses, like those places in an ordinary conversation where it "runs out of steam" and requires a move from one or other party to restart it. This is one of many examples:

*HV:*  And how long does he sleep during the day? Does he go over four hours?

*M:*  (      ) he he has done=

*HV:*  =he has done. [Ye:s Ye:s]

*M:*                   [(          ] wake him up

*HV:*  You do, yes, that's a good idea, I think. (1.7) Ye:s (1.2) Well, Shirley (the midwife) said something about his weight.

*M:*  She wasn't very happy with it [(I don't think)]

*HV:*                                 [Ye:s Ye:s]

The health visitor's reluctance to introduce a new topic is marked by the pauses and the elongation of the "Ye:s" in her third turn. It might be thought that this would create space for mothers to raise their own concerns but, in fact, as here, they rarely take the chance. On the few occasions when mothers did pick up from these lapses, they generally returned to the previous topic and continued talking about that. There are two ways of reading the silence of the mothers, which may not be mutually exclusive. One is to see it as a point of passive resistance to the health visitor's intrusion. The other is to see it as a reflection of their puzzlement about what will count as legitimate behavior in this context. They are aware that, whatever the pretense, this is not an ordinary conversation, but they share the analyst's difficulty in establishing exactly what it is all about. Rather than appear foolish, they wait for more clues.

If neither party picked up from the lapse, the health visitor was likely to use this as the basis for moving toward a closure of the encounter. Unlike conversational closures, these rarely contained any summary of the work that had been done that could inform the mothers what the visit had been all about. The major concern of the health visitors was the arrangements for their next visit, which, as we saw with openings, assumed compliance by the mother. There was only one instance of a challenge, which also raised the issue of purpose.

*M:*   Oh, so far we've had no problems at a:ll

But the health visitor evaded the implicit challenge that visits were only required if the family had identified problems rather than being a matter for her initiative, by interacting with a toddler, sibling to the baby:

*HV:*   When do you want me to come again? (0.9) and come and see your mummy.

*B:*   (mmm)

*HV:*   Can I come again next wee:k?

The use of talk with children to handle difficult moments in these encounters, particularly where utterances might imply criticism, is another recurrent feature of these visits. Although the mother is no clearer about the purpose of the next visit, it is, of course, now very difficult for her to find a way of resisting it because the health visitor has constructed the child's gurgle as an invitation.

This has been a very brief summary of the data, but it should illustrate the basis for our contention that the main objective of the modern home visit by health visitors is simply to visit. The encounter is not used to conduct any clear and systematic health assessment or health education, although these goals may be pursued covertly or opportunistically. The health visitor may, for instance, test a child's motor development by engaging him or her in play, but the element of assessment in the activity is unlikely to be made explicit. Equally, she may take a mother's remark as an occasion to give advice on smoking or diet, but she is unlikely to make this a positive objective of the encounter. Indeed, the most difficult topics are conspicuously absent. Health visitors never seem to ask, "Have you felt anger toward the child? Does she cry a lot? Have you felt like shaking her? Does your husband (or boyfriend) shout at her? Does he come home drunk?"

### The Modern Politics of Health Visiting

If these arguments are correct, they raise some rather obvious questions about the value of an expensively trained and reasonably well-paid professional going into homes simply for the sake of it. In the absence of recordings from past health visitor/client interaction, we cannot state conclusively whether this apparent lack of content is simply a modern phenomenon. However, there are reasons for thinking that health visitors may once have had a much more conscious agenda. The widespread reports of early hostility to health visitors, for example, suggest that they might well have behaved in an investigative fashion with obviously disreputable clients (Smith, 1979, p. 117; Lewis, 1980, pp. 106-107). The workers in the scheme that was set up in Huddersfield in 1906, and had considerable national influence, had to be reminded that they were "not to cross the threshold unless an invitation is given to enter, not to sit down unless a seat is offered, to remember that every 'room' of a cottage has as much right to privacy as any lady's drawing room" (McCleary, 1933, p. 91).

It also seems unlikely that health visitors could have made such an effective contribution to the take-up of diphtheria immunization in World War II if they had not been making a very deliberate promotional effort (Ferguson & Fitzgerald, 1954, p. 167).

Some clues as to a possible change may, however, also be found in the changing tone of public statements by health visiting's leaders. We have already noted the CETHV's view of the centrality of the search as needed for the work of health visitors. They characterized this as "activity that is purposeful, unique, focused on health, self-initiated, expert and non-stigmatizing" (CETHV, 1977, p. 27). It involved the systematic screening of populations to identify needs and then to work with those affected, both as individuals and as groups, to change either personal or collective behavior.

Compare this with the approach now advocated by the then-general secretary of the Health Visitors Association (Goodwin, 1988). The CETHV had acknowledged the importance of searching along various dimensions of need—normative, felt, expressed, and comparative, in a categorization derived from Bradshaw (1972, p. 69). The new health visiting, however, only recognizes those felt and expressed needs which are validated by health care professionals. This is reflected in three particularly significant changes. First, the health visitor's objectives will now be determined by reference to an annually compiled community health profile based on epidemiological data.[12] Second, the health visitor/parent relationship will be put on a contractual basis, which will provide for home visiting only by prior agreement. As a result, the main worksite will shift from the home to the clinic, where screening, group education, and self-help programs will be carried out and parents will be expected to take principal responsibility for initiating health-related actions in relation to their children.

The cumulative impact of these changes amounts to a considerable ideological shift in the basis of health visiting. Instead of beginning from her experience of visiting individuals and aggregating this to map the needs of a community, the health visitor will now start from the official picture of the community and seek to find the individuals who fit its categories, as documented by those data on mortality, morbidity, and related factors that others have considered worth collecting. The result will be to exclude other views of need, particularly those that may arise from what is, in effect, the systematic ethnographic study of a community by an expert in public health.

The language of contract in British health and social services has been imported from the United States, where its combination of authoritarianism and populism reflects the values of a very different society. As Nelken (1988) has pointed out, its abandonment of the vision of universal concern and provision may seem consumer oriented. In practice, however, it forces the recipients into a narrow conception of autonomous individualism. Here, it leads to the discarding of any ideal of client advocacy, that the state might have any duty to see that the voices of those unable to speak for themselves can be heard. Such an activity would be an illegitimate extension of state power and contribute to the perpetuation of dependency. Autonomous clients can and must speak for themselves in the formulation of their contracts with the state.

The new health visiting exemplifies a critical weakness of this contractual theory. Its practitioners will only assess children at times and places chosen and stage-managed by their parents. A child brought to a clinic can be cleaned, fed, and dressed for the occasion. Any peculiarities in the child's behavior can be attributed to the unfamiliarity of the setting. The point is not that parental care should routinely be treated as suspect, but that its inadequacies are most vulnerable to identification in the home.[13] By treating the family as a self-sufficient unit of autonomous individuals, this strategy ignores the abundant evidence of physical, economic, and cognitive inequality. Its effect is to give priority to the views of those, such as parents and especially men, who have political access to the process of defining social problems and legitimate responses, neglecting those, such as children and, to a lesser extent, women, who do not.

Agenda-free health visiting can be seen as the precursor to such changes. The loss of confidence in its own mission left health visiting vulnerable to ideological reconstruction. This process has been shaped by the more general political changes that have occurred in the United Kingdom since 1979, especially the emphasis on the limitation of welfare expenditures and the declining legitimacy of public social provision.

The reliance on community health profiles compiled from existing data obliterates the intelligence that health visitors could furnish to the policy community about local perceptions of health and social need. If the National Health Service (NHS) does not receive this information, it can claim absolution from any obligation to respond. Where agenda-free home visits were a means of containing problems by not seeking to dig them up, the new style simply prevents them from coming to light by not looking for them at all. It is an ingenious method of cost containment at the expense of the poor, the housebound, and the inarticulate. Moreover, narrow financial motives for the limitation of public expenditures can be concealed behind a rhetoric of privacy that colludes with existing inequalities. The language of contract creates an illusion of self-determination that can be used to assign responsibility for the consequences to those whose "choices" have had negative outcomes.

As the British experience has shown, population surveillance is not incompatible with liberal democracy. Indeed, as a number of areas demonstrated in the 1950s and 1960s, the health visiting model could be extended successfully to other disadvantaged groups, like the elderly and the chronically sick and disabled. But the acceptance of home visiting rested on a fragile basis. It arose out of assumptions by the British state about the need for healthy human resources for military and industrial purposes. Once warfare became a matter of technology, rather than numbers, and employment was a matter of surplus, rather than scarcity of labor, the concern inevitably became diluted.

The rash claim of the welfare state that it had abolished poverty undermined further the legitimacy of health surveillance. It began to open up the possibility that the condition of the poor resulted from their own choices rather than their structural circumstances. If they failed to articulate their needs or to use the available services, that was their problem, an attitude which, in turn, limited the collective obligations of others to those who might otherwise be seen as paying the price of their own prosperity.

Home visiting could be revived as a valid instrument of social policy only in the context of its redefinition as an element of the democratic process, as the means by which a liberal state guarantees fundamental entitlements to all citizens. Surveillance as a technique carries no inherent moral charge. As Dingwall and Eekelaar (1988) have argued elsewhere, the public/private opposition is a false dichotomy. The existence of a private sphere is conditional on the self-restraint of the public. To the extent that commercial privacy has perpetuated avoidable inequalities of gender, color, age, or whatever, state intervention has always been justifiable. Its extension to the family is the logical consequence. The search for need is the means of redressing the disenfranchisement of those excluded from the normal political process by age or infirmity.

While surveillance could be a vehicle for tyranny, as Dr. Herbert Rubinstein saw, it could equally be a means of educating a polity, of bringing members of one class into contact with the conditions of another, and of confronting professionals with the realities beyond the cozy environments of their clinics, offices, or consulting rooms. The privatization of welfare is a screen erected by those who will not see. But democracy is a seamless web: A state that abandons its concern for the home life of its citizens in pursuit of a chimeric ideal of privacy is colluding in the perpetuation of everyday oppressions and inequalities that are ultimately likely to subvert its public order. The fate of home visiting is a key marker in the politics of welfare.

## Notes

1. This section summarizes an argument that is fully documented with supporting citations in Chapters 1, 2, and 9 of Dingwall, Rafferty, and Webster (1988).

2. This paragraph condenses arguments developed at length across Eekelaar, Dingwall, and Murray (1982), Dingwall, Eekelaar, and Murray (1984), Dingwall and Eekelaar (1988), and Strong and Dingwall (1989).

3. The reference to "medicalization" here is a slight anachronism. In the language of the time, it would be described as a sanitary intervention. Although it was directed by the local medical officer of health, it would often be at odds with local physicians and came out of a tradition that owed as much to engineering or bacteriology as it did to anything that we would now recognize as medical.

4. As Lewis (1980, pp. 13-21) shows, the continued decline in the birth rate during the interwar years led to a rising concern about the fitness of better-off women to bear and raise children.

5. Full details of the sampling and methodology can be found in Robinson (1986). The original transcripts were prepared according to the conventions of conversation analysis and will be presented here in a much simplified form.

6. In some areas, in fact, health visitors do also provide some pre-natal visiting and, of course, women may have been visited previously following other pregnancies. The point is that the primary visit has a particular significance in the occupation's own theorizing as a critical moment for establishing the terms of the professional/client relationship and for assessing the needs of the family and the appropriate intensity of future visiting.

7. Most of the data on this come from settings where the client is, to some extent, dependent on the professional as with doctor/patient relationships in socialized or insurer-controlled practice. It is possible, however, that the same system can be found with an inversion of roles where professionals are more dependent on their clients in private practice (Strong, 1979; 1988). There may also be rule-governed two-party encounters: Dingwall originally noted the controls in remote signaling using morse or semaphore, but aspects of religious ritual such as catechism also share some of these features.

8. These ideas can be traced further through Goffman (1972; 1975); Dingwall (1988); and Strong (1988).

9. There is a small number of male health visitors, who have not been represented in any of the samples used for taping studies. From observation, Dingwall (1979) has

suggested that their interactional behavior is rather different, having a more official tone and relying much more on the visible use of scientific expertise.

10.  In a number of cases, recording difficulties excluded parts of the closure sequence.

11.  In this and subsequent extracts M = Mother, F = Father, HV = Health Visitor; [ ] marks overlapping talk; ( ) marks passages whose transcription is impossible or uncertain; (( )) marks interpolations; = marks contiguous utterances; : marks an elongated syllable, e.g. Y:es. Pauses are measured in tenths of a second, e.g. (0.3).

12.  It is not clear whether these will be normative or comparatively defined.

13.  The independent access of the health visitor may become even more critical in the identification of many routine health needs because the small size of modern families and the fragmentation of child care caused by the growing participation of women in the labor force means that parents lack the experience of previous generations in recognizing those problems.

## References

Atkinson, J. M. (1977). Sequencing and shared attentiveness to court proceedings. In G. Psathas (Ed.), *Everyday language: Studies in ethnomethodology* (pp. 257-286). New York: Irvington.

Atkinson, J. M., & Drew, P. (1979). *Order in court*. London: Macmillan.

Bradshaw, J. (1972). *A taxonomy of social needs*. Oxford: Oxford University Press/ Nuffield Provincial Hospitals Trust.

Council for the Education and Training of Health Visitors. (1977). *An investigation into the principles of health visiting*. London: Author.

Dingwall, R. (1979). The place of men in nursing. In M. Colledge & D. Jones (Eds.), *Readings in nursing*. Edinburgh, Scotland: Churchill Livingstone.

Dingwall, R. (1980). Orchestrated encounters. *Sociology of health and illness, 2*, 151-173.

Dingwall, R. (1988). Empowerment or enforcement? Some questions about power and control in divorce mediation. In R. Dingwall & J. M. Eekelaar (Eds.), *Divorce mediation and the legal process* (pp. 150-167). Oxford: Oxford University Press.

Dingwall, R., & Eekelaar, J. M. (1988). Families and the state: An historical perspective on the public regulation of private conduct. *Law and policy, 10*, 341-361.

Dingwall, R., Eekelaar, J. M., & Murray, T. (1983). *The protection of children: State intervention and family life*. Oxford: Blackwell.

Dingwall, R., Eekelaar, J. M., & Murray, T. (1984). Childhood as a social problem: A survey of the history of legal regulation. *Journal of Law and Society, 11*, 207-232.

Dingwall, R., Rafferty, A. M., & Webster, C. (1988). *An introduction to the social history of nursing*. London: Routledge.

Donzelot, J. (1980). *The policing of families*. London: Hutchinson.

Eekelaar, J. M., Dingwall, R., & Murray, T. (1982). Victims or threats? Children in care proceedings. *Journal of Social Welfare Law*, 68-82.

Ferguson, S., & Fitzgerald, H. (1954). *History of the Second World War: Studies in the social services*. London: Her Majesty's Stationery Office/Longmans, Green.

Goffman, E. (1972). *Encounters: Two studies in the sociology of interaction*. Harmondsworth, England: Penguin.

Goffman E. (1975). *Frame analysis: An essay on the organization of experience*. Harmondsworth, England: Penguin.

Goodwin, S. (1988). Whither health visiting? *Health Visitor, 61*, 379-383.

Halpern, S. (1988). *American pediatrics: The social dynamics of professionalism 1880-1980*. Berkeley: University of California Press.

Kempe, C. H. (1975). Family intervention: The right of all children. *Pediatrics, 56*, 693-694.

Lewis, J. (1980). *The politics of motherhood*. London: Croom Helm.

McCleary, G. F. (1933). *Early history of the infant welfare movement*. London: H. K. Lewis.

Nelken, D. (1988). Social work contracts and social control. In R. Matthews (Ed.), *Informal Justice?* London: Sage.

Newman, G. 1906. *Infant mortality: A social problem*. London: Methuen.

Robinson, K. M. (1986). *The social construction of health visiting*. Unpublished doctoral dissertation, CNAA/Polytechnic of the South Bank, London.

Rothman, S. M. (1981). Women's clinics or doctors' offices: The Sheppard-Towner Act and the promotion of preventive health care. In D. J. Rothman & S. Wheeler (Eds.), *Social history and social policy* (pp. 175-202). New York: Academic Press.

Rubinstein, H. A. (1976). Letter: A protest about Kempe's views. *Pediatrics, 57*, 577.

Sacks, H. (1972a). An initial investigation of the usability of conversational data for doing sociology. In D. Sudnow (Ed.), *Studies in social interaction*. New York: Free Press.

Sacks, H. (1972b, Spring). Unpublished lecture notes transcrbed by Gail Jefferson, Lecture 5.

Sacks, H., Schegloff, E. A., & Jefferson, G. (1974). A simplest systematics for the organization of turn-taking for conversation. *Language, 50*, 696-735.

Schegloff, E. A., & Sacks, H. (1973). Opening up closings. *Semiotica, 8*, 289-327.

Smith, F. B. (1979). *The people's health 1830-1910*. London: Croom Helm.

Speier, M. (1969). *Socialization and social process in children's conversations*. Unpublished doctoral dissertation, University of California at Berkeley.

Stinchcombe, A. (1963). Institutions of privacy in the determination of police administrative practice. *American Journal of Sociology, 69*, 150-160.

Strong, P. M. (1979). *The ceremonial order of the clinic*. London: Routledge and Kegan Paul.

Strong, P. M. (1988). Minor courtesies and macro structures. In P. Drew & A. J. Wootton (Eds.), *Erving Goffman: Exploring the interaction order* (pp. 228-249). Boston, MA: Northeastern University Press.

Strong, P. M., & Dingwall, R. (1989). Romantics and stoics. In J. Gubrium & D. Silverman (Eds.), *The politics of field research* (pp. 49-69). London: Sage.

Wolff, K. (1950). *The sociology of Georg Simmel*. New York: Free Press.

# About the Editors

JABER F. GUBRIUM is Professor of Sociology at the University of Florida, Gainesville. He has conducted research on the social organization of care in diverse human service setting and is currently studying the impact of institutionalization on life narrative. Gubrium is editor of the *Journal of Aging Studies* and author of *Living and Dying at Murray Manor* (1975), *Oldtimers and Alzheimer's* (1986), and *Analyzing Field Reality* (1988), and the coauthor of *What is Family?* (1990).

ANDREA SANKAR is Assistant Professor of Anthropology at Wayne State University, where she is Director of the program in medical anthropology. She is also Research Scientist in the Department of Anthropology at the University of Michigan. Sankar has a long-standing interest in the field of home care and has published widely in the area. Her recently completed book, *Helping Someone Die at Home,* is forthcoming from John Hopkins University Press. Sankar's current research concerns the caregivers of AIDS patients.

# About the Contributors

EMILY K. ABEL teaches at the UCLA School of Public Health. She is the author of *Love Is Not Enough: Family Care of the Frail Elderly* and of a forthcoming book entitled *Who Cares for the Elderly? Public Policy and the Experiences of Adult Daughters*. She is presently doing research on the history of family care for sick and disabled people in the United States since 1800.

STEVEN M. ALBERT is Research Anthropologist, Behavioral Research, at the Philadelphia Geriatric Center. He is completing a study of caregiver culture based on ethnographic research with adult children caring for an impaired parent. For his doctoral work in anthropology (University of Chicago, 1987), he conducted research on ritual knowledge and seniority among the Lak of Papua New Guinea. He has recently been awarded a National Science Foundation grant for methodological research in cultural anthropology.

JUDITH C. BARKER has conducted fieldwork in the Pacific and returned to the University of California, San Francisco, where she is now Assistant Research Anthropologist in the Medical Anthropology Program. Recently, she examined the management of chronic illness by frail elderly and the responses of community nurses to common disorders in old age. She is continuing to develop her interests in long-term care, especially in-home health care and migrant populations.

JULIET M. CORBIN is Lecturer in the Department of Nursing, San Jose State University, and Research Associate in the Department of Social and Behavioral Sciences, University of California, San Francisco. She is the author of numerous papers and the coauthor of *Unending Work and Care* (1988) and *Shaping a New Health Care Policy* (1988).

ANN E. P. DILL teaches social gerontology and medical sociology in the Sociology Department of Brown University. She received her Ph.D. in sociomedical sciences from Columbia University, and then entered the Rutgers-Princeton Program in Mental Health Research, sponsored by the NIMH. Her research focuses on models of community-based care for the elderly, the chronically mentally ill, individuals with AIDS, and others with long-term care needs.

ROBERT DINGWALL is Professor of social studies at the University of Nottingham, England. His major publications as author or editor include *Aspects of Illness* (1977), *The Sociology of the Professions* (1983), *The Protection of Children: State Intervention and Family Life* (1983), *Divorce Mediation and the Legal Process* (1988), and *An Introduction to the Social History of Nursing* (1988). He is currently collaborating with W. L. F. Felstiner of the American Bar Foundation on a study of the civil justice systems of the United Kingdom and the United States as revealed in their management of litigation arising from occupational exposure to asbestos.

NANCY N. EUSTIS is Professor in the Hubert H. Humphrey Institute of Public Affairs at the University of Minnesota, where she teaches courses in social policy and evaluation research. Eustis has conducted several major studies in long-term care for the elderly and is currently researching the quality of home health care. Formerly, she was Research Sociologist at InterStudy in Minneapolis.

LUCY ROSE FISCHER is Research Scientist at the Wilder Research Center in St. Paul, Minnesota where she is directing the Minnesota Senior Needs Assessment Survey. She is the first author of *Older Minnesotans: What do they need? How do they contribute?* (Wilder Foundation, 1989). Her recent projects include a study of HMOs and home health care (published in *Journal of Aging Studies,* 1990); a case study of DRGs and family caregivers (articles in *The Gerontologist,* 1988, and the *Journal of Geriatric Psychiatry,* 1990); and an interview study of home care clients and their workers. Fischer has published articles on intergenerational family relations and is the author of *Linked Lives: Adult Daughters and their Mothers* (1986).

JAMES A. HOLSTEIN is Associate Professor of Sociology in the Department of Social and Cultural Sciences and member of the Discourse Analysis Research Group at Marquette University. His interests include the sociology of mental health and illness, family troubles, and descriptive practice in social control decision-making. Recent publications include the coauthored book, *What Is Family?* which deals with family discourse and the social construction of domestic life.

ELIZABETH HUELSMAN received her master's degree in medical anthropology and is currently a doctoral student in medical anthropology and gerontology at Case Western Reserve University. Her major research interests include familial caregiving, doctor-patient interaction, urban anthropology, and gerontology. She is undertaking a project in Toronto exploring familial caregiving, its development over time, and the role of secondary caregivers in the families of frail older adults.

LINDA S. MITTENESS is Associate Professor in Residence of medical anthropology at the University of California, San Francisco. Her long-term research interest has been in the cognitive organization of health and illness in late life. This interest has most recently focused on the meaning and management of urinary incontinence in the elderly. Related publications have appeared in the series *Research in the Sociology of Health Care, The Gerontologist,* and the *Journal of the American Geriatrics Society.*

KATHLEEN M. ROBINSON is Lecturer in Nursing and Health Studies at the Open University in the United Kingdom and holds an honorary appointment with the Department of Clinical Practice Development in Nursing in Oxfordshire Health District. She has worked as a nurse in acute and continuing care and as a health visiting practitioner; she maintains a particular interest in using research findings to inform nurses of current nursing practice. Her current research into district nursing is an extension of the analysis of health visiting described in this book and is intended to generate comparative work that can be used by both practitioners and teachers.

LEAH ROGNE is a graduate student in sociology at the University of Minnesota and a predoctoral fellow with the Midwest Council for Social Research on Aging. Her dissertation research is on elderly pacifists. Rogne's published work includes a coauthored article on civil disobedience in *Peace Action in the Eighties: Sociological Views* and the coauthored book *Better Nursing Homes—By Design*. As a Humanities Scholar and member of the North Dakota Council for the Humanities and Social Issues, she helped establish arts and humanities programs in that state.

ROBERT L. RUBINSTEIN is Senior Research Anthropologist and Assistant Director of Research at the Philadelphia Geriatric Center. He has conducted research with the elderly in the United States and has done fieldwork in Vanuatu in the southwest Pacific. His major research interests are personal meaning, gender and aging, and the home environments of older people. Rubinstein is the author of *Singular Paths: Old Men Living Alone* and many articles.

JOEL SAVISHINSKY is Professor of Anthropology at Ithaca College. In addition to recent work in gerontology, he has conducted research in Turkey, the Canadian Arctic, and the Bahamas. He is the author of *The Trail of the Hare: Life and Stress in an Arctic Community*. Since 1983, he has been studying aging in both nursing homes and community settings, and has done related fieldwork in upstate New York and London, England.

MYRNA SILVERMAN is an anthropologist on the faculty of the Department of Health Services Administration in the School of Public Health at the University of Pittsburgh. She is conducting research on the role of family and institutional supports in the care of the elderly, health care alternatives for frail older adults, and women and retirement. Silverman is the author of numerous articles and of the recently published monograph, *Strategies for Social Mobility: Family, Kinship, and Ethnicity Among Jewish Families in Pittsburgh*.

ANSELM STRAUSS is Professor Emeritus of Sociology, University of California, San Francisco. He is the author or coauthor of numerous books, including *Awareness of Dying: The Social Organization of Medical Work* and, more recently, *Unending Work and Care* and *Shaping a New Health Care Policy.*

G. CLARE WENGER is Senior Research Fellow at the Centre for Social Policy Research and Development, University College of North Wales, United Kingdom. She is Chair of the Commission on Aging and the Aged of the International Union of Anthropological and Ethnological Sciences. Wenger's writing has been focused mainly in the field of social networks and includes *The Supportive Network: Coping with Old Age.* Her main interests are in normal aging and cross-cultural studies of aging.